MW01628527

R and Earle in the plaza, Álamos.

Photo by Joan Gould.

Trauma & Drama

A Spanish–Style Home Restoration 1987–1989
Álamos, Sonora, México

The Chronicles of Earle David Winderman

Compiled by Joan Gould Winderman

Park Place Publications
Pacific Grove, California

A series of letters written by the author, Earle David Winderman,

and digitized for publication by Joan Gould Winderman.

Where dates were not specified, a best guess was made, considering the content.

Please excuse any inconsistencies that occur.

Editor Joyce Krieg, Park Place Publications

First Edition December 2016

Printed in the United States of America

Published by

Park Place Publications
Pacific Grove, California
parkplacepublications.com

ISBN 978-1-943887-37-8

*For Earle's sons: Marc Winderman, Paul Winderman,
John Winderman and Michael Winderman,
and Megan Gould Peterson, "Earle's favorite daughter"*

RUNNER - Photo by Don Wolf.

As much as he loved to wear masks,
Earle was a thoughtful, serious person.

Earle David Winderman

He was one of those men who was at home in the world—
one of those rare individuals who could fit in any surroundings.
As one friend, Gene Riggs, put it, "You can take him anywhere."

At various times in his life,
he "became" French, African-American and American Indian.
And then he decided to become Mexican … and thus begins our chronology.

Earle David Winderman, Joan Gould, and Runner.
Being welcomed to Alamos by Larry Lamar, 1988.

Introduction

Born August 20, 1925, in the Bronx, New York, Earle brought an impressive background to his "retirement" in Álamos. I spent almost 45 years of my life living with Earle trying to separate his facts from his fiction and so did not get caught up in good and bad or wrong and right. I identify with the struggle Will Wyatt had trying to identify the real person behind the alias B. Traven, one of Earle's favorite authors. He and Dave Kirbach founded The B. Traven society in Álamos as a sham club to cover their bullshitting meetings. Traven was a master at disguising his real name. He wove a deliberate web of mystery about himself, which you can read about in The Man Who Was B. Traven.

Earle was a puzzle to everyone. Most of all to his sons. At their age they were not bent on understanding power like I was. My father and first husband knew about power. I fell short but never gave up. Earle knew more than most people about it and he was always fair.

He was gracious if he lost. Just a blip in the road. He was on to the next challenge, always secure. Power or leverage was something he understood and what I needed to know about. He never wanted to hurt anyone but he had to prevail. Like his father (an orthopedic surgeon), his motto was "do no harm," while getting the job done.

In some circles we were known as the Earle and Joan show, or the Joan and Earle show, I forget which. He was a mystery to everyone and a pain in the ass to some. "Oh Earle," could be heard wherever he decided to regale a group or person. But that was applause to him. He was his own audience. He was always playing a role. That is one of the things he liked about his wolf hybrid, Runner. Runner made up games. He did, I saw it. That was true. A sign of intelligence in dogs and men.

We met in 1975 when I placed an ad (one of two in the free newsletter of a hardware store) saying I was looking for some good male company. How ambiguous can a person be? Earle thought he was just that and he was. We hit it off until I suggested we get married. He said, "You're not tough enough." I took that as a challenge.

He was working at that time on his doctorate in Community College Development, a necessity in his position as Vice President for Financial Affairs at Lincoln University in Oxford, PA.

So I went my own way and decided to go for a graduate degree and become a Reading Specialist (I was then working as one non-professionally in an elementary school). Earle offered to pay for my degree out of the blue. He had decided he could keep things going without a commitment. I took that in and never thanked him, as I knew he hated spending money. He said, "Go to any school, it doesn't matter, all you need is a piece of paper." I wanted to know as much as I could about teaching Reading, I didn't want just a piece of paper. But I took the money and went to Temple.

After I worked a few years as a Reading Specialist in West Chester, PA we began to talk about moving to the Southwest together where it was warmer, Earle was ready to retire. He had a serious arthritic condition, which required several back operations and lengthy painful recoveries. And he was ready to cut loose from the pressure of his job.

He was in his fifties and had endured enough pain. He said it was time to do what he always wanted to do, read whatever he liked and for as long as he wanted. He liked to browse: he had read all of Shakespeare several times, mysteries, spy novels, Will Durant's Story of Civilization, Greek Tragedies and many modern American novelists. And it was now time to again immerse himself in another culture, learn a new language. To jog for hours if he felt like it. He had French and German down. Spanish would be the next adventure. His photographic mind was itching for a new challenge.

Before his education began he was a medic in the U.S. Army during World War II and spent D Day in the second wave of American soldiers to land on the beaches of Normandy. He missed the Battle of the Bulge by contracting pneumonia, and ended up receiving a Purple Heart.

After the war he was shipped home and continued his education. He earned a BA in Comparative Literature at Columbia, and another degree, after he went back to France where he married and fathered one son, Marc in Paris and another, Paul, in Germany. He worked part time teaching Comparative Literature at the Sorbonne and Wurzberg, Germany. His third son, John, was born in California when he returned to the States.

After he returned to the States he had a number of jobs as a fund-raiser and became good at it, enough to be hired by John Price Jones to work with Bobby Kennedy to raise $62,500,000 for the ransom of the Bay of Pigs invaders. Castro insisted that he wanted medical supplies in addition to some millions of dollars. They got the cooperation of the Kennedy administration and the men were ransomed.

Then he was offered the job of Vice President of Financial Affairs for a black college, Lincoln University, in Oxford, PA. Before that he was divorced from his first wife and had married his second. Their son, Michael, was born shortly afterwards. Earle remained at Lincoln for 20 years during the Civil Rights Movement working, in addition to his regular duties, with James Farmer the President of the Congress of Racial Equality (CORE). He used to tell of his exploits while at Lincoln meeting many young African students who later became leaders in their own countries.

He was tasked with squiring around Langston Hughes on his yearly trips to Lincoln to lecture students. I checked this out with his acolyte Ja Jahannes, born as Jay Johnson, a brilliant student who Earle guided toward his two Doctorates and a career as a colonel in the U.S. Army Air Force.

He was ready to quit working and he knew what he wanted to do: retire, go to Mexico, learn Spanish and become Mexican. That is what learning a new culture meant to him.

I got a job in Sells, Arizona (15 miles from the Mexican border) and he retired. We moved to the Tohono O'odham Indian Reservation and teacher housing. Earle soon went off and bought Runner, a hybrid wolf pup, in Tucson and began the lengthy process of training him 24/7. They walked the desert every day. I even caught him baking dog biscuits.

Later when he read of a casting call (he was always reading ads looking for sales, odd items and jobs) in Old Tucson, a movie studio 60 miles north of Sells. He went with Runner one day to apply as an extra. He had tried a few other job ads but when he showed up with his wolf he had not been hired. He had been only playing though.

He did get the job of an extra playing a rich Mexican with a beautiful animal (smudged a bit to look realistic in Old Mexico) in the movie Tres Amigos.

Earle dressed and ready to perform with an Indian fellow actor playing a Mexican, in the movie "Tres Amigos".

When he heard the director was having a hard time finding Mexicans to play the bad guys, he offered his assistance in finding Indians to play Mexicans.

They were hired and for a time he became famous on the Res as a job source. It turned out though Indians who lived 100 miles from the set and had no cell phones, to say nothing of cars in those days were hard to corral and made to show up on time on the right day.

Earle befriended Bernard Siquieros, then the head of Papago Education in Sells, and set about putting together a Community College (his doctoral thesis) in conjunction with Prescott College for Indian teacher training on the Reservation.

When that was accomplished he announced he was ready to move to Mexico where he had always intended to end up in retirement. That was not my plan. I had my first and only real professional job and we lived 15 miles from the Mexican border among English speaking Indians.

ONE OF EARLE'S QUIRKS was a professed disdain for Art. He claimed it was just a scam, and he didn't trust art or artists. Yet when he had the opportunity to take a free class in clay mask-making for children during the Ortiz Tirado Festival in Álamos, he discovered another hidden facet of his personality—he actually was an artist, the masks of life mere facets he was able to don at will. He turned these works of art out unconsciously and gave them away to anyone who expressed interest.

Four masks by Earle; photos by Joan Gould

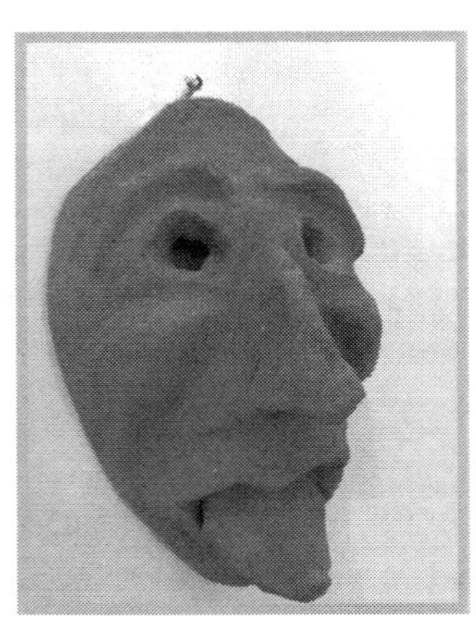

INTRODUCTION CONTINUED:

That was enough for me. Not Earle.

We had been traveling throughout Mexico during this time and Earle decided that Álamos was going to be the place. He found a ruin and proceeded to make plans to buy it. It has to be said that one of the other reasons, among many, for moving to Mexico was to find a place where he could continue to build up the fortune (his "fuck you" money) he was intent on amassing. Living there would be cheaper. Interest was skyrocketing.

Actually he really didn't want to buy a house, he considered buying as a waste of money; he could make more money in the stock market.

But I wouldn't budge without a house and land. He knew that. He really wanted to just roam Mexico in an old car that would break down a lot so he could meet and visit with Mexicans. We always had to spend the first three hours in a town looking for the cheapest place to stay. That had set off my alarm system. I was yet to learn how to break through his tactics to keep me in check and get what he wanted. We traded blows (virtual) and it was hard work. Come to think of it,he did buy an old junker. It did break down. And he did manage to get Mexicans to help him get it up and running. I didn't keep him from doing what he wanted to do at all.

So that is how Earle came to buy a ruin in Álamos, Sonora, Mexico, sign over half to me if I came down, and write these chronicles of his time spent, not alone, he had Runner. At this time he was also busy mixing my money with his in an effort to increase my incentive and his need to get that "fuck you" money. He wanted to die wealthy and I went along for the ride. He even threw in marriage at one point (1994). I must have passed a test somewhere along the line.

The letters are presented in Earle's unique voice and mostly in chronological order. He kept a record of this daunting project in this series of letters, added to almost on a daily basis, that were sent to me as I remained working on the Reservation in Sells, Arizona. His constant companion during this time was Runner, hishybrid wolf, often referred to simply as "R" in his letters.

What follows is both a detailed description of what Earle called the "trauma and drama" of a major construction/restoration project, and an intriguing snapshot of day-to-day life among the American Colony in Álamos, Sonora in the late 1980's.

Joan Gould Winderman
2016

TIMELINE OF HOUSE RESTORATION*

1987	EARLE ARRIVES in Álamos, Sonora, México
	RENTED HOUSE
	SCHOOL FOR SPANISH
	BOUGHT HOUSE
	WORKED ON HOUSE
	HUNTED DOME MEN
November 28, 1988	DOME MEN ARRIVED
December 1988	DOMES COMPLETED
1989	HOUSE COMPLETE / JOAN ARRIVES

* While every effort has been made to present Earle's letters in date order, many had no date, and the reader is tasked with sorting out the information to their satisfaction.

Earle's Chronicles to Joan Gould Álamos, Sonora, México 1987–1989

Dearest Joan,

Am completing my fourth day in Álamos and working to routinize my life. Class from 8:00 to 10:00, a walk around the market for oranges, bananas, etc., to serve as lunch plus buns for breakfast. The young doctors seem to be gone and I share the house with the landlady and her 25-year-old son. Lots of Spanish spoken here plus a nightly rerun of Little House on the Prairie, most of which I cannot as yet comprehend. I seem to run into 50 new words daily in class, few of which stick for no more than five minutes, but with practice and constant repetitions they may.

So far, I've been spending my time from about 11:00 a.m. to 5:00 p.m. under a portales facing an absolutely crazy tropical garden. Runner has the companionship of a same age German shepherd bitch and an eight-week-old malamute/lab puppy to sniff and play with. The shepherd is giving him watchdog lessons. Every time a stray dog goes by the fence, all three dogs run there and bark, though Runner seems to prefer guttural growls to honest barking.

I eat at 7:00 PMat another house along with my two classmates, young Mormons from Utah and a local veterinarian. A month of great cooking costs 50 dollars. The lady was most apologetic for charging that much. It used to be 42 dollars but with inflation, etc.!! Saw two houses, one the former mayor's, needs work but a good lot, don't know the price, and another that gave me claustrophobic feelings, for 15 thousand. The vet has a friend with a large semi-ruin for sale that I've yet to see.

Mrs. Gordon is back and told Gustavo to sell the house with the skinny kitchen for anything. If it goes for about 15 thousand it would be feasible to keep the front part and gut the rest and redo. The place across the street from the Tesoros hasn't moved at 60 thousand dollars, just what the owner put in it, and if it doesn't sell he will be forced to chop back some more on the price.

Found three ticks on Runner. The dinnertime vet will be bringing a special shampoo to use this weekend. Ran into a couple in the jardin and found out that his grandfather was my grandfather's nephew, which makes us? He's a reporter for the Sacramento Bee. She's a psychologist. I'll be joining them for the TGIF party tonight to take a break from trying to cram Spanish. I think that if I can force myself to focus about six to eight hours a day with books and tapes and a couple of hours of painful conversation for a minimum of a month, I'll be in pretty good shape. Next week, I'll try to read (with dictionary at my side) El Diario Yaqui, the Navojoa paper.

The weather's been warm, gracias dios, because there is no heat in my room. All things considered I am reasonably pleased with the way things are going. However, things would be a lot better if you were here. I miss you something fierce and I expect Runner does as well. He established his supremacy with the biggest dog on the street, so now they all have to leave him alone. We discovered an ancient metate in the vacant lot across the street. I'm trying to figure out how to acquire same and have my landlady's son put it in the truck. It looks too heavy for me to lift. My address and phone number is below:

Serdan No. 7, Álamos, Sonora, Mexico

Tel. 8-01-63

I'm generally home between eleven and seven, and after eight every night. Dinner is at seven, más o menos. Will close now with all my love and test my embryonic Spanish to buy an envelope and locate the P.O. Hastas Luego, E

Mid-February, 1988

Your letter arrived a few minutes ago, hand-delivered at 3:30 with a knock on the door. I quit cold in the middle of the 17th FSI tape, seven more to go, and a delightful first break. I also saw the Olympic ice skating, etc., on TV every night in Spanish. Hell, I don't even have the English vocabulary for assorted twists, jumps, turns, etc., but it was fun.

Our lives (Runner and mine) have become routinized. Class from 8:00 to 10:00, Mercado for Runner meat and breakfast roll, fruit, etc. Home to study and read and read and study, dinner at 2:00 and a walk two times around the cathedral square, then dinner for Runner and about an hour of TV and chitchat with the landlady and son, then study and read. It is coming along slowly and I think that I have to hear a word said to me two or three times before I feel that I can use it. My speech is very halting paloma español, if that's the equivalent. My class is good and very demanding. A mixture of grammar (verb tenses) and conversation. Since it is one-on-one I can't hide and my comprehension has picked up enormously.

I've been to the Tesoros once since I've been here and tagged up with the American colony. I see Bet Nuzum's son-in-law (Chacho) a few times a week and he is pushing me to speak exclusively in Spanish. He and some friends go to the beach every Saturday and dig up thousands of clams (three varieties) and oysters, which they sell live at the Sunday open market. They gave me an eight ounce cup last weekend with a lime-chile sauce. Great. I explained that I haven't been by to visit because I know I'd get all fucked-up on pot and couldn't get my study hours in. Will go by when I finish the FSI tapes, continue with class and practice using the language.

A man, Manuel, behind the capilla with a lot that we looked at also invited me over for an evening of Spanish. Maybe I'll give it a shot next week when I have a little more confidence.

My housing is working out, a fenced driveway for car and Runner and a playful pup. The German shepherd gave birth to 11 pups yesterday. Runner and I discovered them at 7:00 ayem when I was having my pre-school coffee fix and he gets his matutinal shit in the vacant lot across the street. The shepherd growls at the three-month-old pups and both she and Runner ignore each other. It will be interesting to see how he reacts to the pups when their eyes open and they start to move about. It's fun to watch him play games constantly with the little pup in the jungle-like garden.

My eye never did heal so went to an ophthalmologist in Navajoa. The problem was a corneal cut. Got antibiotics, an eye patch that made me look like a scruffy pirate, and a suggestion that I forget vanity and get bifocals. Did! Also reexamination indicates that the cut healed nicely, though will still be on antibiotics three times per day for three more days. Glad I went. It could have been serious.

Checked the furniture I ordered. The six chairs are framed and virtually finished. Didn't like the table so they'll make a bigger one. Total price under $60. Just hope everything fits in the truck.

Ran into Hilde. The Gordon house, the one with the railroad kitchen, sold for $27,500 early this week and she says she has a "live one" for the one with the pool. I'm tempted to put in a bid for $25,000 though this figure was rejected a year ago. If it gets away there will be another.

It has been fun thinking about writing to you and now that I've done it, will close and get back to work after a walk to the P.O. to mail same. Miss you and love you. ME

P.S. Wish I wasn't so obsessed with learning Spanish and pushing myself. The "jogging" analogy is correct. Look forward to talking to you on the phone.

January 1988

Right after I mailed yesterday's letter I came home and saw Chacho and the van parked in front of my house. He came for his wheelbarrow, which I borrowed months ago to make adobes. I was embarrassed but he didn't seem put out by my negligence. Then I mentioned the equipale that needs fixing, the couch log, garbage disposal and dishwasher that need fixing. He said he's giving a look-see at the appliances after I explained what they were. He'd never seen a garbage disposal before. I discussed the problem. He checked a wire or two, looked at the bottom of the motor, pushed a red button and announced that it was fixed and it was. Here I am, a product of the most appliance-owning nation in the world, and couldn't figure out that the garbage disposal unit would have a safety switch that cut it off any time it's overloaded with things like lime peels, glasses, silverware, etc. And a Third Worlder like Chacho studies it for less than a minute and determines what's wrong. The dishwasher will offer more of a challenge. He drove off with the equipale and will be back this week to fix chairs, etc.

Ole Bill came by to invite me to dine on barbecued elk. Richard and Craig were the cooks. Teri and Rudy brought salad and better potatoes than El Caricol, and Joannie, whose mother sold the toothbrush house and recently bought the one across the street from the Mansion where we saw people polishing the red tile sidewalk.

After dinner we left Armida's to go to that house for coffee and dessert. Teri calls the house the marble palace because of all the marble floors. The red floor motif carries inside to the portales and into most of the rooms. Turns out the floors are local terracotta brick that has been sanded and sealed and waxed. Joannie said they are much better than tile and the maids and gardeners know how to care for them, while they may not know the requirements for cleaning the tile. You apparently place an order (they come in different shapes) and the guys custom make them and fire them hotter than normal building brick. Having gone thru the custom brick bit and learned the process, I'm sure you could design your own, heart-shaped for the bedrooms, a combination of diamonds and ovals for the TV room to stand on while watching the World Series and Super Bowl, skillet-shaped for the kitchen, book-shaped for the library and in the configuration of two or three sheets of toilet paper complete with indented serrations for the bathroom. Based on dome brick experience, it would take about two-to-three months for delivery. Interesting, no??? As far as I can determine, the brick probably comes cheap, the finishing expensive, acid, sealer, chemicals and labor.

Monday

The week begins with a brick morning. Just got back from class. Allan Pendergraft learned that his car was vandalized in Mesa and will be going home prematurely to deal with assorted insurance problems. My crew is busily at work, one maestro plastering the bathroom, the other finishing off the cupola on the main house. Will then do the guest house cupola. The dome interior got pretty badly cement streaked from the three-day rain and it's going to take awhile to get it cleaned up for sealing because each brick must be sanded and scraped.

Plastering in baño going nicely. I'm anxious to see how quickly the guesthouse goes with two maestros and peons going at it full time. Nellie is busy doing her thing and R is out watching Manuel garden.

After dinner and coffee, I took a walk with Rudy Hale. He plays Spanish flamenco guitar and takes lessons from a maestro from San Francisco. He got his instrument and we sat in the park while he played. Jose, the music teacher and Peter Brown's house-sitter, sat with us and studied the fingering. Rudy is quite good. He's a igh-priced lawyer CPA and says that studying guitar is about the only sane thing he does. They'll be going back this week and hope to come down for another brief stay in a month or so before Teri has another operation on her leg. I haven't finished Amaro (the book). Allan says I can return it next year. He's pretty down about the car thing.

Got a spot of serious plumbing done today. Replaced a valve and leaky pipe in front of the house from street level to roof and a new toilet flow control. The old one leaked. Another wall of the baño is plastered. More dome work tomorrow plus interior plastering. Might get some plumbing roughed in and start trenching for sewer and drain pipe. The crew's gone and I'll kick back and worry about what to do about dinner and read the night away.

Tuesday 5:00 p.m.

Dearest Joan,

This place has been busy. Just got in from class and Chacho's waiting with a jug of wildflower honey. Said the only way he can fix the equipale with leather lashing and was it okay. It was and off he went. Then Joannie of the marble palace and Richard and his dog Jan showed up. She was supposed to fly out with the Preeces but gave her seat up to Allen Pendergraftt and will drive back with the Hales tomorrow. I made coffee and R and Jan raced around and around the pool like they were both berserk. Jan's an Australian shepherd and couldn't keep up the pace. He wandered around, had a drink and promptly fell asleep after the heavy-duty panting ceased. R was slightly out of breath. Then Joannie said she was thinking about a leg of lamb thawing out for dinner at the Hales at 6:30. Be there. They left.

Pancho and Lalo came by and loaded up 300 bricks. More coffee and then he left. Then Rudy Hale came by and said dinner was at 8:00 as the lamb was laggard about thawing. Fine. He left. Pancho came back and visited some more. Just left. I'm having a hot limeade with honey before assaulting the garden for lettuce to bring to the Hales. More to come. AH, THE SOCIAL WHIRL OF ÁLAMOS!!!

Wednesday, 7:15 a.m.

Pigged out properly last night. Borrowed a Clancy book from Rudy, and R and I trundled down the hill to our pad. The crew is hard at work. I have a "white" wash soaking. Not too cold and I thought I'd best run my long johns through just in case while I have a chance.

The lettuce glut is upon me along with much radishes. El jardin is verdant and looks great. Hales and Joannie won't be back for a couple of months. .

Thinking about doing the fireplace with exposed brick. Collalo does good work and to run clean mortar lines all around would only take an extra day. If it doesn't look good, it can always be plastered over.

Friday

The big thing in my life yesterday was getting the legal guys paid 10,000 pesos duty. Also got your letters and enclosures. Read them three times so far. Contact with you is so tenuous and I get so wrapped up around here that letter writing until the day of the phone is the best we can do.

The work goes well. All three cupolas are in place and the final cornice was poured yesterday. Domes about finished early. We are still waiting for the interior of the dome today after the three-day deluge before it can be cleaned of cement streaks. The bathroom is plastered and final cement skim is needed on the dome. I have a crew plastering the neighbor's wall. The number one maestro estimates five more weeks for the guesthouse, a week of which will be ditch digging and plumbing. He knows of a supply of old brick for the floor but doesn't know how many or condition of same. When I have wheels I'll check. If not, I'll place an order to have new ones made ASAP.

It has been damned cold here but I guess it's worse in Tucson. Met a lady who came in yesterday and she said they had frost. What is this sunbelt shit? I'm sweating Tim and truck parts. Would like to come to the States in a few weeks for plumbing fixtures, lots of paint and varnish, etc. Better quality and can save hundreds of dollars. Also want to bring down an air conditioner. I'm afraid that there's a minimum of three more months, which includes front room roofs and portales (six or seven weeks) according to maestro and a week for pool with crew of two maestros and two peons. I'm not going to push things. I'll take it easy and steadily progress. May do that TGIF. It's at the Perkins house around the corner and I can get a chicken chopped. Off to the P.O. Write soon.

Love, R & E

Saturday, February 13, 1988

Dear Joan,

Staring out the window missing you and wondering whether or not this house trip is the smartest or most stupid thing I've ever done. For a guy who works hard at not making huge commitments to anything, I sure picked a doozy for openers. Finished my nightly harvest of assorted lettuces and spinach, gave up on 1,000 radishes in the ground, two big. Will pull 'em and save a few for seed. Have got to talk to Manuel about timing. There are 50 cabbage plants and a frightening number of zucchini, all happy and healthy. The glut overwhelms me. Even with a stagger planting, suspect that we'll produce far more than we consume.

Will try to catch up with Stephanie for a rundown on what herbs and spices thrive as well as some of the exotic edibles whose seeds she collects daily and get 'em all going. Much against my gardener's credo, we may even have to contaminate the space with flowers to use the entire area. It simply looks a lot better fully planted instead of partially with fallow bald spots. Think I'll change clothes and wander downtown to see what is happening. Later, love.

Ran into sculptor guys, had some beers and got home early (no dance). Will crash when R finishes eating.

Slept 'til eight and it was lovely. Did Tianguis and went to the museum. The work they did was amazingly beautiful. The instructor said that this was the first workshop he ever ran where all students finished. One of the ladies ran home and baked her elephant as did Hector, of Hector and Bill. Then while the stone was too hot to touch, waxed the figures with shoe polish and a small brush. The result is amazing. I wonder if marble is finished the same way.

Four of the guys came over for beer on their way home. We talked about how rough it is to be a professional in Mexico. The periodontist, Yanahara, said that in a good year, he makes 12M (that is 12 thousand pesos, I think) after six years of practice. The orthodontist from Obregon said his income is about the same. They're both trying to emigrate to Canada. The gentleman and wheat farmer from Obregon said that they pay upwards of 100 percent interest and must earn in the neighborhood of 200-to-300 percent profit to "make it." Pretty crazy and admittedly risky.

The Obregon wheat farmer built a neo-colonial and said that properly painted and treated pine beams are good for 50 or so years when properly maintained. He's a civil engineer who was called back from Mexico City two years ago to run the family farm. Now he's thinking of going into the construction business because of the opportunity that exists due to an acute housing shortage.

They left at 3:00 and R and I ran. Went downtown. It's pre-Mardi Gras Sunday. This is the night where everyone buys eggs and plastic sacks of confetti and bops everybody. I got egg-bopped once and a few hands of confetti came in my direction. Ran into Gaspar. He proudly told me he egg-bopped one girl nine times. It will be interesting to see how long it will take to clean the confetti carpet off the plaza. If any wind comes up tonight it will take as long to disappear as a foot of snow in Westchester. So far no firecrackers, but I'll approach downtown going gingerly tomorrow and on Fat Tuesday. Time for bed. 'Til tomorrow.

Well, my love, the shit hit the fan today. We were going to start digging the plumbing trench for the sewer under the common wall to hook-up with the neighbors. I thought the situation was a go. Collalo went over to check out the connections and the neighbor said that they wanted a payoff in dollars, amount to be determined. My understanding had been a tradeoff. Rain runoff from our yard was flooding their patio and house. The same problem we had until a French drain was built. With the sewer connection I would have stopped it. I have two or three fall-back positions: connect up to Gen Reynold's sewer, build a septic tank, or go through the city hall and, if Gustavo is correct, gain eminent domain access. The latter is time-consuming. I don't want to bother Gen but I will.

Collalo tells me that the sewer hook-up vs. septic tank will cost the same. I'm supposed to meet with the neighbors at 9:30 a.m. with Gustavo to negotiate. If things get nasty, I can explain how I had to secure permission to French drain and that if they deny me access I will never stop the water from my side of the wall from periodically flooding them. The lady is a bitch and gave Gen a couple of years of shit over a boundary dispute. Great.

Now to find the elusive Gustavo. Hilde's gone and either he's still in bed or out. He had the flu. Maybe taking coffee at Mamacita's. And the search goes on. A true pain in the ass and a lousy way to begin a week. Joanie drove Teri down from California; the latter really limps badly. The former told me that the man who did the brick work will be working at her house today. I'm going to try to catch him and see what I can learn. Off to Gustavo again to see what there is to see. To be continued ....

Could not find Gustavo. While looking, ran into Gen Reynolds downtown with her cavalry. Four ladies of indeterminate age on horseback. Told her my problem, can connect to her sewer if necessary and can also use a sump pump to connect to the big house, also if necessary, dig a small septic system. Options, options. Spoke to the lady and she backed off immediately and said it was her husband or neighbor who wanted the money. I said that I wanted the right-of-way in writing. She said her word is sufficient. Bullshit, thought I. We went around in circles. I told her that the city water man said that I ought to get permission in writing. Calalo was there to verify. I also told her that it was an American custom. I think she's convinced that she can't hold me up, but I still want Gustavo to clarify or I just may hook into Gen's sewer line and flood her ass just for the hell of it. We'll see.

Calalo is moving. He loves to lay brick. I'm sure the front cornice is going to be done today. It'll look great. While Gustavo-hunting, I ran into Junie, Joanie's mama. She said her sidewalk gets very heavy traffic and requires medium maintenance but that the interior is a piece of cake. I'll talk to the guy who did it later. She said he uses a secret formula that can only be had in Guadalajara?? The secret is his, but who cares.

Four hundred ninety dollars and five weeks later, I have the truck back. The mechanic went to the States, studied Ford electronics and figured out that the computer "brain" was defective; it now runs like a dream. I'm going to Navojoa with Gustavo to deal with the telephone , clarify drainage, get the installation made, window and doors in place (can now deal with glass) and cut the crew loose tearing down the front room roofs while I'm gone. Should take about a week. More later ....

Later, back from Navojoa at 7:00 p.m. and have R's food on the stove. Phone promised this week. We'll see. Gustavo will deal with the neighbor lady tomorrow before 10:00 a.m. One of my maestros, Manuel, only worked one-and-a-half days. People are dropping like flies with el grippe. Gustavo spent three days in bed, totally pissed. Hilde is in the States for a week and his libido is stifled. Pancho was dropped for a similar length and the aging gringo community talks about their contemporaries who are sick-abed. The conversation must have been similar to those held from the days of medieval plague to the Great Flu of 1918. You even see Mexicans with bandanas covering their faces com los banditos.

Finished eating. Great salad stuff. Bad vinegar and oil, what a bummer. Getting a tad cold tonight. Runner just knocked off three pounds of beef trimmings. Wolfed it all down. An amazing performance. Tomorrow he may only eat half a pound. Strange indeed. Getting a mite chilly. The siren call of the heating blanket calls, who can resist??

Tuesday

Pretty cold this morning. Bought Runner meat and went to the Plaza to visit Ole Bill and Armida. The streets were clear of confetti. Mardi Gras ends tonight. May wander down to see the festivities and rush back at the sign of the first firecracker. Tony, the museum director, told me that before he came here he was an assistant curator of an Indian museum in Hermosillo and bought a lot of stuff in a small town shop outside of Obregon. I will check it out for rattles, etc., on the way back to the states.

Calalo is finishing off the roof of the casita and has the two peons cleaning brick. Manuel is sick. I'm waiting for either Gustavo or Pancho to show to try to make some fairly explicit plans for the guesthouse completion. Also want to get written permission to move the plumbing, water and sewer connection along. Would like to get it to a stage where it can be painted and floored, tiled, shelved, countered and fixtured when you can come down and help figure out the scheme.

Bought about five pounds of plum tomatoes at less than 10 cents a pound. Will try to make tomato sauce from scratch later today, something I've never tried. Back to chores, more later.

Later. Gustavo came by and said digging is to begin. The price is one blender (used from the States) and free access on both sides to kill "mochomos", the plant carrying ants that defoliate. We apparently have some that are invading her property. It a question of my going out tonight with a flashlight and tracking them to their lair and getting Manuel to zap them.

Also made arrangements for a glazier to window everything—the beat goes on. Colalo is preparing a list of what I'll need to plumb and sewer-connect. Gustavo knows a good plumbing supply place in Navojoa to get the stuff. Busy, busy.

Back to ground zero. Calalo went over to start measuring and she changed her mind. I'll have Gustavo take one more shot at her. If this fails, go septic system with a pump to lead into our sewer line and let her live with a flooded patio and living room and to hell with her.

Got the bid on interior frames to hang windows, 250,000 pesos (which is $109 US dollars). Believe that the glass may run more than the frames but we take it one step at a time. Gustavo is going to take a final crack at the lady tomorrow. We're also going to the city hall to check location of our sewerage access, if any. We may be on a septic system or drainage field. Who knows?

Wednesday, 8:45 a.m.

Went downtown last night. Early evening was still egg-bopping. There was to be a Mardi Gras dance at City Hall with a nine o'clock start. Hardly am up that late so R & I came home, ate supper, and read a bit. Still not smoking and still preoccupied with a desire, hope it passes soon.

Got peons cleaning all brick. Would rather have them trenching for a septic system but must wait for Gustavo. More later.

Gustavo came and went. He spoke to the lady and she says she is agreeable but her husband isn't. Yesterday it was her brother; however, 5,000 or 6000 pesos would make them happy. Fuck 'em. Will meet Gustavo at the court house and go over records to determine sewer hookup. The house is on a septic system. We'll have the city sewer man by to determine street location and figure out where to go from there. As far as the casita is concerned, we will go septic system.

Believe I have sufficient old brick accumulated to do the casita floor. We're going for it. R & I just got back from jogging and P.O. Hooray!! Two letters. Sorry to learn that from one date to the next, there is no improvement on Gertie's (Joan's mother) condition and can imagine the frustration of not getting straight answers."Omerta" among MDs is probably adhered to with more vigor than with the Mafioso. Fear of malpractice, the fact that you changed physicians and asked questions make them nervous and silent. Stick with the nurses, even if you have Ellie run interference.

Monday, April 11, 1988 - hasn't bought the house yet.

Weird, but I missed you the moment I left, but have since survived the trauma. Went to Lake Obregon but since fishing was lousy, had a couple of beers, came back to Álamos and luckily got the motel room with the hopper and shower vacated by a family an hour before I arrived. Went to the prison on Sunday and bought a belt with holes, too big but will be cut down to fit this week. Also ordered one for the Obregon fisherman who will be at the Mansion this weekend. May go fishing next week. Been to the river twice with Craig and Lalo, the young man on the bicycle, who Craig says makes a much better than average living selling macramé and owls that he makes when broke.

Living here is fun. Little feast at night with Annetta, the landlady, doing most of the cooking and cleaning, she enjoys it, and Craig, myself, Lalo, whoever is buying the food. Last night had elk steak which Craig brought frozen from Idaho. Gourmet shit by candlelight. I goofed on the school schedule; it starts next week so I'm just bumming around and using Spanish, which is good.

No word on the house yet. Gustavo says he has a script with lies he can live with, but could not get Madame Smollens on the phone. To further fuck up my thinking, an Álamos family moved to Obregon and contacted him to sell their house, two blocks from the Tesoros, all original, for between 10–12,000 pesos, net (approximately $5,000 US dollars). Gustavo claims that since it also needs a roof and is about the same size, it would be a better buy. He also claims it has a better view and is on a street where big restoration is a'coming. It is next door to the old museum, a converted mansion, and two doors down from the in-process conversion of an old hospital where a chap named Larson has already sunk 114,000 US dollars and is still going strong. I haven't seen it but will shortly and if I like it would like you to consider flying down for a weekend to check it out. Hilde is slightly pissed off at Gustavo for even mentioning it to me since we made a decision on a house that's three times the price.

Only bad news to report is that I lost my glasses swimming or shampooing. Craig and Lalo spent an hour snorkeling yesterday without success, so into Navojoa today for a new set. Lalo caught four small bass by hand, cutting his fingers on the fins in the process. He claims to have caught 28 the previous week. Remarkable. Water's on, quick shower, off to the bank for money and then to the big city. More later.

Thurs. a.m.

Went to Navojoa yesterday with Craig and Lalo. I needed to get glasses and sawdust for Runner and Rye (Craig's dog, the chocolate lab). Lalo delivered five wooden Álamos chairs to a dentist, made 48,000 pesos, then bought 10 large baskets and 12 tiny ones for 31,000 pesos, which he'll try to sell Sunday to tourists and therefore will not have to make as many owls since the Flying Doctors will be operating on his eye today. Spoke very little English. I learned the craft mentality. The makers figure that wood is free, and hemp, nails and leather are cheap. They can earn 30 pesos for 10 days work as unskilled labor; therefore, if they can make 40 pesos doing a craft they figure to be way ahead of the game. This philosophy keeps prices down if you buy directly.

My turn to cook yesterday. Did pepper, bean sprouts and beef, a big success. Sunday will go to Tianguis and buy a live rooster for coq au vin and add some blood at the final stage a la bourguignon for the hell of it.

Pat and Don came by to visit last night and invited me to a "help clean out the freezer" dinner today. They are talking about getting out this weekend. I'm going to see if they'll mail this letter. It should be quicker. They know the owner of the little house with a second story view down the street from their place, a gringo who lived there quite modestly for ten years. It may well suit Al. Ran into Bet Nuzum, who apologized for not being here to have us over. She issued a rain check. Pem is still fishing the estuary-cum-beach. Plan on catching Gustavo to look at the house previously mentioned, and I have located the mason who is willing to go over it on spec if I'm interested.

Runner is having a lovely time. Now that the pups are older he and the lab hang out in the courtyard or stroll the Plaza with me, a gringo canine mafia. She's much more obedient than our Runner. On the "Come" command, she trots right over without the "who me?" look that our guy always has. Took a break to clean up last night's mess. My kind of town, i.e., no water after 6:00, but the landlady kicked me out of the kitchen so we write a bit, study some Spanish and go to the prison to see if the belt is finished. Then off to the Mercado for dog food, fruit, etc., to take to the river. It's gonna be a hot one, yo creo, so will sign off again.

Here we go. Dinner at Pat and Don's, some 20 year Álamos vets, a retired real estate guy with a 40 acre ranch who would like me to buy four acres, and a shy 50-ish gal who lives in the Chocolate Palace. Don repeats his stories, dull evening, but great food.

Next day. Bunch of stuff happened yesterday. Looked at 10-12,000 US dollars house. Probably a great buy but it didn't feel good. Gustavo caught up with Mrs. Smollens and she would like to accept 30,000 pesos ($13,164 USD) and split closing costs, legal fees and commission and all the goodies from the middle. Gustavo is developing the figures. I may end up paying 31-32 with her netting 27-28. Seems fair. Should have figures by next week. Gustavo also went over the house with a contractor who claims to use an interior beam structure in the side walls to support the roof beams. Will check it out first chance I get.

Spent the late afternoon and evening trying to get Lalo to Fuentes for surgery. The Flying Doctors screwed up and went to Guaymas instead of Álamos. Finally found a tourist pilot and wife from California who flew Lalo and Craig to the clinic at 7:00 ayem this morning. Drove by Don and Pat's; they may have split, so will take this to the P.O. soon before I fill the entire notebook.

Hope the snuffling sniffling, sneezing is history. Local sufferers claim to be better. I sure wish you were with me. My address is Cardenas Number 5, Álamos, Sonora.

Love, Me

June 1988

My Dearest,

Still laboring on our behalf to make things beautiful. Down to a crew of six, four tree cutters and two French drainers. The former should finish up in a few more hours. Each guy spends about 20 minutes up a tree. The guys on the ground pick up and burn the base of the fronds and stack the leafy part for a free truck ride to a nearby ranch for ramada roofing.

Big frustrations of the day. The cement, sand and gravel guy didn't show. Ditch is dug four-by-five. Made my first trip to the construction supply store for copper wire, PVC pipe, chicken wire, staples and three liters of sealant. Will give this project a day and a half to complete. Must wait overnight for the cement to cure. Will use crew (two men) on a water diversion wall and patching. Want to get a tad of interior wiring complete, inspect the roof patch job, and re-putty kitchen windows where needed; the glass is loose in some and could break. Finally, arrange to get it termite proofed and bombed the day before I leave. I'll sleep on the portales.

Interior wildlife consists of one fly, I repeat, only one and a trapped lizard which I caught and released. Understand that the bugs don't come until monsoons begin. Am also having a well pump cover built, promised on Saturday for installation. If all goes well, hope to be out in a week. Good thing Runner is with you. The refrigerator needs a part that is unavailable, so storing his meat would be impossible. It would also be nice to keep cold beer around. Guess you can't win 'em all.

Lalo's brother Pancho was by with 25 pesos he left for the bike. He's living 12 guys to a room in Tijuana. He has a morning waiter's job for food and rent (4000 pesos per week). And his owls are going as fast as he can make them, several orders of 20 to gift shops at $4.00 US per copy and $7 to $8 US sold directly to tourists. He has trained one of his roommates to do the eyes and painting. He will be home to visit his mother for a few days in July ($30 round trip by bus) and then return to Álamos and go on a basket-buying trip to develop an inventory for the tourist season.

Next day

Up at five. Leisurely coffee and review of day's activities. Truckload of sand arrived and was reloaded with a load of palm fronds and a big fire started to burn the rest. Crew arrived at 7:00. Manicured French drain and put on first coat of mud (cement). Finished coat maneuver and hopefully it will set up fast for the waterproof coat, one-and-a-half feet of gravel, back fill with dirt and hopefully area will be cleaned up before neighbors use it over the weekend. Our garage doors will be repaired, on some the weld broke, re-hanged and reversed and a new concrete lintel built and possibly hung tomorrow. I'll throw a big crew at the job.

Will hold off building interior ramp because we may want to use stone instead of brick as the retaining wall. Also considering using stone instead of brick around pump core area, shifting bottom tank and hiding it behind ore stone. Its removal from the present site will facilitate construction of casita bathroom. Have also been considering a San Miguel d'Allende-type roof on casita. What do you think?

Went to Navojoa today to look at fencing wire. Nothing decent. May have to smuggle. Did bring back 1,650 pounds of lime and cement. The toy truck took it fine. Am waiting for Gustavo, who is negotiating for a ruin for Al.

Will try to call you again. Since I haven't been able to get an answer, assume you've been playing at the lake.

Cleared out and watered bamboo stand. Think it will survive. Am also waiting for Gustavo. Was told that I may have a problem with exterior-opening garage door, as a violation of city code. I'll need him to mordita whoever. Too bent up to write more, so will take a shower and pack it in. Love and stuff,

Friday

Up five minutes after dawn cracked and walked four-and-a-half miles. No pain, no strain, just sweat. Mañana will go for five and sit there. It's where I was when I quit the reservation. A gringa stopped her VW bus and introduced herself as Elizabeth Dale. Her husband is Scottish and she an Oregonian with a unique quasi-Brit quality. She's a lawyer, and he? They are planning on making Álamos their permanent home and do kid-visiting summers. Down here now getting a stone wall completed. Experience taught them when work goes on, be there. I've already learned that lesson.

Went out for an hour and found a load of construction stone waiting instead of pea gravel. Wow! In consequence, a day and a half strayed away before the coming of the gravel. This ayem I went to Gustavo's for about an hour and found them dismantling the garage doors instead of cementing the wall, which should have been done yesterday and would have been except for the fact that the cement should have been mixed one day previously. Will get the stone in my yard until you decide where it is to go and have the water diversionary wall done in low brick. If we go stone, the brick can be taken down and the footing will still be in place. Will design it that way.

Those three overgrown bonsai are not plums, they're kumquats, called yoyomos. Been eating them and giving them away. We also have an extra good mango tree. The workers and kids as well as myself have picked it clean. However, we have a spare tree that's loaded and the neighbors' tree over hangs.

Toluca is undergoing gentrification. Three houses are being worked on and the sidewalks are littered with piles of rock, sand, gravel, broken brick and concrete from a roof job and no dumpster dumpers. Looking forward to Sunday and a lazy day at the Cuchujaqui River.

Gonna work the crew tomorrow. Having problems with the roofers, who have about a day's more work to do and haven't shown for three days. Spoke to Gustavo yesterday and asked him to send them back to work or pay them off. There are lots of guys who need work because construction slows in the summer with gringo flight. This ayem, he said they'll be up there by 10:00. It's now 12:30, no roofers. Back to Gustavo and since I'm getting up to leave I'll hit the Post Office on my way. In summation I'm having lots of fun, feel great and miss you mucho.

Gustavo to the rescue. Kind of an awkward situation with the brick man concerning the 2,500 ruined ones. Seems he wanted me to pay for 'em. Gustavo pointed out that if a baker is making bread in an oven and it burns, the baker eats the bread and the customer doesn't pay. After some more chitter-chatter, the brick man said he can sell them to somebody else as fire brick for a chimney. Gustavo checked out the guesthouse layout and bed problem. His solution, and it is both good and obvious, is to build the bed in the fireplace corner and the fireplace in the bed corner. And why not?

He cut off all the water to eliminate further seepage. Plumber will come on Thursday to find the all-elusive leaky pipe. Gustavo will be here to cheer him on. The hour of the dome man approaches after today's legal holiday goes by the boards. We hope and pray. I lost my crew unless they are out loading brick. I thought I had agreed to double time, but maybe they decided that they needed the day off. Manuel, the gardener, showed and he's busy digging and raking his heart out. I've got class (I think) and will wander over shortly even though I suspect that it is a day off. Just as well, there are a bunch of piddly things to do around here.

Runner has been unbelievably antsy in wanting to go out. Bugged me a few times during the night. When we left the front door, he thoroughly sniffed a spot across the street and started drooling. I suspect a bitch in heat was out there at night and he smelled her. Will be leashing him and watching him like a hawk. Time for marketing and then class???

The brick guy came 'round. I sent him to Gustavo. No crew, no class. Ole Bill came by, car problem, saw mechanic and I acted as interpreter, if you can believe it. He needs a hose for his power steering. I'll get him one tomorrow. I've got to go anyway. The town's on holiday so it is a day of sloth. I love it. May lift a few beers with Manuel later. Want to catch the garden hose while there is still sun. 'Bye now.

Thursday Eventide

Yesterday did not go as intended nor did today. Manuel didn't show so I went to the Tesoros. The usual crowd and a busload of tourists. A digression.

The brick man who was unloading a truckload (1,000-1,200 bricks) carefully came by for a 20 M advance for gas. This is the guy I paid 1,400,000 pesos ($614 USD) a couple of weeks ago up front for special brick and who lost 3,000 USD to rain. Tight, tight margin. Of course I gave it to him. Two minutes later, he showed me where he put two of Umberto's brick-handling tools he used to off load the truck. To give you a brief perspective of what's involved in the operation, the guys have to carry separate loads of brick on their backs from the cover down that lousy trail, mostly uphill to where I had parked the truck where we went brick-checking. They loaded with utmost care so they can survive the bumpy road to the highway with minimal breakage and with equal care unloaded them.

Tour guides came into town desperate for a House and Garden Tour. They offered Bet

$125 to do a quick tour. She lined up in a hurry Gen Reynolds and June Martin, who has been waiting for a week for a furniture shipment from L.A. She said that they started out with 20 and by the time they reached her place for the traditional punch and cookies only five were left standing. The Garden Tour raises money for Álamos scholarships. A doctor had been summoned to deal with the five who couldn't make the tour, and since the others were dropping out like flies, had himself a minor epidemic of Turista with 20 victims. Some he gave shots, others pills, prescribed bland diets for all. There was a lot of nervousness involved with a consensus that "They all got the bug in the south and that it was impossible for Álamos in general and the Tesoros in particular, to be in anyway culpable."

Spent several hours in Navojoa. The day started with my going to school and deciding to postpone 'til Monday. Bill was waiting for me at the school with his car that was losing fluid from it power steering assembly (peligroso). So I lined up a mechanic who said it would take two hours to remove the part, which we can take to Navojoa and replace or get repaired. He sent us to a place where the latter can be done. In fumbling Spanish I explained what has to be fixed and could they do it. They could. Then it was a question of how long (hours) it would take. At which point an older man, obviously the owner, came out speaking perfect English. He spent three years going to Fairfax High School in L.A. and staying with his grandmother during W.W.11. His parents were afraid he'd either get drafted or enlist so they got him back to Mexico fast. He's from Álamos and his grandfather built the real hacienda with orange groves, walk-in well, etc., and owned the Tesoros at one time. The Bours family next door are first cousins. He owns a house in Tucson which he bought for his two sons while they were going to the U of A. He said it was cheaper than paying over $300 per month rent. He set both boys up in business in Mexico and he and his wife use the house a couple of months a year. He assigned a man to fix the part ASAP and we were out of there in less than 30 minutes.

Then to search for fencing. Tried three places and finally ended up with a very heavy wire mesh normally used for laying concrete floors. It comes in widths of 6'6" and has to be cut down to size, which they agreed to do, and deliver. It will look good, be Runner-proof and I just hope to hell it can be strong because of its gauge.

Then found the good butcher shop. Got sawdust for Runner and meat for me. Bill bought a bunch of T-bones. And then home, where the possessor of the enclosed (a feather) broke its neck on the back door. If we turn the big room into a greenhouse and wash the windows, kamikaze birds will be common. All for now as I face the nightly decision of whether to eat out or in. Better get this in the mail and start a new one mañana.

We love you and miss you. R & Me

P.S. Guadalupe C. just popped in to tell me that the new maestro will be completing his present job Wednesday and will be free to start here on Thursday. He added that he also knows a bit about plumbing and electricity. And away we go. He also figures that we are two-to-three months away from completion.

Now, Mercado.

More love, R & Me

Finger-Eating in Mexico, Tortilla Technique

When your host serves you a chicken dinner with a side of beans and fried onions, keep in mind that one's fingers should never make direct contact with the food. Should your portion be leg and thigh, break one tortilla in half and, using the two pieces, carefully disjoint the chicken by holding the end bones. Be careful not to splatter your fellow diners or yourself. Using the same tortilla halves, strip the meat off the bones. Get a fresh tortilla, and using one of the halves, place a line of chicken, onion and / or beans in the tortilla. Voila! Instant taco.

While enjoying, the tortilla halves are eaten concurrently. Since they are soggy by this time, a scoop method to capture and eat beans would neither be appropriate nor effective. Instead, use an overhead swoop. With your left hand, take about a quarter of the tortilla. Fold it into a "V" position between thumb and fingers and select a cluster of beans on your plate for a target. Ensnare the bean cluster between the folded tortillas, exposing the edges, bring thumb and fingers in apposition with enough pressure to hold the beans in the tortilla but not too much to avoid squirting problems. The objective is to place as many beans as possible in your mouth. Alternate bites between your taco and your beans. Every third bite can be accompanied by half a chile verde or a whole chilte. The latter is recommended for only experienced consumers of Mexican gastronomic delights. Novices find the practice embarrassing because of side effects such as: consumption of copious amounts of water, ice cube-sucking, tears, and other unpleasant reactions. Come con gusto!!!

— Earle

Monday, June 20, 1988

Miss you guys badly and will wind things up here ASAP. Finally got the papers signed today, ten days late, and big fight with Gustavo. I gave him the check Friday night because I got every and all assurances that the notary would have me in signing condition Saturday ayem, and he had a gringa lined up to take it to the States to cool out Mrs. Smollens, who has been bugging him about the money and worried about a personal as opposed to a certified check. I told him essentially, "no tickee—no washee." I had to have appropriate papers indicating ownership.

While all this was going on I've been busy get things put back together, had the well cleaned, pipes added, new pump installed, electrical shit done for repair, refrigerator problem corrected, dead trees removed, weed trees eliminated, ten years of debris raked and burned. The palm tree circumcision crew started Saturday, four climbers and it's been taking a day per tree. Four more guys have been roof-patching and waterproofing since Thursday. Should be done by Wednesday. Also had interior wall of front and bathrooms fixed and have a mason-type working on the swimming pool heater and pump house. Shit, either the electricity is off or a fan died. Got to check—bye.

Back (obviously). Is possible no electricidad en Álamos a este momento. Paciencia! Good thing I left because the wall man didn't fix the bathroom cabinet interior, which suffered from water rot. Believe I'll put the fence on hold. Had a wrought iron design priced, $2,500. Have an idea of putting a wire fence on a slant to reduce height and preserve the view but haven't thought it through enough.

Bat shit comes off walls easily. Got a guy out there doing it now. Don, the vet pilot, is flying down a compressor and spray guns and offered to let me use it. Can paint interior and exterior in two days total. He suggests bringing paint from the States. Want to start trenching operation in neighbor's yard in the next day or so. One of the yard men pointed out that because of the lot's slope, come the rains, water and mud will run over the tiled area that he had just cleaned. Will build a low brick wall to divert mud and water but must get permission to run a drainage pipe through our wall and into the Bours' orchard. Gustavo hopes to get that done tonight.

Still no electricity. A major problem has been getting door and shutters, etc., to function. I've been the oiler and just about used up an entire can of 3-in-1. After much effort, got the lock and door open on the shed. Pleasant surprise. Found a new hopper and sink and a miscellany of pipes and plumbing fixtures that the Smollens brought to do the guesthouse. Have been living in the kitchen and dining room for two days on a borrowed Sonoran cot from Armida. As a consequence, the light pours in and I've been getting up about 5:00 and hitting the sack before 10:00.

The shower works great but needs you to pick out a soap dish. Also, the two car garage isn't. The doors open inward which necessitates parking six feet away from the doors to close the damned things. Will redesign and get them to open outward and play around with the ramp area so two cars can be off-street parked. Still no electricity so will go check and see and notify or whatever. Much amor, E.

P S With the help of Gustavo, solved the electrical emergency. One of the wall men blew the wiring to half the house while trying to cement in a damaged outlet. Gustavo solved the problem in one minute and everything is working just dandy. For awhile I thought it was back to the Somar Motel. Things are winding down now. The palm tree quartet knocked off after completing the second tree and I estimate one-and-a-half days for the balance. The roofers and my two general workers split and a somewhat chastened wall man is using the balance of mud before Tecate time begins.

Got an approach for the portales potbelly from a mansion-living center-city gringo who called Mrs. Smollens to try it and was referred to me. I told him that I was interested, would talk to you and then went home and looked at it. It is a good one if your bag happens to be potbellies.

Either the heat is less intense or I am acclimating. Fans and showers do the trick. However, a bedroom air conditioner is an essential luxury. A few space heaters are also very much in order as well as an electric blanket. 'Nuff writ.

Love again and hope that all goes great, E

Summer 1988

Work has started. Took maestro number two off wall plastering and have him and two peons roof plastering on the dome and sealing the old roof to avoid another catastrophe in case of rain. The dome men are still behind and trying to catch up. At 7:30, I have to go and load the truck with cement.

Don't know what happened to Umberto; he's having ulcer problems and maybe his pride is hurt because he couldn't do the domes the way he thought he could. Personnel problems suck. The toothbrush house looks mighty good to me at times like this. (Suzanne Chartrand's present house was for sale when we were looking.) Will just muddle along and hope for the best.

If Guadalupe Camarena comes by today I'll ask him about maybe finding another maestro and crew to continue on the casita and later the pool to see if things could be moved along a bit faster during the next week. There is no way I'm going to start on the front rooms 'til after January1.

Off to get cement. Bought another 1,500 pounds of cement. This place ingests it, 22,000 pounds so far. Came back and made coffee for Guadalupe and told him my problems. He is going to try to line up another maestro who worked for him for years to try to speed things up around here. If Umberto continues to no-show, I'll let him go. He may or may not have a stomach ulcer but things have to keep moving. I will speak to Armida first.

Nellie, the one-morning-a-week cleaning girl, arrived and despite my efforts she faces a real challenge. She has started night school to learn English. The ex-seminarian-cum-artist gave her a scholarship with Medellin to increase her employability at one of the hotels or as a maid. Nice kid, works hard, and would be worth considering for full time when and if we can get this place together.

The garden is jumping. Learned yesterday that it rained four inches. That could well be half the annual rainfall in Sells, AZ. Ran into the Preeces during plaza festivities yesterday. Bill said he'll call you this week. Told him you bought tile and got the same deal he did. Sounds good. Sorry about my panic over it but I expect Gustavo went to a different place. I'm off to the Mercado to get out of Nellie's way and get my daily ration of tortillas and Runner food, milk, bananas, etc.

Will get this in the mail en route and hope that it arrives before you leave.

We love and miss you, R and Me

P.S. Guadalupe C. just popped in to tell me the new maestro will be completing his present job Wednesday and will be free to start here on Thursday. He added that he also knows a bit about plumbing and electricity—and away we go. He also figures that we are two-to-three months away from completion. Now, Mercado

More love, R and me.

Sunday

Dear Joan,

Whilst drying off from twenty laps preparatory to getting dressed for Sunday night street food, decided to start a fresh, crisp, new epistle summarizing the weekend so far.

Goofed off and swam Saturday noon, got somewhat garbed appropriately and did the Tesoros for perhaps the second time since you split. Pember and Bet just returned from three months' absence. Pember looks the same, quite proud of his scars, flashed the leg, the one where they get a vein. I suggested that he and Ole Bill get together to see which one has the biggest scar. Bet says she was terribly sorry to have missed you and looks forward to your October visit, as does Runner. Gen and Pancho were there along with Gen's youngest son, Douglas. He is a dealer in Vegas, the bounciest of the three boys. The day he came, Lincoln departed for the three weeks Doug will be here to visit kids in Colorado. We moved the party to Polo's for steak. I promised to be in the Plaza between 7:30 and 8:00 p.m. so they can try out a new camera on pictures of R and their little, fat kid. I agreed with the proviso that we get prints. More later.

Got home about 8:30, fed R and bedded down. Polo and kid never showed. Sunday at 8:00 collected Ole Bill and did Tianguis, chicken, fruits and veggies, etc. On my way home, ran into Candy Joe and we decided to go to the good restaurant he was bragging about. I felt like goofing off for the day and doing some exploring, so we picked up his wife and we went to a tiny town near Huatabampo and looked at an exhibition of Mayo weaving.

Then we went to the house of a Mayo chief, or so Joe claimed, and looked at masks, carvings, drums, etc. The home was two rooms crowded with people and dogs and thick with artsy stuff. It had carved jaguars poking out of the cornice in front and a sign in Mayo and Spanish inviting people to come in and look. The chief (?) was fairly young and very enthusiastic about his stuff. Maybe 100 or more wood and skin masks, many over 50 years old, his personal collection. He said that he's trying to get guys to replicate some of the older ones for sale but doesn't expect to have any until October. It was all artifacts and squalor except for a large TV/VCR and enough tapes to start a store.

Since we were close, we went to Huatabampito. R played in the ocean. Good beach and reasonably clean. When R realized I wasn't going in the water, he tried to get something going with three boys in the 10-to-12 age category. We then drove about a mile and house-looked. Some elegant, others one room and palapa-roofed. Joe said that most of them belong to Navojoa farmers.

Then we went to Yavaros, about eight miles away, a big fishing port larger than Rocky Point, and walked around. The shrimp season had just started; the crop pays 7,000 pesos per kilo. We were offered shrimp, giant blues at 10,000 pesos a kilo, less than $2.00 USD a pound. Had a beer at Tesoros, paid my monthly bill and Ramon told me he pays 15,000 pesos a kilo but the price will decline as the season progresses. Wish I could eat the damned things, but we can pick some up when you come down, freeze 'em and you can have pig-outs in Sells.

At the goat place, about a pound of meat was served caldo style in a broth. You add onions, lime, chile verde and salt to taste and either spoon the stuff out or make tacos. They served limitless commercial corn tortillas and some of the people were making a couple of tacos to take home from the most generous meat portion.

Then home to Álamos, a hosing of R to remove sand. Then downtown to dinner and bed. Also, did 20 laps. Leg has healed but will still try to take it easy. Limping is boring.

Lalo is back on the job. Claimed he fell and injured a hand. It looked slightly puffy. More later. Gustavo called, will be here with Douglas in tow to place confirmation of tile order and to see if truck is loaded before we mail (telegraph) dinero.

Tuesday

Couldn't quite put the tile thing together yesterday. We'll give it a shot today. Planning on meeting Douglas and Gustavo at the bank, where we'll pick up cash to carry to the telegraph office. Did call Dolores Hidalgo; they have the stuff and are getting it boxed and prepared to ship.

The big thing coming is a weeklong music festival. Ran into Allen who with Carlos, the student captain of the soccer team, are in the process of forming a group for the occasion. Lalo is stepping up to sing a song or two and predicts the new peon will once again win a prize as the best young musician in town. Lalo told me that his father was for years Allen's guitar maestro and taught the Tesoros guys and others. He died of alcoholism before he could teach his kid, but like the Bach family, there's something to be said about inherited talent. Lalo claims he is completely self-taught but his problem as a performer is his "timido." Miles Davis never looked at his audience.

Anyway, if I have the energy I'll go and see and listen a few nights. Last year I went a couple of times but couldn't hack it because I was too beat up with the gnats. Things are somewhat more under control now, though I still occasionally crash at 9:00 p.m.

It's really a cool morning and I have already fished out leaves from the pool. Have a routine going that's fairly simple. Figured out that the brown stains on the pool sides come from the pipes that hadn't been used for years. Pember says that there's stuff you can get in the States that solves the problem. Put it on the "things to bring" list.

Took care of banking, wiring money etc., and waiting for Gustavo to come and place final phone call to Dolores Hidalgo confirming everything. Still out a little over $700. Did not get my Schwab statement and am curious as to whether or not the annuity has started to flow into my account. Patience! Patience!

Up bright and early. Did the pool: swept, checked chemicals, etc. This weekend will clean the filter, also stretch on a new screen. Had a copper ring made to cut down on rust and bought new mesh. Cindy the dog has passed heat so R is calm. Mornings are chilly and it warms up nicely, low 80s during the day. I think the monsoon season is tapering off. Just an occasional sprinkle and no fireworks in the sky.

Work is going along. The sala edging is about complete and will have plaster patching done in the bedroom. The window ledge is in poor shape. Calalo is still busy in the bathroom. An incredible amount of carpentry is required to construct the frame to lay the brick up to the ceiling. Picky, tricky work involved. Lalo has about finished the doors and I will have him clean and re-paint jambs, window bars, etc. Will then have Calalo install the hot water system for casita, washer and complete wiring while Manuel brick floors the bathroom.

Problem I hadn't considered: much of the old brick comes in slightly different sizes, so to get them approximately the same it is necessary to cut them down. A time-consuming pain in the ass.

Got my phone bill, so off to bank to pay same.

Larry and Kay Lamar are back for a week or so. He's the guy who called you to get hold of Bill Preece to fly his 90-year-old artist mother down. He had half a lung removed, big C. Prognosis is excellent. He quit smoking over a dozen years ago, as did his wife Kay. They live on a ranch a few miles out and run the whole thing on solar energy. Interesting operation which you'll have to see. Off to el banco, more later.

August-September 1988

Monday 7:00 a.m.

Joan,

We're off to the races. Four men are assassinating the bougainvillea with machetes. They'll dig the roots, transplant the roots, and pray. The gravel you love is being moved and I made the decision to level the guesthouse and start fresh. Some of the original adobe is pretty soft and Umberto said it would be faster and better to start from scratch rather than add-on. He estimated that it will take about six weeks to complete.

We checked out the Mansion bathroom. No problems. Ours will have considerably more space to work in. Went to Navojoa and spent about $1,000 USD on cement, etc. Will check on brick fabrication progress Thursday and pay another $800 USD, the first half, the balance upon delivery.

Been trying to phone you unsuccessfully at Polo's. Did meet a man named Walter Taylor, an archeologist who has been digging in northern Mexico for over 50 years. He is a retired academic who has evidently written a few books on ancient Sonoran Indians. He invited me to join him for drinks and dinner later in the week.

Runner thinks he's the job site supervisor. He's just sitting and watching the men at work. He finds my sitting and writing boring. Got to go.

We need a crow bar. Aha, something interesting happened. Visited Gustavo to talk about a telephone and mentioned the tearing down of the casita. He came with Pancho to look. There is a distinct possibility that its total demise might be to extend job time, tearing down, hauling out, new wiring, floors, etc. With work scarce and premium wages being paid, Umberto may have tried to hustle an extra week or two. He'll have to be watched.

Gustavo checked the walls and they are strong. So, they will be extended and the original, fireplace included, preserved. Very interesting. Need a bunch of wood tools. Pancho offered to lend me some with the understanding that I replace any that are damaged. Fair enough. Currently awaiting a couple hundred 50 kilo sacks of cement, lime, etc. The crew is tearing out part of the brick path and assaulting the cement roof with pick and crowbar.

The gardener was by to tell me, or rather ask me, if I liked beans. They are different than any I've seen before, long and skinny. I was waiting for them to fatten up. I'll try some tonight.

Runner is still out there watching the roof come down. I join him from time to time. It seems that every owner of a bitch in town is propositioning me for his services. I try to explain that the pups might grow to become peligroso and they back off. The latest was the corner grocery store owner, whose dog plays with Runner daily. Another thing we have to do is measure the truck and the car to determine whether it is possible to open the garage to accommodate side-by-side parking or extend it into the garden. Our neighbor, Genevive Reynolds, said she's too lazy to put hers in the garage and some kids took it joy riding and wrapped it around a tree. It still lives outside.

Just checked the casita. The first layer of concrete and brick is about gone and they are shoveling dirt to get to the next layer of brick and then come the beams. Will quit now to go banking. I'm down to about $25 USD in the account. Later, Babe.

Later! Semi-successful in the banking world. It took an hour and a half to make a VISA transfer. I also wanted to pop in $500 USD cash to bring the balance up to 4 million pesos but by the time I got through the line they were no longer accepting dollars. Back mañana at 10:00 sharp. The beams are coming out now and being stacked against the palm trees. They've carefully saved a lot of the brick which will be incorporated in the reconstruction. Still waiting for the cement truck, after which I'll need a new shovel from the hardware store for cement mixing, and so it goes. Will drop this in the mail later. New address is Box 25, Álamos, Sonora.

Love, R & E

Tuesday

Dearest Joan,

Missed the P.O. so continue another day of Álamos chronicle and it was a big one. Went into Navojoa to buy pick, shovels, nails, lumber, etc., with Bill, the ancient, sick electrician who can't read because he needs glasses, and Armida, who had to see her lawyer.

The work crew has been busting ass. The beams are out. A few were so badly rotted that it was a miracle that they didn't go. Front wall is gone, doors and windows stored. The wall leading to the bathroom has been taken down partially to allow for a door and the extension. Tomorrow forms will be made for the foundation of the addition which may even be poured. Wow!

A threat of rain passed but we found a back-up solution for wall brick and located sources already made just in case. Armida gives you her best. Will be trying to line up a truck to haul off tons of adobe which smothers the sidewalk in front, as well as bring in clean, cement-grade sand later tonight. Lord, the days seem long and endless. If I don't tonight, I'll be hot on the trail after checking on the cement tomorrow. Will also be trying to figure out the electricity scheme tomorrow to determine what to bring down from the States.

Tom Cook dropped in this afternoon. He and Mary may try to hitch a ride back with me. I'm planning on leaving Friday or Saturday as we discussed.

Bought yards and yards of heavy duty black plastic to serve as temporary cover in case of rain in the dining room and bathroom. All fixtures, cabinets, and furniture will be shifted to the front rooms and kitchen when the roofs come off. I'll keep an island of living space in the kitchen and the contractor will figure out some way for me to use the bathroom. He may have to remove and/or shield the stove and one counter.

Was advised to bring down a 50 pound bucket of tile glue, which I will do. It is supposed to be much better than the local stuff. Incidentally, a few tile have come loose in the kitchen and must be replaced or re-glued. Grains of sand compared to the enormity of the tasks ahead. Runner still thinks he is the supervisor and camps under a tree to watch the action.

Had all the work I needed done on the Toyota. It looks almost new and it has been cleaned inside and out. Tomorrow at 11:00 a.m. I've got to haul a load of lumber which will undoubtedly crud it up some. Can't be helped. All for the moment. Off to hunt a truck.

Continuation—lined up Gustavo's bro Poz who will deliver a load of sand tomorrow to move out a load of busted adobe. While I was on the phone talking to you, the police came by to ask Gustavo to serve as an interpreter for Tim of Tim and Lorrie. The latter is in jail for threatening to kill Lorrie's uncle, a big domestic conflict. As happens, when police come to a person's house, passersby stop to watch. As I was leaving, mi amigo Manuel and two of his cowboy friends were there and invited me to join them for a beer. I think Manuel is in love with Runner. One of his friends, who he had mentioned to me before, lives on an ejido ranch with large stands of amapa and a bit of palapa palm. He'll let Manuel know how much new amapa costs. The lore of amapa is that it can only be cut during the full moon if it is to endure hundreds of termite-free years. Since I have a full construction plate at the moment, if new amapa is doable and not prohibitively expensive, I'll try to arrange delivery by December. Perfect palm-cutting takes place in late October so I'll order enough for a casita portales and a roof-top palapa. Busy, busy, busy and lots of shooting from the hip. At Lincoln we used to call it strategic planning designed specifically to accommodate unpredictable variables. It's now 10:00 p.m. Faithful wolf has crashed and I'm off the join him. We love you, girl.

Wednesday

Drinking coffee and getting ready to go to market. Runner's outside making sure that everybody's working. Will be meeting with Gustavo to set up nominal supervision until Runner comes back and leave him some contingency money for materials, etc. Will also take a look at the truck/trailer combo he told me about. Slight problem regarding the guesthouse fireplace. Parts are infiltrated with roots that will have to be dissected out to avoid major structural damage, if not total replacement. It is a result of years of neglect. Coming across a lot of similar surprises, nothing major, but still a pain in the ass.

Took a break to hit the market for fruits and veggies. The wild chiltepines are coming out of the mountains now and some of the merchants have pickled them in garlic/vinegar. I want to find out what to do with them and maybe buy a liter bottle and decant in smaller jars for gifts. If they are like the dried ones, one the size of a cranberry will either cauterize your piles or perform a hemmorhoidectomy within 12 hours of consumption.

Met a Swede named Peter Hed going to market. He's been living here nine years and likes it. Off to the P.O. to mail this and maybe get your letter. Love and stuff, R & E.

Saturday

Dear Joan,

Another epistle begins. Couldn't mail the last so will see if I can find somebody going stateside to do it for me. Post Office closed today. The Obregon fisher folk showed, did the house tour and are now at the museum. I'll take them to the Tesoros and send them on their way. Fishing has been lousy and flies grab them on the water. I'll wait 'til next year.

Caught a pilot on his way back to Phoenix to mail letter. Went to a crazy party to raise money for a local prep school. The garden in which it was held looked like a Hollywood movie set. The students served food (terrible) and drinks and did the entertainment. Dancing, singing etc. Pretty awful. Left Runner with landlady. He howled and then tried to undo the chain with his paws. Finally she called the chocolate lab, who calmed him down and stayed with him until I returned. I received the most effusive greeting ever, jumping, wriggling and dancing between my legs.

The water shortage seems to have all the Americans uptight. It was all I heard about at the party. I was advised to sound the well to determine depth by the people who live on the corner of the street the house is on. Will do it today. Lalo's eye was not repaired. They jabbed it twice with a needle to do a nerve block for anesthesia and struck out. They'll take another stab (pun unintentional) next month.

Thursday

Saw Hilde yesterday. Gustavo developed preliminary figures. We are talking 28,000 USD for Mrs. Smollens, 32,000 USD for us, which is okay. Had a young contractor walk the roof, etc., to determine just how bad it really is. It is bad. The portales beams which Gustavo estimated could be saved may be too far gone. The wood is punky and he could push my penknife into them up to the hilt with no problem. My present thinking is to go with amapa if I can round them up in sufficient quantities. Must decide whether to use the good ones in the house if they can be stripped or whitewashed as in the Polos' house. Also whether or to use amapa in the portales to replace the rotted pine, or continue with concrete.

Decisions decisions! Of major concern is the time it can take to run the paperwork, which is very complex to say the least. If it goes on too long, the rainy season comes and roof work is impossible. If it's neglected the roof may go and take out windows, etc. My feeling is to discuss this with Gustavo and see if my earnest money or a portion thereof could be used to temporarily shield the roof against rain, with Mrs. Smollens splitting the cost in exchange for an option to buy that covers a period sufficient to complete all paperwork to result in a clean title.

My Spanish class is going well and I'm beginning to feel more comfortable learning all kinds of construction and ranch terms. Runner is quite happy and beginning to show an interest in the lab pups who opened their eyes a few weeks ago. He's also beginning to play a little with Craig's horse. He barks and the horse is supposed to chase him.

We are still into communal cooking. Craig went fishing at San Carlos and brought back about 10 kilo of fillets, a fish called salmon. It's not even remotely related to the ones we're are familiar with, but good.

Have been trying to phone you and it's most frustrating. A couple times I couldn't get a line to the States. Tried for three hours at Polos' last night and you were out. Really miss you and my scribbling must sustain me.

Big news this morning was a drug bust in the wee hours of a dealer staying at the Mansion, complete with Federales armed with machine guns. A little excitement for the guests.

Saturday

Great talking to you on the phone re: tax matter. Did nothing. Sometimes you win, sometimes you don't.

Can do amapa beams, located a few stashes. Gustavo has started paperwork and I'm going to find a lawyer to review everything to make sure I get a clean title. I am tentative about certain legal aspects such as joint ownership, etc., and want to do the smart thing for us. Will be checking the house today and taking assorted measurements. Will also start making a list of things to bring from the States, such as roofing nails, and maybe wire, piping, etc., which are supposedly of better quality.

Also need a lot of information on moving stuff into the country. Thinking of visiting consular office in Tucson to get the straight dope. Some people bring stuff in problem-free. Tom Cook said he was turned back twice with a van load of stuff. Others have used stripped down RVs, filled them with furniture, and moved entire households in a couple of trips. The old school bus at Ziggy's shop would lend itself to that operation if it is not already sold.

Also want to touch base with the US Dept. of Agriculture to learn about termites and talk to Tucson roofers concerning materials and design. Need to talk to pool people. Was going to ask Pember Nuzum to look at it but learned this ayem that he's sick and may need a pacemaker. A shame. Will sign off now, hit the market and measure the house. Later, love.

House size interior is about 1,500-to-1,600 square feet. Must check, may have goofed in transcribing figures, and it might be 100 square feet bigger. Had a bit of rain the night before and there's a puddle four inches deep on the low spot over the bathroom/dining room. Must be fixed before summer rains hit. Plan to put tin on bad section, i.e., front rooms, dining and bathroom, to keep house dry until September/October, weighted with brick and pitched to drain rather than risk possible cave-in. Tin can later be incorporated in permanent roof to cover foam insulation, since there will be no nail holes.

Been reviewing details concerning legal aspects of ownership, pretty complex and possibly time-consuming. Will be signing a purchase contract and making a deposit to cover roof expenses ($81,000 USD or so) pending receipt of clean title. We will have to decide on joint ownership, you or me, when I return. The latter two options will require your presence before a Mexican notary.

Runner injured his leg. Went to Mocuzari Lake and he cavorted in the muck and mire. His lower three-quarters were covered in a black, stinking mud, so ran him a few miles behind the car to bath him in the Mayo River. The next day he started limping. Hop it is just a sprain. If not better by tomorrow, off to the vet.

Talked to the contractor yesterday. If the front portal cannot be saved and must be replaced in toto, can have five arches built at $100 USD per and go the rest of the way with amapa beams and either brick or wood struts for a ceiling. An interesting possibility. Sure wish you were here to help kick some ideas around.

Sunday a.m.

Runner still limping; doesn't seem as bad as yesterday so will keep him off his feet to the extent possible. Will drive to Tianguis and later to the prison to buy a belt. Poor guy. It was a tad chilly last night and slept under an Indian blanket that weighed a ton. Must get cracking and see Gustavo about contract and earnest money to cover roof. Later, Love.

Back from the Tianguis. One of the benefits of living in Mexico is cheap food. Bought a bucket of oranges for 70 cents that converted into one-and-a-half quarts of the world's best orange juice.

Missed Gustavo so will drive by later. Will also re-check house measurements and have Richard thoroughly massage the portal beams. Lalo set up his basket operation outside the front door. Very clever. He borrowed our two wood chairs and a bentwood crèche that Craig is bringing back to his pregnant sister to help enhance his display. In addition, he is sitting in the hallway strumming a guitar to further entice tourists. No sale so far. A bus just pulled in front, blocking him off from the Plaza. He argued successfully and the driver moved.

Lunch: egg burros with homemade tortillas. Eggs are extra large, bright yellow/orange, stand-up yolks at 45 cents per dozen. How does that grab you? No more forgetting to buy fresh eggs outside of Tucson.

Monday after class

Runner's leg is better. Class was rough. Future past and past imperfect tenses, much study needed. House interior is 1,550 square feet más o menos. Mrs. Smollens owes three years' taxes and three years' bank trust maintenance. Gustavo was to contact her and get her to rush a check to the bank before the house can be sold. Why he waited 'til yesterday to do this is a mystery. When I return, I'll immediately send Gustavo "earnest money." I forgot to bring a check, which he'll need to show the bank there's a buyer. It just ain't simple. Couldn't find an exiting tourist to take the mail. May beat it home. Miss you mucho, love and stuff, Me.

September 1988

Dear Joan,

Trip down with my saving angel mechanic was uneventful, piece of cake. The car was not inspected, $2 at the border and a wave bye at the second check point. Álamos has been and may still be in the middle of the mayoral inauguration ceremonies, a three and possibly four day fiesta, mucho musica, caballeros and beautiful young girls strutting in their Sunday-goin'-to-meeting raiment.

The rains came and the world is verdant. The gardener cleared out all the debris and floats in a sea of assorted zinnias. He did the kitchen garden in staggered stages and some of it is tasselling out. A bunch of beans, again successive plantings, are popping. Limes are coming on. Thirty plus inches of rain did no appreciable damage. The guavas lived and the old bamboo jungle is pushing to touch the moon.

When we arrived, Runner jumped into the pool, which has a few feet of green rain water and a solitary frog, for a dip. His claws couldn't grip the algae-greased concrete to get out. I started stripping to attempt a rescue and saw an aluminum ladder, which we lowered. He studied it for a few seconds, swam over and climbed the rings like a natural man. It was spooky.

Friday morning we went to visit Merv Larson, the guy who's redoing the hospital, who is a long time friend of Jim Coon, the mechanical savior. He's already got big bucks tied up and unbelievable plantings going. He's even brought things from Africa to see if these work. His company did Loews Ventana, the place you and Gert stayed at in Phoenix, the Desert Museum, and just landed a $100,000,000 contract to do a new zoo in Tokyo. He needs some bamboo and ours is an especially good variety according to Jim, who told him we have just what they are looking for. I offered and he'll be over to dig some and will I ever pick his brain in exchange.

Visited Armida to locate her nephew Umberto , the contractor. He and his crew are finishing a job and will start next week. This week we'll be measuring and buying materials, drain the pool so it can be patched and painted, buy the fencing and chat with a dome person. Gustavo advised me to buy and store everything I can lay my hands on if I can. Last night's TV predicted a 5000 devaluation to the dollar peso by November now that the election madness is gone, so I'll be busy dickering for beams ASAP. One problem which may be major, Umberto wants to finish the pool and fence and get on with the guesthouse with no break, and I told him we have no plans to roll. I can copy the Mansion bathroom; already spoke to the lady, but have no idea of what provisions to make for the darkroom and how wide to do the casita, una problema. I told him I would think about it, but my inclination is to stall for a couple of weeks until I can show him some shit on graph paper.

Emergencia!!! Took Jim to the bus depot in Navojoa. He had to get back to meet his mamma. Because of the holidays, busses were at capacity so he took a cab back. We went to the Tesoros and there is a train out tonight that hits Nogales. He will be on it. Also, an American who runs a flying school in Scottsdale is instituting a charter service. Seventy dollars from Phoenix, but he left yesterday and nobody seems to know when he'll return. The Mexican airline which reopened only goes as far as Hermosillo. Pity. So it looks like a Cuchajaqui day. Did it yesterday; it was great. Bought Runner food and staples in the Navojoa supermarket. Didn't find prices of canned goods, etc., appreciably cheaper. Interested in outcomes of the devaluation; more later or mañana.

A las lunes. Still sweating Jim problems. After four phone calls to the depot, we figured out that the holiday would close it but assumed the trains would run. Tried for the 10:30 p.m. SRO Express. It was late; we waited along with several hundreds of local folk. Learned that it wouldn't arrive until 5:30 ayem; returned to Álamos, squishing a possum en route, and crashed at 1 ayem. Got up early and checked an American going to Phoenix. He said, "No room." He lied. More phone calls. Lalo's bro, Pancho, suggested Obregon's bus depot which runs a local to the border and agreed to go along to help mordita the ticket seller and bus driver. Depot chock-a-block with desperate people trying to go back to jobs in the north who had already bribed the ticket-takers.

Off to the train station to catch Mexico's mail and milk train, also SRO. Left Jim on line with a friendly local couple who spoke English and agreed to look after him. On the way back noticed an addition to a motel under construction using domes. Pulled in, admired the domes and met the maestro who was imported from Queretero by the architect to do domes specifically. With Pancho's help I explained our project, learned that the price was something I can live with and that it would take him about a week to make 'em. He's coming out tomorrow to take measurements and prepare a materials list and advise the locals on how to prepare the walls for his specialty act.

Returned to Álamos to have Umberto meet him at 5:00 p.m. Couldn't find him but left word with his mother, wife, and Armida, his aunt. Gustavo, who is planning to complete the little house he showed us, might want to do a room or two and will also be here. The "major domo" is planning to go home for two to three weeks, which will give me a chance to line up materials and get walls built to accommodate domes. The timing is tricky but I'm going to try to orchestrate everything with a major assist from Gustavo to cover my absence in Arizona. May just get the house shelled and rely on the dome man to suggest main room dimensions and build walls accordingly, and worry about interiors and bathroom—sink, hopper, shower placement—after we play the graph paper game. Fading fast and must meet a 6:00 a.m. trucker to contract for a trash removal. Miss you, Me.

Álamensen Notes, Martes

Up at 5:30. Appear to get up earlier here. Expect it has something to do with the weather. Do things early, hide home in the afternoon, and get moving again. It was chilly last night and I needed a blanket. Bad news. Termites had their way on the curved wood chairs. The originals. I will return them to see if they can be fixed and am awaiting Gustavo, who will mix me a potion to apply to the new ones.

Another Álamos bulletin: Shit's out of the garage. You could eat off the floor. You can also park a truck which, heretofore, had been living in the street. The plumber came by and the pool is being pumped out. It has been running for about four hours and still has a ways to go. Someone at the door.

Back. Pancho was by trying to sell furniture for a friend who needs money. Told him that was your department. He was followed by Manuel, the young rancher who tried to sell us an L-shaped lot behind his house last year. He told me that the rain saved his cattle. The town of Concordia in Sinaloa is where furniture is made. That's where the Cooks went to furnish their villa. He also offered to keep me company when I go to Navojoa in a couple of hours. The pool is drained and dirty. Will get someone to clean it out and the plumber will work on the drain so that it can be filled in as well as install the new system smuggled in from the States and repair one leaky faucet. Off to Navojoa. To be continued.

9:00 p.m.

Just returned from Navojoa where I dropped the domer. He measured everything, three domes. Dining room starting at major beam where original house ended, requiring removal of the new beams, guesthouse and bathroom. Tomorrow I go with Umberto, the local maestro, and order 10,000 bricks. They are not a standard size and must be custom-crafted, baked, etc., which will take awhile. In the meantime, the old roofs must come off, build a bit higher in the casita and dining room, and steel reinforced concrete beams made to interface between the wall and the dome. The latter will be nippled with cupola skylights. They'll cost a bundle, but that's the price one must pay for beauty. Just realized that this is the first English I've used today. Wow! Must feed Runner and self. Goodnight.

Up at 5:30

Cool last night and needed a blanket. Have some minor banking to do and plan a mission of mercy for the Cooks. Their American car died for lack of parts and gave Tom a lift home with a load of groceries. A major "shlep." I plan on taking them marketing. Also, will start cleaning the pool for patching and painting and see if the chairs can be saved. Later, will meet with Umberto to try to put the brick thing together. Currently waiting for a girl to come by to mop, dust, etc. Plan on using her about once a week.

Screwed up and forgot to take the drip irrigation material to measure. If I'm lucky, Don the vet will fly in and since he's done it, I'm sure to get some advice. Also plan on visiting Ron Slaughter, the guy who bought Casa Azul and was redoing all the tile, to learn what I can. Still haven't figured out a good way to solve the timing dilemma while I'm gone. My options seem to be a contract with Umberto to finish the prep work for the dome man at a fixed rate or keep him and his crew on an hourly rate and hire Gustavo or an American lady (Judy McClain), who does this sort of thing for Americans who want their houses worked on during their summer absence. Ron used her and I'll check out his degree of satisfaction. There is also the question of availability. We'll see as this day progresses. I really wish you were here and miss you much. Will get this in the mail and hope it arrives before me. All my love, Runner and me

P. S. Just had a good idea. Rather than have a few truckloads of rock and cement carted in to do the pool and driveway, I can use the shit that comes off the casita roof and walls for fill. There should be more than enough and it would eliminate hauling in and out. I'll then concentrate on amapa beams and fencing over the next ten days.

Take care and more love.

Monday, September 19, 1988

Dear Joan,

Been a full day so far and it ain't over. Bob Dunn's down for a week. Said he spoke to you to see if you were free. Pity you weren't. We miss you. Ole Bill came by. Says he isn't feeling too well. He's always in bed and I assume asleep when I look in on him. Dan Reynolds was by to bring me money. Gen was headed for the bank and I gave her a check since I was broke. Then Don Coleman drifted in. We played in the pool. I'm going over there. He's roasting pork and I'm doing applesauce.

I've made a discovery and must credit you for making it possible. Apples can keep for a long time, since you were here, and survive without getting moldy. Avocados can't. Little did I realize that the bag leaking in the fridge was your attempt at miscegenating apples and más. They don't mix any better than apples and oranges.

Paid my IRS quarterly, only four days late this time. Just can't seem to make more than half my payments on time. Also mailed the TIAA tax form you sent; it indicates October 1 payment. We'll see. I still haven't got the monthly Schwab statement. Who the hell knows where they sent it? Already called and asked for a duplicate. Also got the July-August electric bill, 70 pesos, which includes air and pool. Es nada and they are peak months.

Must check applesauce and head on out. Dick is coming quickly and I don't like to deal with cattle gates in the dark. More later.

Apple sauce is done, used a piece of piloncillo instead of sugar. Needs a shot of nutmeg. Maybe Don has some. I'm letting it cool in freezer before leaving. Don asked Cooks to come. Be interesting to see if they do. I'm afraid that the Mrs. weirded out. Nobody has seen her for a month. Tom does all the in-town shopping. I don't know if she's alive. Doug Reynolds was over to say hello. He used to run with their kids. Then offered coffee, no booze, no cigarettes. He stayed for a minute and split. He smokes, said they looked fine. We're off!!!!

9:45 p.m. We're back and waiting for R to finish din-din. No Cooks but Veronica was there, and reminisced about the good old days of Álamos when "the season" was hat and glove lunches for the ladies and the Nuzums were the new kids in town. I gather these early residents are now dead, gone or institutionalized. Population under 5,000 now. A mildly interesting evening, but staying awake and alert was a wee problem which I have solved since R has dined. G'night.

September 1988

We're talking bricks, 9,000 to 10,000, and having problems. Had inconclusive conversations with three yards that make a top quality product which is governed by the clay they use.

They are all producing at capacity with large order backlogs because bricks can't be cured during the monsoon season. We need ours by October 20 to meet the domer's work schedule. Will be meeting with another brick-maker tomorrow night. If he falls through, will have to try Navojoa and Obregon yards or rent a machine to cut standard bricks to the required size. My mistake was not ordering them in June, but then I was uncertain about getting a dome man. We learn. We learn.

Had dinner at Armida's and there was Ole Bill, 76-year-old American from southern Idaho who is recuperating from open heart surgery. He's still mighty frail. I helped him open a bank account and took him to the JFK Institute. He wants to learn Spanish and is bored out of his gourd and needs something to do. He'll start class on Monday. He's a master electrician and has worked all over the world and would like to help wire our place in a couple of months when we are ready to roll. From a perusal of the darkroom, we can use all the help we can get. He guesses that the entire house can be rewired to meet American standards in a week to ten days after the construction is completed. Great.

With the exception of a couple of hours with him, and five minutes with the Cooks, it's been a heavy Spanish day. They have to use their car very carefully and plan where they park, because their reverse gear is gone. Found a tick crawling on Runner's ear so we are back to a nightly check. He really seems to enjoy it. Weary and bed tempts. With a tele-transported hug and kiss, goodnight.

Thursday

Up early per usual. Diddled around to let plumber in at 7:00. They've got the pool cleaned and are currently chipping away at the old drain to add new pipe to decrease depth. Pool construction comes to a sudden halt when this is done and the new pump and motor is hooked up. Then we wait until the casita roof comes tumblin' down to provide the fill debris. Later, plumber completed drain elevation. The deep end will be shoulder high. It was three meters deep and is now reduced to 1.5. We are either going to need conversion charts or learn the metric system down here.

Learned that if I hit the market by 7:00 a.m., can get meat scraps for Runner. Gave him a good hose bath today. He rolled in something dead in the lot across the street and stank. The market is fun to wander through slowly and pick out the perfect tomato, banana, etc.

Our limes are coming on fast and the guava trees not only survived but appear to have thousands of baby guavas growing daily. Margarita, the Casa Azul maid, played with Runner and asked about you. Went by looking for Ron Slaughter. He was buying shit in Navojoa. Spoke to Gustavo briefly. We were running in different directions. He told me about a truck and trailer for sale for $4500 USD. He wants the truck. Will look-see and talk more later on tomorrow. I'll be seeking the sacred brick this afternoon. Also located a good stash of amapa coming out of the portales of a government building. More than enough for our portales but whether they are big enough for the interior rooms remains to be seen.

Someone at the door. More later.

Later hath come. Picked and ate first lime and, biblically speaking, it was good. Also, checked corn patch. Mostly one ear per plant. Lack of fertilizer? Species? Must find out. Flowers are attracting legions of butterflies that take on, from a distance, the appearance of airborne blossoms. No, I'm not stoned. A bunch of papayas are growing nicely and I'll have some bananas poked in. They are pretty and give instant growth. The porch vine has purple flowers and red berries. No idea what it is. The tree under the classic mango is a screaming yellow, another unknown. Wish you were here to share it all. You'd freak. No mosquitoes but a most annoying gnat that strikes for about an hour at dusk. They must be related to the Sells bugs that bugged me on my desert walks before I left. You gotta keep moving.

Later, off brick-questing. Eeeeeeyah!! Got a brick man with two helpers lined up to do the 10,000 special numbers. He borrowed my wheelbarrow which is larger than those in Mexico and admired by all construction types. Be going by with Umberto to inspect for quality periodically. This is apparently how you buy brick. We're still looking for 2,500 to 3,000 standard bricks to enlarge the guesthouse, and to form support for the main house domes. Umberto doesn't believe that these will be as hard to find, though we failed three times tonight because of previous orders that remain to be met.

Tomorrow's tasks include getting a post office box and treating new bentwood furniture with oil, etc. The other chairs will be fixed for about $5 USD. I brought them over today and hope to pick them up next week. Still miss you mucho and now beddy-bye for Runner and me.

Love, us'ens

Day started out as a bummer. Had chores to do and people to see but the car wouldn't start. Did a differential diagnosis. No water in the battery. It and some other minor stuff is being fixed at the mechanic at the bottom of the hill. Until then, I'm grounded. Will spend the afternoon checking out circular staircases and finding out when the palapa palms are cut for storage so I can reserve some. Also looked at amapa, perhaps enough to do the portales. Will have Umberto check length, quality and price. On and about my errands.

Bye

Back, car's not done. They were in the middle of cleaning and polishing. Gustavo was siesta-ing. With Hilde guru-ing in India, it looks like he moved in his family. Brothers, nephews, nieces, etc., all of whom were walking tippy-toe and whispering while "the great provider" gets his rest. Gonna sosh it up tonight. Dinner at Armida's and then beer at the Caricol with the Cooks. Imagine I'll be busy supply hunting in Navojoa tomorrow, and Sunday's blocked out to try and arrive at some fairly detailed planning, which should include approximate costs and construction schedule. Will also take measurements, etc., to replicate Mansion's bathroom with a proviso for extra cabinetry and counter space for the darkroom. This is it.
Love, E

Wednesday, October 12, 1988

Dear Joan

Trip down was uneventful. With three gas stops and car insurance transfer, made it down in nine-and-a-half hours. There is now less than ten miles of one lane road between Nogales and Hermosillo and work is going on between Navojoa and Obregon. I was amazed at the rate of progress on the guesthouse. It looks as if we'll make the 20th deadline. However, the dome maestro was by last week and wasn't sure whether or not he'll start his magic on that date or the 26th.

Checked brick about an hour ago—5,000 dome brick were being readied for firing and will be delivered Saturday. The brick men are readying the next batch for midweek delivery. The other brick sits on the portal and is being incorporated in the building. Tomorrow, they will do the bathroom door with each. They had to take down the fireplace—pity, and a few hundred bricks but 'tis only money.

Having a problem getting the fridge going. Bill, the aging electrician, believes that it could be poor wiring in the kitchen. He'll be by tomorrow to check it out as well as to give me a list of circuit breakers, a special junction box for the casita, darkroom, bathroom, etc., to be purchased in Navojoa. A serious (?) plumbing problem—interior will leak. Plumber due tomorrow.

Thursday

Bill was by. Have the electrical needs list. We are hoping that ITE circuit breakers are available in Navojoa to match the junction box. Could be sticky. He also suggested that I move the meter to a front room, closer to the source, because he suspects that the distance travelled on shitty wire might provide insufficient voltage to have it work properly. Had the crew move it and we wait. We also wait for the plumber to fix the leak and rough out casita according to your diagram. Waiting is the Mexican way of life.

Yesterday was Columbus Day here. Went to the bank this A.M. and the line was much too long because of the holiday mañana. The American Colony seems to be gradually drifting back from places north. Days are warm, nights cool and October 15 seems to be the time to start your hot water heater.

Runner is glad to be back supervising construction. Am now running four-and-a-half men to make sure the deadline is met. Should the maestro come on the 26th I'll start on the pool, the fence and the garage extension to accommodate two cars. Am currently keeping the truck at the neighbor's across the street so the garage can be kept open for sand, gravel storage, and brick delivery. Garden is doing well. The flowers are still blooming; green beans are great as is the corn. Gotta go. Más ahora.

The crew just left. A good day. The concrete pillars were cast in the casita. Tomorrow the arched doorway to the bathroom/darkroom will be made. The plumber never showed and he's got a pile of work to complete. Umberto will try to locate a couple of other plumbers. He suggests we go on a bid basis for the casita, leak repair and shifting the water tank.

Am resting the refrigerator for 24 hours to see if the Freon settles. It now sits in one of the front rooms. I hope all the bumps en route didn't do any damage. It would sure be nice to have cold things again. Today was pretty hot. Made a reservation at the Mansion for a single for 20-27 December. Will put a deposit down tomorrow.

If we can stick to the schedule, cabinets, mirrors, etc., will be removed from the bathroom and dining room Saturday. The roof will come down Monday and Tuesday and cement collars built to accommodate the domes. I'm wondering how livable the house will be. I may have to crash at the Somar for a week if it becomes too uncomfortable.

By the way, I opted for a brick bench in the bathroom instead of cement. We can decide whether or not we want to retain any exposed brick or plaster it over in the guesthouse when you get here. Will get Gustavo later and see if he will make a few phone calls to Navojoa for electrical equipment before I head into town.

Have been following Wolf Camp advice and feeding Runner at different times. He looks at me a little strange and is not sure whether he is supposed to eat at high noon or five at night. Wish it could be frozen and it will be. Ate at the Mansion with the very blond family. He's a retired airline pilot; they live near the airport, have their own plane and the son, age 19, starts airline pilot training school in January. They've been here a few years and the son speaks Spanish; the parents don't. They've had some tutoring from Gay and may sign up with JFK (I hope) in November so that I will no longer constitute a class of one.

Must wander down to the tienda, seek Gustavo, shower and, if I am up to it, have a coke or eat at the Tesoros. More later or mañana.

Friday

Mañana in la mañana. Things seem to be routinizing a bit which is good. The crew of five are working away like beavers finishing off the casita. Another day of waiting for the plumber. Met with Gustavo and will be Navojoa-bound to buy electricals after I put some money in the bank. My total payroll runs $160 USD for a six day week. I feel like a neo-colonialist.

Went to the Tesoros last night. Scrabble seems to be big down here so there will be plenty of action for you. Met some folks named Hill that have a center city manse with roof top palapas. When you come down you'll have a chance to check them out and decide on a wrought iron circular stairway, which may take a month or so to build. Would also like a wrought iron fence up there because of Runner and my own fear of heights. Everything takes time. Gustavo has not shown up and it is moving towards 9:00 a.m. Must head for the market shortly and will post this letter en route. P. O. is just around the corner. I hope it reaches Sells before you leave.

Our love, Run and E

Tuesday

Dear Joan,

Big things happening. The bathroom roof is off. Room looks a lot brighter. Appears as if some of the front room roof may have to be opened to build a collar to accommodate the dome. Won't have that problem as we move to the old dining room. Umberto has no firm opinion until he gets into the wall. My failure to insist that the fridge be turned so that the back faced the trunk wall turned out to be a $40 USD fuck-up. Also, the panel box I brought from the states will not work. Must go to Navojoa tomorrow to buy the right one—shit.

The Cooks came by and cleaned out the corn for chickens and the stalks for jackasses on their property. Will get going tomorrow on the kitchen garden. May also pick a bunch of what I thought were green beans. They are black-eyed peas. What do I know?

The plumber should have the gas hooked up properly before Runner and I head to the Tesoros for dinner as their guest. Huge piles of dirt, broken concrete and brick decorate the sidewalk in front of the house. Fresh truckloads of sand and gravel fill the garage. Nine guys working out there today are racing against the dome men's deadline. It is going to be a photo-finish.

Met the photographer lady (Susie Moore) briefly. She told me where she lives. She knows all about doing a darkroom. Will try to make it up there later today with your graph paper plan and the Kodak book for counsel on drains, venting, etc., while plumber and electricians are on the scene and can do any needed routing of pipes and wires while the place is exposed. Moved all my tools and electrical stuff in the living room. Learned that the plumber is a kleptomaniac. Tom Cook says that it is the price you pay for quality workmanship and he has been stealing stuff for years. He said that all I can do is make it a little difficult for him. No sense being outraged.

Runner made no attempt to scale the wall today even though we both heard the neighbor's dogs on the other side. Maybe he learned something from yesterday's experience. The next episode of R& E in mañana—to be continued.

Just made a momentous construction decision. The lintel of the dome housing will be slightly higher than the portales lip to provide good drainage off the dome. The beams in the bathroom were unbelievably bad. Without realizing it I was playing Russian roulette every time I shit and showered. Umberto predicts that many in the front room are in equally poor condition.

The sledgehammer and crowbar teams are now attacking the dining room roof and Alberto believes that he has figured out a way to remove it and concurrently protect the wall cabinets and counters without pulling them. It remains to be seen. The dust level is incredible. As the detritus tumbles, it stays on the floor to protect the tile. It is going to take a maid a week to clean things out when all is done. I'm beginning to feel like I am living in a bombed out house but the garden looks great.

Will be heading down to Armida's to rescue R's food from her refrigerator shortly. More later.

The stove works, as does the fridge. Life is beautifuller as a result of these little luxuries which in another time and place were necessities I took for granted. The sledge beats a tattoo on the roof. I hope that they'll break through before quitting time but am planning on being out of the house when it all comes tumbling down. Concrete is still being chipped and chiseled to reroute the water and sewerage lines. Don't have the energy to wander up prison hill to the lady photographer's. I'll take the plans with me and hope to catch her at the hotel. If not, mañana. To be continued.

Wednesday morning.

Shit's flying today. Amapa beams from the bathroom are marching through the living room to lie against the back wall of the kitchen garden. Dining room furniture has been stashed wherever it would fit. The house is without water because of pipe rerouting. I'm not exactly living in luxury. Met the lady (June Marthens) that owned the toothbrush house that bird-watching MD bought. She couldn't stay away from Álamos and just bought another house on Tesoros Street. She's down with her son and daughter and a well kept poodle. They sat at our table and the two dogs scrupulously ignored each other . Each pretended the other didn't exist.

I'm in the process of cooking my last breakfast. The kitchen will be out of commission for a couple of weeks. Sweet irony, the refrigerator works and it is of no use to me now. Runner let himself out while I was sleeping last night and gave me a huge tail-wagging greeting at 5:45 when I awoke. I'm going to have to teach him to open the door and let himself in. Dogs call from the orange grove and R makes no attempt to climb the fence and play. He does not wish to get stranded.

I've set up the hose so the sun will hit it and warm the water. We bathe in the garden when the crew leaves. It's hard to keep him clean with all the construction going on and his insistence re: supervision.

Waiting for the old man, Bill, to show and off to Navojoa for a buying of electricity things. Then will check and approve dome brick and get delivery started. We are going to be loaded with amapa beams. I think it is possible to do the bathroom with them with herringbone sticks in the guesthouse, should we so desire. The ends are a disaster but they could be cut off and the good part used. Could also do some floors with amapa rounds in lieu of tile. "Que pienso?"

Have a mechanic checking brakes so that I can pick up posts in Navojoa. Best go check him. Later!

Back. One brake shoe is perfect. The other being checked. Learned that the truck's jack and lug wrench are gone. Mechanic suggested I get them in the States, which I will do.

Running a crew of nine today and a few minor things remain on the guesthouse. I'm afraid I've fallen a couple of days behind schedule due to a few unforeseen complications and an arched doorway in the guesthouse which took time to build. Back out now to check mechanic and jobs. Things are going well. They are masking off the kitchen with wood and plastic before the beams come down later. The mechanic is road-testing the truck to make sure the brakes are OK and then to the bank and Navojoa.

Back from big N. Have finally put together all the electrical stuff except for odds and ends that can be bought locally. One of the girls at the electrical place in Navojoa freaked out over R. Phoned her mother who drove up with a camera and they both posed for pix in her office.

You will be pleased with the bathrooms and arched doorway. They put on the finishing touches while I was gone. Looks great. Spoke to Umberto and in the event we don't come out even with roof prep work, he has another maestro he can use to help out for a few days. His feeling is that the dome man will probably show on Monday or Tuesday instead of tomorrow which will give the present crew three more days. The guesthouse will keep him busy for two or three days while the regular crew readies the remaining two rooms.

The truck is fixed: $20 USD for brake shoes and labor. Cheap indeed. My electrical supplies will run about $300 USD. With labor, I'm sure it is going to come in well under the thou I am anticipating. Plumbing costs may go higher because I'm dealing with a known pirate who seems to have a lock on all the business. It's 4:15 and my crew are still finishing up. Clock watchers they ain't, but I wish they would split so R and & can bathe in the sun.

Saturday

Dear Joan,

Post-rain clean-up is over. Candelaria (Calalo), the new honcho, took over nicely and sealed the main house roof and did an excellent job on the cupola. Everyone I've talked to had leaks. Hildy's recently painted kitchen is streaked with water stain. The Keeler's brand-new roofs let in water. The Slaughters had some. Armida had many. Umberto allegedly just fixed them. The rains quit on Wednesday, laying down a total of five-to-six inches according to my bucket rain gauge.

Have two maestros and three peons working. All energy is focused on the guesthouse. The bathroom is about half plastered and the brick cornice work around the dome is progressing nicely. The roof, cornices and cupola should be completed next week. Might even get the fireplace finished and the rest of the inside plastered by next Saturday.

Checked the Slaughter's bathrooms and will do ours the same way. Incidentally, his tile work leaves a lot to be desired, not smooth and uneven grout lines.

Started class again and learned that Calalo built the school and Prof. Medellin's house. Good workmanship, so despite a less than brilliant start, I think I lucked out and things will go smoother. After much frustration and time fiddling around, I finally solved the kitchen faucet mystery. It works perfectly. The rains jumped the garden to a lettuce glut here.

I've come down with a cold and have been drinking lots of hot limeade and taking Contac. The combination must be a powerful diuretic. I was up at least six times last night. Seems much better this morning, "gracias a dios". Been a tad chilly in the early morn but warms up nicely later. May wash R in garden today if it gets hot and go downtown tonight to see what the rest of the world (gringo) of Álamos is up to.

Am hoping the "Tiny Tim" arrives with the truck part today. This is a biggie in my life. Bill was by yesterday to invite me to an elk steak barbecue. Craig arrived and brought the meat from Idaho. Bill also said that Armida's pissed at me for firing her favorite nephew. She'll get over it. Also planning on getting electrical work done next weeks and notifying the city re: hooking up the guesthouse to the sewer system. Gustavo will handle it.

Pancho visits regularly and has located 150-year-old floor brick. With truck in hand, will hit the boonies in search of more. I assume that Don was unable to get the Guadalajara tile on the truck because he'd have let me know and given me a bill. I'm feeling a lot more relaxed about things. The rains, cold weather, no car, your departure, cold, etc. was damned depressing. I've come to the conclusion that stoicism sucks and will do what 'ere I can to make things easy and fun.

Ran into "Wug," he's the fellow who wandered into our house. He's a civil engineer from California who has made some money in real estate and is renting for a month. He and his wife adopted a little four-year-old Mexican-American and is looking to buy a place here. He told me about another American who is being screwed by going the contractor route, which serves to confirm that what I'm doing makes sense. The trick is to go at a leisurely pace and not try to do too many things at once. That's been my problem. I've learned and look forward to stop pressing too much.

Reading Amaro. It's good. Should finish it and return same to Allen Pendergraftt at school Monday. R. is bugging me to go out so off to the Mercado and P. O. to mail this. We miss you, Love, US

Thursday, October 13, 1988

Dearest Joan,

Time to take a break. Been struggling since six ayem doing one damned thing or another. Finished the two bark chairs and the table with bug preventative and a coat of linseed. The bathroom is ready for El Domo and they are now working on the kitchen. The cabinet is off the wall but we ran into a snag. Two water pipes have to be cut if we can't find a plumber. The crew, expanded to five, not counting the truckers, are trying to work around the problem, but it is costing time. There is one other plumber in town, not as good, but pipe rerouting should not take more than an hour and I can use the outside faucet for minimal laving. Won't be able to cook for awhile, so dishes are no problem and coffee can be made with the electric element. Right now, they are placing chunks of wood to protect the stove before they take out the two concrete beams as well as protecting the kitchen window.

Checked brick this morning and they are cooking in the oven. They haven't started forming the remaining 3,000, but promised to start tomorrow. Will check. Unfortunately I paid 12 mil of the 18 mil cost and don't have the leverage I would like. If the price goes up a couple of hundred for the balance, I'll pay but won't appreciate the screwing.

Blocked out the electrical plan with Old Bill and will get the local electrician moving. Navojoa manaña to buy switches, wall boxes, etc. Have cleared the counter and put everything away to minimize dust which will engulf the room in short order. The guys are hammering so will get out of the room. More later.

Well, the crew is gone. Taking out the cement beams was quite a feat and looked dangerous as hell but interesting to watch. I just finished sweeping the floor and dusting. Much like shoveling sand in a cyclone. However, I feel better for it. Went to the market and bought an avocado, salad makings and sardines. I simply don't have the energy to go downtown. Another wire got cut today in taking out the concrete beam. We were able to jerry-rig something by using the new extension cord and running electricity to the back room with the extension cord. Through all the chaos, turmoil and confusion Runner has been good as gold. Think I'll doze off for half an hour, wake up, eat, read, and play with my little story. All for the nonce.

Friday

Did all of the above and got up at 5:30. Finished the Updike book. Really enjoyed it and will pass it along to you. Captured the plumber coming back from market. Told him it was an emergency. He came by with his crew to temporarily reroute all the pipes, which were concealed by the two concrete beams. The electricity ran through the beams through a conduit that was embedded within. I'm wondering how I'm going to deal with this with the dome. Perhaps run them through the roof support beam prior to the dome brick work build-up. Must discuss this with Umberto.

Finished all but two sides of one chair and woke up stiff as hell from all the bending and stooping. Gardener virtually completed the brick work as assigned. It looks good. He's started spading the soil for planting. Just finished hosing down and can't decide whether to go downtown.

The burlap broke on the Sonoran cot. Pancho was by and said it happens all the time ... just buy some twine and reweave it. I bought the twine but can't reweave it. I'll assign it to the gardener and sleep on the day bed. Just liberated a magenta-bodied dragonfly that was trying to beat itself to death on a window. Weird color for a bug.

Just realized that the weekly TGIF party is tonight but I just don't have the energy to be sweet-fucking-charming. Ran into Peter Brown. He went fishing at dawn yesterday with some Mexicans. When they got back to town they filleted "mucho pescado" and made what he claimed to be the best ceviche he ever tasted. It is getting dark now and I've got to sweep up some concrete so I can close the dining room door. More manaña or later.

Later. Went down to the Tesoros for a couple of beers. Can't have more because of my delicate condition. The usual crowd was there and they all asked when you were returning. Gen Reynolds read an article in the Mexican newspaper that said that the government was selling their airline in December to a private company, which may well explain the November shutdown. She also said that there was some new status for frequent visitors or Mexican residents that involves getting permanent stickers for six months on your car so that you can cross the border check points without having to fill out all the papers and stand in lines. If you have the sticker they just wave you through. Can you check the Mexican Consulate in Tucson? It would be a damned handy thing to have.

Runner is having a lively time with frozen bones. It extends his meal time about a half hour with lots of crunching and a blissful expression on his face. He is still shedding but I brush him practically daily and keep it under control. I signed up at the JFK Institute for Spanish lessons on Wednesday. Told El Professor I would like to spend the first week or so leaning construction words. It will help and lord knows the incentive will be there as well as the opportunity to practice. Getting sleepy and R is about finished and the daybed needs making, so, my love, goodnight.

Fall of 1988

Dear Joan,

I don't believe it, but this morning I had walked about 500 yards and then took about 10 jogging strides and my leg cramped. I started for home immediately, covered about 100 yards and then it got worse in a hurry. Terrific pain so I dragged myself home. A very interesting thing happened after I hit the side street. I freed R from the leash to let him get into his "niff and piss" pattern. At one stage, I felt his wet nose on the calf of my cramped leg. Strange, indeed. Home now, took some aspirin and am keeping leg elevated. We'll see what happens. More later.

Friday a.m.

Limping, hurting and taking aspirin. A pure, undiluted pain in the ass. Got R food and staggered home. Out of desperation have Nellie in. When she chooses, she can make the place spotless.

Holiday today. The guys only work a half day and do not come in tomorrow. Lalo is here. Be interesting to see what he does. One plan is roof painting, final coat. Colalo is putting up forms and Manuel is fine-grouting the new brick floor.

Kendall called, will be flying in tomorrow. Problems with his father, who may or may not have broken his hip. The women (Brujas) he lives with went to Slime John to borrow money to take him to Nogales. Kendall then made arrangements to fly him to Phoenix. He met the plane, no Papa, so he's coming down to check it out.

Snake Bob has been busy trying to fix the Hacienda's electrical problem; ours was minuscule in comparison. He's working on outside stuff and coming up with hundreds of feet of buried cable, much of it still salvageable, that doesn't go anyplace or do anything. He's also giving Jose a lesson in electricity. Went by and everybody seems to be digging ditches. Bob says that he's afraid to even begin circuit tracing and wire replacement in the interior because of the enormity of the job.

Will mail this later along with the M.O. enclosure. If you want your father's boat, it occurs to me that there is plenty of room for storage at the Hacienda and Jose will be willing to keep an eye on it. One thing to consider, I cannot back a trailer; you will have to. Also, if you decide to get it, learn how to run the motor. I know less than nada re: power boots. The best solution re: the latter would be to bring Mart down here and get a hands-on demonstration at both lake and beach.

The crew's gone and I've been reading. It occurred to me that I better get this in the mail because the P.O. will probably be closed mañana.

So we limp away.

Love and stuff, R and E

The cupola form is finished and concrete collar poured and hardening. The guys showered, changed clothes and for the first time since they arrived, left the house to see Álamos. I'm going to clean up and do same. Later.

Visited Cooks. Their car died. A rubber water seal got brittle and crumbled. Now, to find or make the part is the problem. They have an Alaskan friend coming down with a virtually new Datsun truck for sale. If they are not interested in buying it, I might be. I offered to take them to Lou's to play their music mañana. Depending on what goes on here, I may stay and indulge in prime rib, etc. I've got five pounds of sawdust going for R and a garlic, jalapeño, onion, tomato and, of course, chopped meat dish simmering and tantalizing. At the end will dump in a can of green peas. An Armida recipe. Admonition, don't rub eyes after chopping jalapeños.

More things to buy and bring: three boxes of Milky Ways at Price Club, one for Guadalupe Camarena's crew, one for Jose Medellin and wife, one for Gaspar and Christina, and masks or something for the Christmas Masked Ball if they have one. A turkey would be a good idea, here or at Cooks. Here needs pot, plates, silverware, etc., cranberry sauces, after-thoughts.

7:30.

Nice and peaceful, with Ormandy's Carmen on the stero. No dome men in sight. There's a lot going on in Álamos tonight. Carnival in Plaza, a tent circus and the inevitable Saturday night dance. The workers have completed the dome and are proud of their work. They are away from home and ready to party. I can only hope that they don't get hurt and don't come home too drunk. We'll be living under the dome and I want a steady hand on the trowel mañana. Guess I'll eat. Later, Runner is growling and woofing. The maestro is back.

Sunday morning

The maestro came back, bombed. Your camera is in such a safe place that I can't find it after repeated searches. He looks like a muscular hybrid between Groucho Marx and Jerry Colonna. He came home carrying a six pack and displaying a personal pint-sized bottle of brandy with about an inch left in the bottom. He announced with pride that he had consumed the contents solo. I drank a few cans of beer, played Jose Alfredo and he sang along, knew all the words. He said he liked working here and would do his very best work. I left him about 9:30. He must have gone straight to bed because two cans of beer were untouched. I read till about 11:00 o'clock and crashed.

R ate four tortillas yesterday. The fire cooked out of the jalapeños meat dish, interesting. It's about 8:00 ayem. The maestro is up and moving slowly. The apprentice sleeps. No idea what time or in what shape he rolled in. I'm off to the Tiangus before the chickens are gone. The day looks threatening. Rain will hold up progress. Been awfully lucky so far. Planned on washing R. When light is right, he has a pink brick dust aura going. Plan on cleaning kitchen and dining room complex after guys finish cupola and steel brush and clean up the interior of dome, the pre-varnish procedure.

Please bring the small vacuum cleaner to do upholstery. Ain't no other way. More to come.

Back from Tiangius. My crew is lolling around resting and trying to overcome inertia to get cracking. The sky still threatens and work is canceled if it pours because the cement won't set up to keep the angled bricks from sliding. However, all things being equal, they will finish easily by Christmas since the difficult one is done. Will head down to the Mercado now to buy milk, and machaca or chorizo for Sunday brunch. Got two chickens and fresh tortillas. The latter run about 10 cents per pound and the former about $1.15 per bird.

Andalé. Came back from walking Ole Bill downtown and read a lamp post announcement that the state and municipal employees are sponsoring a weeklong music and dance festival in the Plaza across from the cathedral. Lots of folklorico stuff from as far away as Hermosillo. Eight o'clock every night. If I have the energy, I will attend. Ends this Friday.

Looks like the guys will be moving into and will complete the bathroom in a week and the very square casita should be a piece of cake because it won't require a bunch of time-consuming brick-cutting.

The museum director, Tony Estrada, came by and thinks he would like a dome. We are trend-setters. Before long, no self respecting person in Álamos will own a house without at least one dome. History is in the making with every brick that's being added.

Gonna siesta for a half hour, pick up and deliver the Cooks and probably return to see the opening night of the festival. No point in washing R because he'll take a dip at Casa Cook. Later. Oh, before I forget, a reasonably large frying pan can be put to good use down here. Also, see enclosure and keep. I might be able to duck surgery. I'll take the article to the VA and see if they are using this procedure.

Monday

Bit of a nip in the air this morning. Went with the Cooks to the Caricol. Decided to stay and eat. The prime rib was just as good as the first time. Got home about nine, fed R, chatted with the maestro, read and crashed.

The form set solidly, and the cupola is rising while brick is being cleaned. Have to find out about glass placement. May have to bring someone in from Navojoa. Will start school for a second week in a one hour per day spurt. Feel I need to use my head a little and things seem to be pretty much under control here. Will have the cleaning girl in tomorrow to get the place in some sort of shape. Maintenance will be easy with construction shifting to the bathroom. Umberto's crew is working on the pool pending delivery of a truckload of brick.

Must also do banking chores, though I will try to just get walking-around money. Rumor has it that a major devaluation will take place today or tomorrow. It would be great but must wait and see what happens. If it does pop, I'll be busy buying everything needed to complete the house before inflation takes off once the government removes controls. Off to class and Mercado. More to come.

Returned home to problems. The first was a futile search for brick. Thinking I could find old, I figured that new can be purchased readily. They can't and it'll be a week or more before I can find some. I need "8s" and six places only had "6s". Also, these are some rough spots on the dome that'll have to be ground down some before finishing. Mistake. But albeit will require a lot of work to correct. Will be meeting with Guadalupe and Professor Medellin at 4:00 p.m. The latter suggested possibly reducing the price, let them get on with the basic structures and paying locals to do the finishing, chipping and grinding. We wait until four.

Woke up this morning and thought I had the world by the tail and now things are coming apart. To make matters less agreeable, city water has been cut off and I can't use the well because the extension cord is busy electrifying the house so that the brick-cutting machine can do the cupola job. Life is tough right now. I'll keep the crew on the pool and keep brick-hunting, otherwise we're talking a two week wait and I can't keep a crew all that busy, muchos problemas. Maybe things will improve as the day passes.

The water shortage is bringing work to a standstill. No way to make concrete. Oh well, and woe is me.

2:50 p.m.

One minute ago the dome was completed along with the cupola. Now begins the brick cleaning, which they advise will take time and probably be messy as hell with concrete and brick dust flying . Please bring vacuum cleaner and also a large frying pan.

Back from meeting. A grinder is lined up for tomorrow. They can finish the interior in about five-to-six hours, varnish it, and set up bathroom scaffolding. It's an easier room because of size and only one bad angle, so could be done in three-and-a-half days. The concrete binder on the top can be done in a few hours and left for last. Still más o menos on schedule. Must wait for Pember to come back and check pool, Umberto does not exactly know what he is doing and expert advice is needed.

Chicken cooking. Dinner tonight and two days' lunch of caldo.

Tuesday

By 7:45 neither Umberto, crew nor grinding machine showed. I went to class. Returned to find grinding machine and Umberto waiting to scout out desperately needed brick. Checked the last pile of old brick of the size needed, but they have too much salt in them. Checked with more brickyards and at the last one, came across a small pile, 435, enough to do the job and of high quality. Ordered them on the spot.

In the meantime, the dome men were struggling with the grinder and you couldn't walk into the room without getting covered with a fine patina of brick dust. They finished in four hours except for the detail work, which will be done by one of my regulars. I told him that a maestro should not be doing that kind of work. They are now in the process of setting up in the bathroom and may get their rigging up and start on a corner before the sun sets.

Off to the market. Bye for awhile.

Cement mixing began before 7:00 a.m. Scaffold is up and the corner is being started in the bathroom. Umberto and crew are putting boards and tile up to protect sink, etc.

Went to the dance festival last night. Sonoran folklorico group of 16 with a few changes of costume performed for about 45 minutes. Another group that looked like tired, overworked housewives and their husbands did a couple of what appeared to be dirge dances. The finale was a spectacular Yaqui deer dance solo. Very dramatic and spectacular he was. The audience of over 1,000 was enthralled.

Time for another cup of coffee and then chase the dome men off the roof while I shit. Even communal living has its demands for privacy. Then off to class and off to market. We need a nail-set to countersink nails on the bentwood chairs. Runner is busy supervising. Umberto tells me that it will take one good worker about four days to clean the dome and a couple of days to plaster. I'll hold off painting until all is complete and then borrow or rent spray equipment. We are short one man today from the regular crew.

The garden is doing well and may have lettuce when you get here. After class came back, reviewed schedule and decided to hire a new maestro to finish off the casita roof. Umberto, who wants to learn, will work on the simple parts of the dome after the maestro has squared things up. Under the latter's direction, he'll do the brickwork canals required for drainage and the interior and exterior dome cementing and plastering. Miguel, the number one peon, will clean, complete the sanding and apply the necessary finish coats of lacquer. Following unforeseen calamities of a major nature, they will, for all intents and purposes, be done when you return.

It looks like it will be hose-bathing for awhile. Today's minor trauma was a water bill for over one hundred thousand pesos to Smollens. It is the third one I've received and I passed the two others to Gustavo and he didn't do shit. Went to the Palacio and they found my sign-up in one file dates to June, but through a goof, it didn't make the billing file. I left the bill and we parted amicably with assurances that the water will not be shut off.

Also arranged for an electrician to show and start redoing wiring switch and receptacle placing, etc. Wish you were here to help make a few decisions. I'm going with high spots in two opposing corners for the dining room dome, no idea about the bathroom, and possibly a double spot arrangement in the casita. Wiring has to be in place before plastering begins. It will be nice to have lights in every room again.

Please bring another box of Milky Ways from the Price Club for the folk across the street where I leave the truck. They won't accept money but they have a bunch of kids. Tonight's festival consists of local groups. Tomorrow it shifts to the Palacio where a renowned mariachi group performs. It will last until Sunday. If not too beat up at day's end, I'll go. All for the moment.

Two bathroom corners are about 20 brick courses done, one difficult and the other square. He's saving the hardest for last, says el maestro. The dining room is being "dug out": dusty, congealed cement, sawdust, the god-damndest mess you ever did see. Another thing to bring: several large jars of Hellman's mayo. Can't get it without lime juice addition here and I think I prefer the US variety.

People keep dropping by to see the dome and Umberto gives them a tour and explanation. I'm going to put a stop to that. It costs me about an hour of work daily but I do enjoy his enthusiasm. I just hired the extra maestro to plaster the dining room and build the fireplace chimney and complete the baño roof. Sometimes the whole operation seems like a juggling act and trying to orchestrate things comes under the heading of work. Off to the P.O.

Love and stuff, R and Me

Between October 12 and 24, 1988

Bright and early. Crew arrived. Plumber due in half an hour, then get reefer to repairman and off the Navojoa to get electrical supplies. Want to get back before one to meet with Gustavo.

A most unsatisfactory telephone experience. After the disconnect I tried again for half an hour. I guess Sunday night is just a bad time to call. Let's hope that Wednesdays are better and further hope that reservations have been made. A bona fide pain in the ass truly.

Big excitement. The gardener, Manuel, came by to tell me that Runner jumped the fence. Dashed out, blew the whistle and he showed with the neighbor's Shepherd and Dobie in his wake. After repeated tries he couldn't grip the top of the fence to return. Went around the corner to the neighbor's side entrance and rescued him. He looks as if had been swimming. After several attempts to return, he whined a bit, poor baby. We'll see how intelligent he is and whether or not he tries to go over again.

The plumber is here tracing gas lines and water lines. The crew is busy finishing up the casita and I really hate to zero in on the fence. May have to this week if I can find a few extra guys. He seems very subdued now and sticks very close. It must have been frightening to be unable to come back. We'll see if he has learned anything. After his experience of needing to be rescued from the swimming pool, he never went for another dip.

Back from Navojoa. Tried four stores looking for ITE circuit breakers. Found a couple and bought some Westinghouse brand which superficially look like they might fit. If they do, will ask the store to order a few more. Got the refrigerator in and man is working on it. Fingers are crossed.

Came home to chaos. One team is taking down the roof. Umberto rigged up a very ingenious way to protect the sink and hopper using the wooden barrier gates from the garage. I can't piss vertically as is my wont but I won't have to poop in a pit and can wash in the garden. Another crew is cutting out the porch bricks, they are replaceable, to run the gas in underground to the stove and water heater instead of over and into the walls from the roof which is a bit dangerous as well. As I have to keep reminding myself, the river cannot be pushed.

Later

Met with the electrician and plan on going to Navojoa on Monday to buy a bunch of circuit breakers and a junction box recommended in the book for darkrooms. Hope I can find the ITE brand there, if not, Obregon. Will wander down to the Tesoros for beers and English tonight.

Sunday

More Americans are taking up residence as evidenced by the Tesoros crowd. The Cooks were there. They invited me to dinner, roast beef night at the Tesoros, but I had accepted a previous invitation for Sunday dinner at Armida's.

Hit the tianguis early. Brought Runner food and a $1.50 USD chicken as well as veggies and some truly delicious fig pastries. Ate three for breakfast. Someone at the door. R. growled. It was Gustavo. I lent him the swimming pool book. His excavation is complete but yesterday's rain put a halt on cementing it in. One and a quarter inches fell. Will run a brick check tomorrow.

It's gonna be a busy week. May be without gas, electricity and water for short periods. Also placed an order for mesquite so can do pretend camping if need be. Will take a break now and retrieve the chairs. Forgot to ask Gustavo for the weak preservative mixture but will find out tonight when I visit to use the phone to call you. More soon.

Just returned from picking up the rebuilt chairs. $5.30 USD for the pair. We can think about leather-seated bar stools for the kitchen and take measurements and order them when you get here. Without the tourists in Álamos in force, he doesn't have his usual two-to-three month order backlog. Am absolutely stuffed by dinner at Armida's. Salad, squash, orange juice, chicken, potatoes and ice cream, sliced peaches and sugar wafers with a couple of slices of cinnamon bread. Planning to indulge myself with a siesta since I don't have a crew working. Will watch the World Series at Gustavo's later and call you then. We do miss you. More manaña, R & E

Note: Armida was Levant Alcorn's mistress for many years before he married Anna Maria. Armida bore him three children. Only one, a daughter, is still alive and she is as beautiful as her mother. During Earle's years in Álamos, Levant Alcorn lived on the other side of the plaza with Anna Maria and their children. Earle had befriended Craig and Richard Schneider, who were renting rooms at Armida's house. Later, Craig brought "Old Bill" from Idaho to Álamos to recuperate from a heart operation. Old Bill later died at Armida's house.

Saturday morning

Dearest Joan,

At 4:50 a.m., rain came for two-and-a-half hours. The crew arrived at 7:00 a.m. and we are concerned about whether the brick-makers protected their work with plastic. The crew is busy building concrete beams on the guest house and deferring opening the other rooms until Monday because of weather. We are in a bind if the plumber doesn't show because gas pipes have to be moved and water access stubbed in at the rear wall of the guesthouse before it can be capped with a concrete beam.

Went out last night with mi amigo Manuel (Manager of Hacienda) for a few beers and then he took me to the best menudo maker in town and insisted on paying the check. He would still like to sell the lot he showed us a couple of years ago for two-to-three thousand and use the money to buy a beach house for his family. When you are down here and we have some time he offered to take us down for a look-see in the area where he would like to buy.

The plumbing team arrived and he is on the roof checking the plumbing. Hay muchas problemas. Discovered that there was never a plumbing plan and bits and pieces were added with no thought given to water and sewerage circulation. Will get it all corrected at great cost. Will do the same thing with gas routing, which was equally screwed up. Come Monday a full crew will be here digging up the garden and chipping walls and floors to get at pipes. It sounds like mucho dinero but essential if problem-free living is an objective.

Rain has been coming on and off and I'm waiting for a break to make a market run. Had the refrigerator checked. A pipe got broken in transit and must be welded and a fresh charge of Freon added. 'Tis but a minor problem compared to the others I'm wrestling with. If the weather clears, I'll get the crew to load it on the truck and get it repaired.

Sun's out. Going on a market run. Sky still threatens and I still have to face the brick problem later. I hope they haven't been lost. They are necessary because a dome with a gas pipe would look shitty. Umberto is finishing off the casita. Am praying that the breakers fit or may have to get them from Tucson, assuming I can't locate them in Obregon. Will know manaña. Will be eating out for the next few days while the gas lines are being worked on.

Bill kept me company while in Navojoa and our last stop was the supermarket. He sat in a little cafeteria with Runner under the table while I shopped. Don't know who was babysitting whom. He told me that a Mexican came by and yelled at him, telling him to go to another table. Runner came out, put his head on Bill's knee and growled softly while staring at the Mexican, who then decided that he really didn't want that table after all. When I came through the pay line, both were sitting quietly, one beside the table the other under. I almost have to fight Bill for R's leash.

Going off to visit Gustavo and will post this en route. Love & stuff, R & me

Monday, October 24, 1988

Wandered through Obregon yesterday and looked at the tile store. I saw the same tile at a building supply store in Navojoa. I believe that there are five tile stores or more in Navojoa, each with its own sources and franchises. Many, I'm sure, are sourcing from Saltillo and Dolores Hidalgo, so that with time and patience you could look at samples and they will eventually show up after an order has been placed.

Spoke to Don, the vet. His brick came from Guadalajara. Learned from Pancho that the wives of the brick-makers use the same clay and turn out flower pots. Up at 5:00 this a.m. and getting organized. The crew came in an hour ago and are hot at it.

Problem: for the life of me, I could not find the yellow pad with your sketches of the bathroom, garden layout, etc. All I can figure out is that it is in your purse or suitcase and may never again surface in my entire life. My main concern at the moment is that the dome maker show. Worry, worry. Will wait until noon and then see if he can be tracked down in Queretaro through the guy that brought him to Navojoa.

Later, no domo. Drove to a site where he had worked for a Navojoa architect and Umberto spoke to the project's maestro, a friend. We learned that the architect was due either later today or tomorrow. We'll get the domo's phone number or address and see if we can find out what is happening Also learned that the brick won't be ready for a few days ... no maestro, no brick. At least I come out even.

Will be hiring another maestro tomorrow to see if I can't get things moving faster, i.e., finish the new casita bathroom wall, start working on the pool, etc. Plenty to do as I'm sure you must have observed and the sooner I knock off these basics the better I'll feel. As a fall back for the domo, Pancho is willing to travel to dome country and bring one back. We'll wait on that one awhile and keep hoping.

Did my banking today to make sure I have lots of cash since I'm getting low on concrete and lime and must get about 75 sacks of each in Navoja. More later.

Tuesday update

Busy, busy and not much sleep. At 4:00 ayem Runner opened the door and leaped the wall. I got out of bed groggy and cold, took the flashlight and there he was dancing in the grove with a timid male Dobie and a friendly Shepherd. He couldn't get back. I got dressed, drank coffee and cussed him out until daylight, waiting for the neighbors to wake up. He was exuberantly happy to see me. We lock up tonight.

I am looking at different types of fencing on the wall with Pancho and I guess I'll go with the sticks even though it totally obscures the view of the Sierra when you are sitting. I'm not convinced that wire would be better and may switch. Peter Brown was by while we were discussing fence and told of a friend's dog that was impaled on a stake fence. The resiliency of wire eliminated that danger as well as the possibility of heavy winds destroying the wood.

Got to Navojoa and spent about $900 USD on supplies. Learned from the man that needs more domes in Navojoa that the man is not due till next week because there is a two-day holiday this week. Day of the Dead Fiesta. I may go with Peter one night at Chacho's invitation if I'm not too beat up. Also bought wood preservative to work on chairs and table. Will finish with a linseed oil finish. Still no brick and the two house rooms need a few more days. Ran into a problem with the exterior bathroom door that may have to be opened and a concrete beam built to replace the embedded amapa. Will bust the plaster off and check it.

The trouble of coordination here is ridiculous. Last Monday the brick should have been ready, Umberto should have had the rooms ready and the domes should have been started. Not one of the three happened when they were supposed to. The Mexican Way, I suppose. The electrician came by today. He's the same guy who's wiring the domes in Navojoa so I'll go along with what he suggests for switches and outlet placement. He's put in the junction box and will start rewiring Thursday. Or so he says.

Crew left now and I took a garden bath and shampooed Runner. They must have irrigation ditches in the orange grove because he was wet to his belly when I rescued him this morning. I'm running out of steam and haven't the energy to dress and go out and eat, so will close now with love and chow down.

Wednesday

Crashed at nine-ish and up at 4:40. Becoming like Mart. I don't need this. I've been sipping multiple cups of coffee and blocked out a storybook about what little we know about Indians and wolves. I'll play with it for a few days and mail you a rough draft. If it works, let's make it a collaborative project.

The lights went out about half an hour ago. Will check the outside breaker box after I put some clothes on and go potty. I try to get the letter done before the crew comes to work. They are scurrying around the bathroom walls and it would be like shitting in a theatre-in-the-round with an audience.

Fished a good book set in the Australian bush. The protagonist is an Anglo-Abo. Not much of a plot but a great deal of info about the land and its people. Started Updike's Coup. I think it will be a winner. Hippity-hop to the hopper. Later, lass.

No hay electricidad, que lastima. Breakfast consumed, dishes done. Crew working and am waiting for 8:00 o'clock to go marketing and buy turpentine at the hardware store when it opens. Planning on spending the day chair-finishing. Checked the beams; we have three-to-four inches thick and none of them are Sabino wood, which was used a hundred years ago along with pine and amapa. Ours are pine. I 'm going to clean one up and sand it and then figure out what to do with it. Maybe get a super heavy table built, or shelving? A little bonus to recycle ... a gift from generations past.

Runner is giving me the wolf-eye and nose-nudge. I'm heading for town in awhile.

Back from town and did one chair. It took about an hour of steady, uninterrupted work. I'm taking a break now; all the bending gets to me. Been working under the portales to avoid inhaling the bug killer's fumes. Work is going on at Gen Reynolds' which supposedly explains the electrical cut-off. It should go on shortly, they tell me, but I'm not holding my breath. Off to the P. O. to mail this and see if your letter came. We love you, R & E

Saturday

Slept in until 6:20 and it was good. The crew is busy. Manuel is fixing the cot. I've got to finish the chair and then line up a truck for brick delivery. They are apparently pretty fragile and cannot be moved in batches of more than 1,000. Also believe that both plumbing and electrical problems have been solved. They will run on the roof and drop down into the interior through the wall.

I'm mighty glad it is Saturday. I need a break. Plan on doing a little spading in the garden this weekend and get things ready for planting. Will also play with my story some. Wish you were here to talk about it with me. With a good shot at it tomorrow, I hope to have a bunch of words to send you.

Hilde is back so will pay her a visit and learn about life in India. Peter Brown wants me to go shopping with him in early December. Depending on my schedule here, I may go to get an idea of prices, buy some equipment and maybe some tile. You will be here before then and we can measure and count. He's going down to pick up tile and furniture for his place.

Pancho is talking about going along to buy some lamps for his house. He knows the area and has some cousins there. Getting along towards eight o'clock. Time to go to market and get about the business of the day. Curious to learn what you found out about the purported new train, Preece's air service and any other third party modes of transportation that comes this way. We miss you. Runner is busily supervising Manuel's repair of the cot as I'm writing. All for the moment, on my way.

A new squash appeared at the market today. Bought one to fry with onions on the assumption that the stove will be working this weekend. The crew is busy mixing cement and hauling to Umberto, who is finishing off the brick work in the dining room. It, as well as the bathroom, have been and are being made lightly higher than originally specified to enable the rain to run off onto the portales and into the garden. The flowers are still holding strong. Armida will be by on Monday to pick a whole bunch to decorate graves. I'm going to pick some dried ones for seed. The black-eyed peas are vine ripening and guavas are getting bigger.

Discovered something about limes. Those being sold in the market and used in restaurants have turned yellow and are fully ripe. I guess that they are shipped to the States green because of their keeping quality and unlike bananas, don't ripen off the branch. The ripe ones seem to be a bit juicier and perhaps a bit sweeter. Back to work now and will sign off and get this in the mail before noon when the P. O. closes.

Love & Stuff, Us'ens

Monday, October 31, 1988

Dear Joan,

Yesterday was a great goof-off time. Slept in 'til 7:30 and it was grand. Runner snuck out and skipped the fence to play with the neighbor's dogs. This week we'll do something. Spent the day cleaning up, completing the chairs and worrying about a damnable leak that the plumber has not as yet found. The garden box is all complete.

Did street food with the Coltins . They will be flying up to Scottsdale to get their kid started in school. Then they'll go to Vegas to play the slots a bit, then off to California to talk to their mining partners and to pick up a bigger two engine plane. Then, Tucson to visit daughter and grandchildren, at which point they'll call you to see if you want a lift down. Getting you back up will be the problem unless the trains will work.

The crew is busy putting on the finishing touches and dome brick should start arriving momentarily. I'm waiting until 10:30 to go to the bank, get some cash, make a deposit, etc. It was another 1 M week and, assuming the dome man's arrival, fencing, etc., there will be a thousand or more week. Perverse as it might seem, I'm enjoying all the activity. The sense of power maybe, having six or eight guys doing your bidding and watching things happen. The demolition is over and the rebuilding is taking place. It is cleaner and quieter around here.

At six tonight I'll be going to a Day of the Dead party. Ran into the Chacho family and Cammy reminded me and gave me specific directions. She also reminded me to pick up the carriage wheel (that is the iron wheel on the portal wall). I don't think it will fit in my truck with the caps, so I'll use Gustavo's flatbed. Did no writing on the story yesterday. The creative mood wasn't there. Hope to get an hour or two in later in the day. Time to go banking. More anon.

Deposited my last of the cash I brought down, which is just as well since you get a slightly better rate of exchange with personal checks. Also, I don't like to keep a big wad of money around the house.

Ran into Gustavo and mentioned my leak. He said problems like that fascinate him, particularly because the plumber couldn't solve it. He'll be by this afternoon to see if he can figure it out. Met an American who has been building from scratch for four years. His problem is that he only comes down a couple of weeks and things have a tendency to lag when he is gone. He wanted to do amapa but could not find them, so he resorted to concrete. Hope we don't have to go that route on the two front rooms.

It was downright chilly this morning at 6:00 with the total skylight concept in the dining room. An interesting phenomenon, no bugs that sting or bite are attacking my pale, frail, ass. The screens are useless but it is not uncommon to be visited by stray butterflies. No wasps or bees have come to visit as yet.

Armida and Bill came by to visit. The former picked a bunch of flowers for grave decorations and then took off in search of a gas man. Her tanks are on empty and she needs one for the stove and two for separate water heaters. We will need a separate water heater for the guesthouse and its placement may be tricky. Will figure something out when the time comes. More later.

Later hath come. A palmas man for palapas came by and I explained that I will defer until the circular stairway is built and until the guesthouse is finished. Then Umberto asked about procuring new amapa on his ranch. He said "maybe," but it will be expensive. We took measurements and asked him to give us a price. I can see that next week I'll have to get real serious about finding some. I spoke to a fellow that lined up 150 this summer—used—by going hither, thither and yon. But they are expensive, he claimed. My old landlady, Micha, whose German shepherd is coming in heat and makes all kinds of overtures towards Runner, told me he acted like the surrogate father to her last litter. I'm going to watch him like a hawk and go to Navojoa mañana, hire some more guys and get a fence built.

Pancho was by. He'll go to Navojoa with me Wednesday afternoon. Class in the morning. Waiting for the crew to split so I can play with the garden hose. With any luck I should be able to take hot showers in a real bathroom in a couple of weeks. Oh, the luxury of it all. Am also running out of clothes, but one of the girls who works near the school will do laundry. At least she did last year so I'll give her a shot. I seem to live mostly in blue jeans and T-shirts and my pillow case laundry bag is bursting. 'Nough written for awhile. Time for a coffee break.

Tuesday

Went to the fiesta. Cammy and Chacho lined a road, a few hundred yards, with stubby candles in brown paper bags, no wind, and placed them in lieu of lanterns up to the house where the festivities took place. People of all ages present. Homemade apple wine and food was served, nothing I ever tasted before including a chocolate corn mix instead of coffee. Interesting and different. Fires were built and the men hung around them and talked while the women gathered for what seemed to be an interminable period and prayed. One gal did the ritual and the others responded in unison with Hail Marys. They were still going strong when I left.

The Nuzums were there as was June Martin and her daughter. They are the former owners of the toothbrush house (now owned by Suzannne Chartrand) who moved back to California. They missed Álamos and bought another house a month or two ago. They have a dainty white poodle which I mentioned previously, that Runner considers to be unworthy of interest. Gay was there with an interesting friend named Stephanie who is down here to collect seeds. She has known the Grays and Robin Coon for years. She had just attended a bi-national meeting in Hermosillo concerned with preservation of the Pinacate region which straddles the border. Vivian Juan (Papago Queen in Sells when I was there) was apparently there as the spokesperson for the O'odham nation and blew them away with tribal concerns. The plan of the meeting was to get President Reagan to sign a bill that would preserve the area's environment from any future development.

Bet Nuzum came by before seven. I offered coffee made in a cup with the heating element since the stove is covered to protect it from mortar spills It is obvious that she regards you as a kindred spirit and I get a feeling that despite her years down here, she doesn't have too many people that share her interests in art, culture, books, etc.

Umberto informed me that tomorrow is a paid holiday and if I want the crew to work, I've got to pay double time. I'm heading up to Gustavo's to verify. Still sweating the dome man who has three other projects besides ours. When he shows we'll be the first because we have or will have all the special brick on site, as well as the walls prepared to receive the brick. The other client in Álamos is still sweating brick and I'll get the balance of my order from one of his kilns. More in awhile. I want to try and catch Gustavo.

Failed to catch Gustavo. Will check back at 1:00 p.m. The brick-maker is getting pissed because they have to be moved off his lot so he can start up a new batch. Always and forever, the waiting game. In my absence, another yard or so of wall extension went up in the dining room. I imagine that the brick work will be completed in another day and the cement beam caps in one or two more. We'll see.

It's interesting to watch Umberto and the crew work. They hit the easy stuff, work, and I can almost feel him thinking about how he's going to deal with the problem areas. Right now he's about to contend with the area where the electrical conduit comes in. He is going to have to lay his brick in a manner that will permit the conduit to come up and over where the dome meets the existing roof and then connect with the other side of the house. Looks pretty tricky.

Back from Gustavo. Pay double time for the guys to work tomorrow. Bricks are coming in. He'll be down later to see if he can solve the plumbing problem.

Will enter into a seed exchange with Hildy, at least in the veggie arena. Fleurs are up to you or I can keep going with zinnias. She said that Manuel is the best gardener she has had in 18 years but that he has little initiative; with directions he can make anything grow. Also, I feel lucky indeed. She's been mulching, composting, fertilizing, etc., and maybe has about six inches of topsoil. The subsoil is caliche and impossible to break through for drainage root rot is a constant problem. This year she is experimenting with square foot gardening and will set up gravel and sand drainage a foot or so below the garden's surface. It's a bitch.

In the hour I was off visiting, the wall is virtually complete and they've started the palm work for concrete beams. They also swept out the bathrooms, which may be a mistake when the dome man gets going. Suppose plastic can be used to protect the tile. Currently have five guys working and will add another one or two to off-load brick. Will probably reduce the crew to three or four to knock off the guesthouse wall and roof, install doors and windows and fill in, repair and get the pool going. This should use up all of November and come December, do the two front rooms, finish off the guesthouse and get the patchwork and painting finished in January. And then the big remodel,re-tile,rearranging of the kitchen can begin or can be deferred until the fall or whenever. At least, the place will be habitable.

Friday

Tomorrow is here. It began with a Runner round-up from the neighbor's. At least this time he did not have to be hosed down from irrigation ditch wading. I'm killing time before going to Peter's place for my "matitunal deposit" and then off to market. Will play "catch Gustavo" about noon and do dome man hunting in Esperanza. It means "hope" and at this stage, that's about all I've got. I learned that the guy Umberto knows is working on a project in Huatabampo and won't be back until the weekend so????

Coffee finished and nature calling, we are off. No Esperanza today, always tomorrow. On the positive side for a change, we have eliminated the need for a hot water heater near the gas tank to service the guesthouse shower and sink. Since all the pipes are exposed, I'm having Victor run the hot water pipe through the portales floor—it is all chewed up anyway—to the ground where at the appropriate time, it can be extended to service the guesthouse. He suggests that I buy a roll of pipe insulation for the job in the US because it is one of those dumb things that simply don't exist in Mexico.

Spoke to the laundress-cleaning girl's mother and had a cup of coffee with her and a good dose of Spanish. I told her to send her daughter over on Monday when I'm sure I'll have water, both indoor and hot, for the floor and shelf-dusting and scrubbing. Manuel Murrietta offered me 10,000 pesos for the portales pine beams but Pancho, who has about 50 of his own, told me to hang on to them. He is going to trade his with carpenters and cabinetmakers for furniture, doors, etc. Seems like a good idea. Amapa beams are still elusive in the size we need.

Álamos is going to be loaded with culture this weekend. The museum is going to have two hours of music, a lecture and a video on Mayo Indians and an exhibition of "El Mundo de los Mayos," their art, I guess. A solo exhibition of a lady named Elsa Maria Cacho will open Sunday at the City Hall. Also on Saturday a big bash in the Capilla district from 2:00 to

11:00 with music, a volleyball tournament, plays, poetry, multi-media presentations, food and things for sale. Big doings for these parts.

Clipped the enclosure out of the newspaper. Give Remy a call to verify the procedure. If it stands up, I can give you a 10 M check on Thanksgiving and another after the first of the year. These letters are getting to be entirely too long so, 'nuff written—Love, E

Sunday

Up early as usual. It wasn't as chilly. Still no water in the house. Must haul it in from the garden in gallon jugs. Tomorrow I'm going to start the crew on the guest house rear bathroom wall. Will be taking down the existing adobe and starting from scratch. We have enough amapa beams to complete the roof. I'll have the plumbing and electrical work roughed in and wait for you to make tile, wall and floor, counter, fixtures, lighting, etc., decisions over Thanksgiving. Will then put the crew in the pool to hold them and keep them busy. It seems like most of the heavy construction is out of the way. It will only take a couple of weeks to do the front rooms and I can wait on the portales and the kitchen redesign, clean up the mess and maybe do a few things in the garden. All for now—off to El Tianguis. Got there late last week and the fresh chickens were gone.

Sunday evening. Lord what a frustrating day. It can be called Catching Gustavo Trying to Catch the Architect with Telephones Working Intermittently. Contact was sort of made. The results uncertain and will remain that way until Wednesday. The domo didn't show

Didn't show in Navojoa. The architect is going to try to track him down. Gustavo is going to Hermosillo for two days and will keep trying.

Monday

Today's problem is plumbing. There is a mysterious pool in the bathroom. I noticed some dampening in the grout last night and assumed it was the chronic problem. The men arrived and Umberto took one look and has his crew digging away on the outside of the bathroom. They've hit mud and are still going strong. He is afraid that the leaky pipe is under the bathroom floor. I sure didn't need this.

I guess I'll put Spanish class on hold. I can't seem to control my life and time with all that is happening. If there is light at the end of the tunnel, I still can't see it. A lesson? If you tile something and use an exotic tile and something like this occurs, you can't replace it. We may need a new bathroom floor before this day is over.

Time to go to market and notify Prof. Medellin about my problems and defer school until???

Just got back. Three thousand bricks were being transferred out of the bathroom; the toilet has been removed as well as the sink, and they are digging into the wall to track pipe, hoping that they won't have to go into the floor. If necessary, they will and I've already granted permission.

Need a month's laundry done. On my way to the Tesoros to join the Cooks for dinner. I ran into Patrick, a former seminarian and aspiring artist, who is staying with Armida. He has a friend who needs a job as a maid. I told him we wouldn't need one for a couple of months and that hiring her would be your decision. He is teaching her English and I'm going to see if he can get her to do my laundry every two weeks. 'Bout all for now.

Tuesday, November 8, 1988

Life ain't improving. There is a helluva lot of water under the bathroom floor and probably under the front room and dining room. Capillary action just hasn't brought it to the surface yet. The bathroom floor is going to locate the ruptured pipe. Moisture has come up the wall and started popping shower tile and soaking the bathroom cabinet. Big problems. Will continue to hope for the best but it becomes harder with each new discovery.

The latest plumbing—uncovered old and rusty pipe. I surmise that it was on the verge of leaking for several years but since the house was unoccupied and the water disconnected, nothing happened. When the water was turned on and the pipes put to use, they simply ruptured. There is evidence of prior embedding or sheathing them in tape and concrete to contain or slow down any leaks. I guess it worked for awhile. Now it will be new pipes as needed. This reduces my problem to simply finding a place to shit.

Also, Umberto estimates that it could take a month for the substrata beneath the house to dry. Hope there is no more tile popping on wall cracks while this occurs. It occurred to me that a lot of the stuff in my letters is pretty picayunish but I've got to tell somebody about my hard trials and great tribulations. If you find it all boring, don't read my epistles. I will say this. My life seems simplified and I'm noticing things I've never paid much attention to before.

Patrick was by with two girls looking for work. I loaded them up with laundry. I pay for the soap and chlorine and we agreed on 5000 pesos as the price. I then met one of the girl's mothers who runs the taco stand across from the Somar. She invited me by to practice Spanish and help her kid, a JFK student, with English. May do it. JFK has 25 English students working their butts off. It is their passport to work both in Mexico and as illegals in the US.

Umberto has stopped the leak but keep discovering pipes that need replacing. He is currently checking out the hot water system. May as well go first class and install copper pipe or PVC instead of the galvanized variety to be sure that this problem does not re-occur.

Well my love, the day has ended on an upbeat. Victor, the owner of Black Power, told me of 15 amapa beams, wrong size, but checked out the plumbing and agreed to do the job. He has the tools, can solder copper, etc. My regular crew will chip away at concrete and tile to give him a clear shot. As a bonus, I now have hot water, cannot use the bathroom or shower but can wash dishes. I made arrangements with Peter Brown to use his hopper and have a key to his house for my more serious evacuation endeavors.

Runner and I are staying home tonight. It has been a helluva day. We miss you but this is a war that's best fought alone. Got the bathroom ready for plumbing and require six grey tiles and one with a design. Must start on search. A bit more serious problem is that the subterranean water shifted the foundation separating the shower stall from the wall and cabinet. Umberto believes it can be saved and the fact that the room is open expedites drying and firming. It is a bitch.

Got your letter. Terribly sorry to hear about Gertie and delighted that she seems to be okay, scary as hell. The crew just quit so I am going off to the shower, more on my return.

It is getting just the least but chilly to hose off in the garden but should be able to take a hot shower shortly if I can a get the plumber and buy match-up the tile. That is tomorrow's task as well as getting info on the dome man. Glad to get the bathroom sketch for Umberto. Plenty needs doing. Cindy is no longer in heat so R is much calmer and has made no attempt to jump the neighbor's fence. The zinnias are fading. Hilde has some African daisy seeds which I may have Manuel toss in. Also got some Big Boy tomato seeds from a gardener I know who received a whole bunch from his bosses in the mail from LA.

Every once in awhile like while re-reading your letters , I wish you were here or I there quite strongly. Runner feels the same, I'm sure. Pretty well writ out so will put some clothes on and visit Hilde to find out when Gustavo is due back, have a beer at the Tesoros, fix dinner and either read or write and listen to election returns. Later.

Well, it's Bush for four years. Buy stock.

The laundry ladies came by and with some difficulty, I explained that I need a dusting and floor scrub job and I would notify them when I have water. Every surface is covered with a patina of dust from construction. I don't know how to deal with the upholstered stuff. I beat cushions outside and watch clouds rise but what the hell I do you do with arms and bodies????

Went to the Tesoros and about 8:30 told Pember and Bet that I was going home and having a barbecue sandwich on the main square. They asked, "Where?" and I invited them to dinner. It blew them away. They said that in their 20 years here it was the first time for 'em.

Pember said that his friend and dentist is coming in a week and they made plans to take him there for dinner one night. They each had two sandwiches. I've always had the impression that through Chacho and seniority they knew this town and were fairly well assimilated. Strange indeed, don't you think? Anyway, we are invited to dinner at their pad. I have a feeling that Bet is courting me because of you. They'll be going to San Carlos for a meeting of the Arizona-Sonora commission. Bet is the U. S. arts rep. I have no idea of what she does.

It's after 10:00. I've heard all the election news necessary to last four years. Who cares how California goes. A hug, kiss and cuddle and goodnight.

Wednesday, November 9, 1988

Did marketing and made morning call to Peter's john. Plumber is here and making a list of needed supplies which I will pick up ASAP. Will do a wire and wood fence that according to Umberto won't last long, he's strongly recommending pipe and says solid would not only fuck up the view but would screw up air circulation and probably blow down. So be it.

My concern is Runner containment so we are gonna compromise on this one. Haven't checked Gustavo's return yet. Want to solve the urgency of plumbing and fencing. Freeze my ass off when I get up at 6:00. May move to one of the front rooms if the electric heater can't work manaña. Primitive living and element exposure is fast losing its charm. On my way, more later.

Cannot buy the necessary plumbing supplies in Álamos nor can I match the tile, get the pipes and wire for fencing. The goddamned architect cannot be reached until 4:00 p.m., so there is no sense in going to Navojoa since the stores close until 3:00 p.m. It may be necessary to go in tonight to see the architect. Frustration resulting from sheer impatience builds. Umberto just came by to show me an eight foot span of totally rotten pipe. It did not brighten my life. The guesthouse bathroom wall is going up and it is anybody's guess as to whether or not the shower stall wall can be saved when things dry out.

Of a more serious nature is whether or not the whole damned bathroom floor has to be ripped out because of settling, and to top off these tragedies, the architect that used the dome men gave up on him and is finishing his projects with cement slab roofs. The other folks here in Álamos are dealing with new construction and can afford to wait since they are in no great hurry. The architect knows of a dome man in Esperanza that works the Guaymas San Carlos area. The town is five miles north of Obregon and I will try to go this morning with Gustavo. The only other solution is to commission Pancho to go south and find one or go myself and drive, since Runner can't go on busses and I'm reluctant to kennel him if that is possible in Navojoa. Of course, it leaves unsupervised help for a week; not a good idea. I'm pronged on the horns of my own dilemma, I guess and simply don't know what to do. Shit. Maybe the Esperanza guy will come through or Umberto's friend that worked in the south is competent; only time will tell. Think I'll buy something to eat, have some wine and crash. Tomorrow's got to be better.

Friday, November 11, 1988

Dear Joan,

A slight problem. Nobody seems to know when the dome man is coming. There are two other people looking for him. I'm going to meet with one of them today and see what has to be done to bring in another guy. I also learned that there is a local man who spent 15 years in Guadalajara and can do them, but I have no idea of how good he is. I will check with the others with the same problem, including an architect, to determine the feasibility of the route. In the meantime, I'll get the bathroom under roof, fireplace and bed built in the guesthouse, etc.

Other than that, am having a good time. Went to Navojoa with the Cooks. Still haven't found the proper fencing wire. Tom brought in an amplifier for repairs. They took me to lunch at a spectacular seafood place. Mary did frog legs, Tom broiled fish and Kendall ordered what could well have been bass in a beer batter. It's called "rebozado" style and since none of us knew what it meant I ordered it. Great.

Stayed home last night and tried a new carrot recipe. Partially cooked them in water with sugar added and then sautéed them in butter and dusted 'em with bouillon powder. It's a winner. I'm getting better at frying cubed potatoes jazzed up with onions.

Been reading Wilder. I forgot how good he is. The Flying Doctors are in. Met a few yesterday and they remarked that I looked like John Huston. Shit, he looks like me. The crew is busy working and I'm off to the market and then Gustavo to seek his counsel and help line up a meeting to find a dome man. Later, love.

Gustavo must have taken off for the weekend. Place is locked. Went marketing and watched a 4 K race. Met Mrs. Preece who was out for a morning jog, and joined it. She told me that they got all their furniture at the Concordia factories and bought their tile in Nogales and flew it down. She said that is the year it took 'em to do the house; they flew down 24 times to check progress and still encountered mistakes and slow-downs.

I'm waiting for the guys to finish and get on the dome problem. I should have started doing something a couple of weeks ago but everybody kept reassuring me that he would come because the money here is much better than in the south.

It is getting a little colder in the mornings and a roof will help. Got my Tesoros bill, about $45 for a month. Not at all bad because I ate there and ran up a bunch of beer and wine tabs. Went to visit the Acosta family and learned from Mrs. A., an American gal, that an architect in Navojoa controls the dome man's movements. Went to Polo's, no answer at office. Tried his home, and wife said he was expected later. Came back for a garden bath and to wash R's head. He picked up something pissing under a big truck (grease?). Of course I'm kicking myself for not having taken these steps a couple of weeks ago, but! To be continued.

Gustavo called the architect at 6:00—still not home—but spoke to an associate who said the dome man was due tonight. We are to call back at about 10:00 this a.m. and Gustavo is going to try to arrange a meeting in Navojoa.

Saturday, November 12, 1988

Dear One,

Yesterday was pure frustration. Gustavo, Pancho and I went to Esperanza, and after a couple of hours of searching to find the local dome builder, only to learn that he had died last February. We then located an engineer in the town of Cócorit, in the heart of Yaqui country, who directed us to the home (and it is a beaut) of a contractor who's into building for gringos in San Carlos where domes are occasionally used. Gustavo will phone him this weekend and I may run to San Carlos Monday if warranted.

At 1:00 p.m. today I'm going to hunt up a retired maestro of maestros from Guadalajara with Umberto and Jose Medellin to see if he would be willing to take on the job He lives on a ranch about ten miles out of town. Will also check on another dome builder who has contracted to do the masonry work on a supermarket at the beach. Perhaps he can locate one of his former colleagues in the south. Pancho is also going to call his cousin in Guadalajara, who is an architect's secretary, to see if a maestro who is available can be found recommended by the latter. All this activity and no closure, verily a pain in the ass. More later. Got things that need doing and got to go ....

Just got the mail. My problems here are miniscule by comparison. You sound pissed at the medical care Gertie has received and it does sound sloppy as hell. I'd contact an ambulance-chaser immediately. Won't cost a penny on a contingency basis and win or lose you can be damned sure that that's an oversight that the doctor will never make again, so in the future no patients will have to suffer.

Got two purchase slips from Schwab. Seems that Skip spent all the money I received on the buyout. I told him to cool it until I got back because I had to put aside money for capital gains tax, finish the house, lay some bread on you, etc. I'm going to have to call him Monday, maybe from San Carlos, and give him a royal reaming and get his suggestions on what to sell to raise cash. To make matters worse, I haven't received my Schwab statement and don't know how much money I have left. Shit. Sometime it seems as if my little world is caving in. If I can get the goddamned domes finished I can put this place on hold and get back and give you a hand with your folks, but until that is solved I'm riveted here. Shit!!!

Bring the wolf tape with you. A VCR would be available at Gustavo's or Bet and Pember's. Got to go again.

Back, paid the crew, advanced the brick-maker 100,000 pesos so that he can buy wood to fire up the kiln to finish the rest of the brick. Planted the garden, 14 short rows of assorted stuff for future transplanting. Will keep it wet continuously for awhile. Will start moving out the zinnias and replace the area with some African daisies Hilde gave me and a packet call "Western Wild Flowers."

Forgot to mention that Runner woke up with some sort of exudate so I went to the vet pharmacy and am treating it. It could be dust infection, but I want to be on the safe side.

Discovered that Manuel can't read so I dealt with the garden, proper depth, spacing, etc. Will transplant when things come up. Your brick border was a good idea. Still haven't fenced, too preoccupied with other things. Have the casita window opened to the ground. Took one guy a day and a half with mallet and chisel. The wall is up to window height and the concrete broad beams laid so that the gas tank cannot be seen. Will have to decide whether or not to go ahead and have the bathroom roofed pre-doming or work on the pool. With drying taking place over the weekend. I'll know whether the floor and tile walls of the bathroom can survive.

My main concern is getting the hopper hopping. I'm taking Lomatil for insurance. The quarter mile walk to Peter's pad can get scary. So far no accidents, but in Mexico one never knows, does one.

Crew's gone. Victor hasn't shown up for the plumbing costs, labor and materials. I'm filthy, so it's hose time for me and R's weekly shampoo and off in search of a dome man. Quick change of plan. Remembered that I forgot to eat, so fixing something. Will ablute absolutely later. Running out of time and am pretty sure I'll be back before 3:00 with plenty of sun remaining. Food and duty call.

The next episode in search of a dome man: met with the maestro of maestros. He did some 40 years ago in Nayarit and has since made some ovens locally using the same technique, but said that it would take him a month to do one today. I then drove him from his ranch to look at two that the man who never returned did. Good work, he said. That, we knew. Tomorrow, between 9:30 and 10:00, I will meet him at Polo's. He will call both his brother and sister. He has a nephew who's a civil engineer and another an architect and he said he would put them to work locating a maestro. I have to see Gustavo so that either way he can call him when they line up somebody so the arrangements can be made for him to come. Transfer of funds and maybe a quick trip down to move the body and check the work if indicated. The next chapter of search tomorrow. Now to bathe; after all, it is Saturday.

Sunday

Did my weekly Tianguis run early and bought my usual stewing hen, which soups up and yields a meal and a half dozen sandwiches. Met the old maestro at Polo's at 10:00 and called his brother in Guadalajara. He explained the problem and left it that the architect's son would look for a dome man and call back at 4:00 p.m. Was back at 4:00 p.m., no luck, but the search will continue. Another phone call at 4:00 p.m. Monday should, according to the old maestro, bring the results we want. We'll see.

Spent Sunday on the square to watch the weekly young girl fashion show and eat world class tacos. Forgot to mention that Armida invited me to dine Saturday. She had shrimp in green olive sauce. R ate all of the shrimp but left three or four olives on his plate. Kept the garden moist and am waiting for seeds to sprout. That's what you do in Álamos for excitement.

Up at 5:30. Couldn't make it to Peter's so did my daily in the garden and buried same. Today the hopper goes in. Thank God no rain. Life will get better. Will be having a scrubber/duster in for a half day if she shows. Upholstery is going to be a problem. Can beat the cushions, but arms and back are a problem. What to do???

The crew has arrived and are busy completing the brickwork required to finish the casita bathroom. You were right about using a large picture window in the front. It do look good as does the arched doorway.

R's eye has cleared up. The medicine worked. May go to Navojoa today to buy things. Will also go and check brick. Either my body is adjusting or it is warmer this morning. I did not have to drink coffee swathed in blankets. I will buy my own Sonoran cot in Navojoa and a pad designed to go with it. It will be a good thing to have on hand and stores easily. Armida's going to need hers in a couple of weeks.

If I go to Guadalajara, will pick up an equipale set for portales use. Both Peter and Pancho agreed to come with me should the trip be necessary to hand-carry the dome man. Also have to contact a Dr. Acosta (MD), who's ready for doming. The more work I can promise, the more the attractive a package I can offer to get him up here. Learned from Peter that cypress trees are protected but might be able to locate old beams for bathroom. Sun's blasting in the room and I better get downtown to make sure I can get R food. They run out early. If I missed, have learned to keep a reserve in the freezer. More later "Andale."

Did Navojoa plumbing supplies; looks like the bathroom floor can be saved. Also bought fence wire, you may not like it but it will do the job. It's not what I wanted but after four hardware stores and three construction material places, it was the best I could find. Still fiddle-fucking around. Two 4 o'clock phone calls to Guadalajara. Another to be made at 2:00 p.m. tomorrow. If I can't score, will run up to San Carlos on Wednesday, and failing that, head south as soon as possible. It is all very depressing. My immediate concern is rain. I've got mops, buckets and plastic ready if it hits tonight. Life here ain't hell.

Post-phone call continuation. We were cut off after a 30 minute attempt to get through; I just plain quit. All the preceding is probably redundancy. But, and it's a big but, I was mighty glad to learn that Gertie and Mart are okay and that I can expect you on the 23rd. Assume you'll be returning with the Preece people. 'Bye until tomorrow.

Just a note because I want this in the mail and hope it gets through before you leave. Got the crew working. I can now use the bathroom. They are finishing up the guesthouse and reinforcing the back bathroom wall with brick. It might cost us six inches of space and $100, but Umberto recommends it for structural integrity because the original adobe is wearing out. As you recall, it was an exposed fence wall and probably 100 years old.

Waiting impatiently for the magic group of two to arrive for a phone call to Guadalajara. If today, will have Pancho available to deal with financial arrangements, transportation, etc. While my Spanish is getting me around now, I lack precision and cannot deal effectively with tense changes. It will come, I guess. All for now.

Love, R & E

Monday, November 28, 1988

Dear Joan,

Phone calls cannot be made on Sundays. Tried for two-and-a-half hours and finally, frustratedly, quit. Wanted to find out how your flight went and to tell you that they are here. Professor Medellin brought them by my house, two live dome men. They had been on the bus for 16 hours and made Álamos by noon. I fed them, checked them into the Somar to shower and sleep, and took them to Lupe Camarena's ranch with an introductory note from the latter's nephew in Tepic.

Then back to Professor Medellin for negotiations, which were interesting. Camarena and Medellin were definitely protecting my interests re: price and time. The dome men wanted to start, break for Christmas, and return and finish. The guy that did the other domes simply roughed them out, didn't do drainage canals and other details. We messed around discussing hiring them as independent contractors or as weekly workers like my regular crew. After much back and forth, we agreed that they would work from daylight to dusk, seven days a week and Lupe knocked 300,000 ($132 USD) off the original asking price of 900,000 ($394 USD) per room for a total of 2,400,000 ($1,053 USD) plus room and board on the promise that they'll bust their asses and be finished by Christmas. After my last experience with the no-show guy, I was afraid of a Christmas break, for fear that I'd never see them again.

They will also be living in the glass room and doing their own cooking, which seems to be the pattern for traveling artisans. They had just completed a beachfront place in Puerto Vallarta and that was their modus operandi. At the moment, they are crawling around the roof of the dining room taking all kinds of measurements. As luck would have it, I took them on a nickel tour of Álamos yesterday evening and ran into Umberto buying a Sunday taco in the plaza. I made intros, let 'em out of the truck, and took off. Later learned from Armida that Umberto was very enthusiastic and told her that now we'll really get rolling, or the Spanish equivalent thereof.

In the meantime, his crew has started building beams for el baño and we'll go on an old brick search after we find forms to rent or buy. Feeling good and relieved that finally things are happening. It's going to be a busy three weeks, but domes will be up to greet you when you return to Álamos. Off and running.

Back from a purchasing run, bought the rebar for the beams and ten 15-foot or more pieces of wood (logs) for the dome men to build scaffolding. The present set-up isn't nearly high enough. Must also do a brick check and locate wood to construct forms. Things are moving, whoopee. Later.

We have peculiar-shaped rooms, not square but sort of rhomboid; this sets up special problems and costs time. The domer, he's like a kid with a new toy, watching, asking questions, etc. I don't know at this stage whether to go back to the States this Saturday or see this through. They have jig-sawed one corner and are working on another to compensate for the room's shape. I fed 'em ramen noodles for lunch. They loved 'em. Tonight caldo de pollo con legumbres and many tortillas.

Just got back from trying to rent a brick-cutting machine. The guy could not be found. It would expedite things because they are hand-cutting now. Not getting much work out of Umberto. He's like a kid with a new toy, watching, asking questions, etc. I don't know at this stage whether to go back to the States this Saturday or see this through. I'll just take it a day at a time and see what happens. Had the girl in to clean up—a mistake, concrete and dust are flying again, more in awhile.

It's time to buy tortillas. Back. Bought 1.1 pounds of tortillas and was advised that the daily requirement is 2.2 pounds. During my absence, Lupe Camarena showed up to observe progress. He was also here at 8:00 a.m. He showed up five minutes ago with a brick-cutter. It works like a charm but the dust it throws is incredible and, as I learned from you, dust is the enemy.

Two corners completed up to five full brick courses. They tell me that once the corners are in place, they will be able to roll. Sure hope so. The more I think about it, the more I want to stay. Dilemma. Will try to locate a periodontist in Navajoa or Obregon and may as well try and do it now or I'll be going back to Tucson four or five times a year, a pain in the ass. More on this subject later.

It is after four and the brick guys are still at it. They told Pancho they hope to finish (rough) the dining room by Friday. Once the bricks are in place and the cement sets up, they clean each seam with steel brushes. They said that in the south most people apply a coat of lacquer to the interior. I must find out more about it and why it is done—structural or aesthetic reasons?

Had Manuel re-burlap the Sonoran cot for one of the guys to sleep on. He loves doing things like that and does an excellent job as well. Will go to Gustavo's to call you later and hope I can get a line out. If I can, most of the previous will be redundant. All for now.

Dome-making observations. A thin, goopy cement is used and some of it dribbles out when bricks are pressed together. The maestro eyeballs every piece and if a special cut size on angle is required, he yells to his apprentice, who slices the brick and delivers it. The position and angle of each brick is checked visually and then by touch as it curves and angles to the zenith. It's 5:30 now and they're chugging away while there is still light. He has one more difficult corner to master and true up, which he may leave for tomorrow and better light, which is fast failing. Muy interesante. Also, it seems to be the apprentice's job to try to anticipate brick needs, much as good OR scrub nurses have instruments at the ready before surgeons ask.

Tuesday

Morning has come. Awoke to the sound of cement being mixed, the apprentice's job, while the maestro was heating coffee water. A bonus for me as I staggered into the front room. This was critical because they are starting on the stove corner and it has to be covered up with wood and tarp to protect it from cement globs. Breakfast will wait. After much discussion, they are not satisfied with one corner so they are going to rip it out, a couple of hours work down the tubes, but beauty doesn't come easy. Umberto showed up. He located 400 old bricks, but the guy wants 1000 pesos (44-cents USD). We agreed that it was an exorbitant price, so we are still looking.

I was sure glad the plane trip was smooth as silk. I have memories of small plane rides thirty years ago that were rough and scary. Will head downtown later and see about getting Armida's help in making an appointment with the Japanese periodontist. It does make a world of sense for me to hang around just in case.

Forgot to tell you about the dumb thing I did yesterday. Went to the bank to transfer funds and then Ole Bill came in and I helped him clear a check. The place was packed. I left and got as far as Peter Brown's house before I realized something was missing. Runner!!! Ran all the way back. He was right where I left him and didn't realize that I had gone. Wow. It's about 7:30, so will be out canvassing butcher shops for his food and hit the tortilla line for what will become the daily kilo. The dome guys flame them over the stove. Ya gotta be quick and they come out sort of toasty. Muy sabroso. Later.

Did my marketing chores and set up my short order restaurant. Since the pan only holds two eggs and two potatoes (if you move them around a lot), I had a flurry of activity going. In the middle of all this, Bill, Peter and Poncho showed up. The former solved a major problem with my lousy, locally bought can opener. I have trouble keeping up with the bean demand. He's going to lend me a crock-pot. I'll get a recipe from Armida and do two-to-three days at a clip. I also want to make salsa en masse for the same reason. The little 100 gram cans last about a meal, so it makes sense to do a pint or so at a shot. Also, the guys insist on doing their own dishes, a nice touch. Time has come to clean up the cantina; will then head downtown to call the periodontist for an appointment. To be continued.

Armida accompanied me to Polo's to make an appointment with el periodontist, no answer. She also gave me a lesson in bean-making, has a kilo cooking which I will pick up later for dinner. Just did lunch, canned frijoles, salsa, two ramens (they love 'em) and chopped carne tacos. I'm stuffed and indolent. They are up on the roof. They've laid two corners with about 25 brick courses each. I figure that they will complete about one-quarter by six tonight. We worked out an eating schedule. Rolls and coffee break at 7:30, breakfast from 9:00 to 10:00, lunch 2:30-3:30, dinner anytime after 7:00. Got to keep the help strong and happy to be done by Christmas.

4:00 p.m., dishes done. They've been an hour on a killer corner. They've already ripped it out once and are on their second shot. Slow progress and they have three more bad ones, two in the baño to struggle with. I think they'll be happy if they can get it done before dark. Umberto is at a critical stage of beam-making, so I imagine his crew will be quitting late tonight. I'm on my way down to Armida's to try to find the dentist and pick up frijoles. Bye.

No dental appointment. Try manaña in typical Mexican fashion. For what it's worth, Gen Reynolds recommends the guy highly. Time to do dinner. I get to do meat and salad. They squish and refry a monstro pot of frijoles, courtesy of Armida. More manaña.

PHOTO GALLERY

A Spanish–Style
Home Restoration 1987–1989
Álamos, Sonora, México

Photos by Gene Riggs and Joan Gould

HOUSE AT TIME OF PURCHASE – PHOTOS: GENE RIGGS

Numero 6 Toluca, Álamos, Sonora, México 85650

RESTORATION IN PROGRESS – PHOTOS: GENE RIGGS

RESTORATION COMPLETE! – PHOTOS: JOAN GOULD

Wednesday, 7:00 a.m.

Tricky corner started. Peter came by and joined us for our dinner party. He's afraid he picked up a bug, giardia, beaver fever, in the south so I gave him chicken soup and a few books. He's planning to split in a couple of days since he's not feeling too good and claims that it takes about a week to perform the necessary lab tests before they start treating him. He's had it before. Too bad.

Ran into Stephanie in the street. Full of enthusiasm about her trip to Chiapas with Kendall and Bob. Was heading up to the latter's for drinks and asked me to join, but I declined. My days of gadding about evenings are over for the duration.

All four corners of the dome are in place. The basic structure should be about half done today. I learned that the clear varnish they put on after its completion is needed to provide a seal and eliminate a perpetual rain of brick dust. Peter says his old bricks shed constantly but you get used to it. I'm going to have Umberto learn the technique and mixture, and apply it to our old brick. Dust is the enemy in all forms, colors and shapes and must be stamped out ruthlessly with the same true grit and patience one requires when engaged in mortal combat with cucarachas.

Breakfast was a big success. Eggs, tortillas and beans and more beans. The tortilla ration must increase to 1.5 kilos. Guadalupe Camerena came by, judged the ongoing work with a cool professional eye, and said that these guys are better craftsmen than the man that never showed. I also gave him 250,000 pesos to wire to his architect nephew to cover from Puerto Vallarta to Álamos expenses for both men. It includes meals, phone calls, motel, etc.

We also re-rigged the brick-cutting machine to work on the portales to cut down interior dust. It will make a big difference in the quality of life. I may get Lupe to do the casita fireplace if he is willing. Might as well get the consummate, albeit retired, maestro out of pasture for another job. He told me that he can replicate any fireplace from a picture. If you see one in a home and garden magazine you like, bring down a picture. It would be a clean way to repay him for helping to procure the dome men. More in awhile.

I've got an hour or two of clean-up, and must go to the market and buy serrano chiles, tomatoes and onions for salsa in copious amounts, too. Lupe checked the work and thinks they are about a day and a half to cupola stage. Progress. The dome now looks like this. And they'll be moving along the sides, continually arching upwards. I imagine that they'll fill in the sides with about five to six hours left of daylight. The beams are up in the casita and the ventilator has been placed. I'm pepping the skylight as centrally as possible. Though bigger, the casita dome will go faster and I'm tempted to look at a spiral and go for it. I saw a picture of one in Ron Slaughter's house. I can ask Margaret the maid for a look-see since he isn't due back until December 15. It's 12:40 and got to shower before Umberto and crew returns, more to come.

The cleanest hombre in all of Álamos writes you. Solved some plumbing problems. Ole Bill and I directed the drippy kitchen faucet. He found a strategically placed pebble and I fixed an improperly seated ring. Nary a drip. Also figured out how to kick up the hot water in the heater and then turn it down. I also bought the proper bushing to enable the safety valve to be added when I catch up with a plumber. I cobbled together a wax barrier to confine water to the shower stall as settling continues. And so it goes.

The gap closes ... couldn't catch Gustavo and am having a bitch of a time trying to locate old brick. Checked several sources and hate to rip up the garden but ... may have to.

Thursday, 12:03 p.m.

Up and at 'em early. The dome should be almost complete by tomorrow. Will go to Navojoa to check cupolas as well as the one on the hill. The debate is six- or eight-sided; I can go either way. Will also do periodontist. The apprentice has la grippe. Got him some medicine. Have to keep him healthy. Though am beginning to feel like a slave-driver. Good to talk to you from Polo's. Things to bring: oil and air filter, and case of oil. Pep Boys always has them on sale with a rebate deal on the latter.

Opened the B5&R letter, your quarterly appraisal and a five page economic treatise analyzing current conditions. They are "cautiously optimistic." Talked to Skip and asked about creating a tax loss on a couple of stocks, about $700 USD total as well as the advisability of my doing the same. Forget above. I will try and reach him at Polo's.

Still no luck with old brick. Pancho, who has been out looking, claims they are as difficult to find as long amapa because they cannibalize the garden and break Manuel's heart. Can't win 'em all, I guess. Nuff writ for now.

Just ran into another brick dead-end. Found old salt brick, weak, couldn't use. Also found old brick at $500 USD a copy un-cleaned, much work needed to get rid of old cement. Will make one more try. This a problem I don't need and frankly, with new brick in the dome I think new brick will look like shit. I might add that Umberto is not too pleased with the idea of old brick either since their size and clinks make them rather irregular and somewhat difficult to work with. More to come.

Shit, still no brick. 4:00 p.m., Umberto's got the concrete beams poured and is busy bricking up to the roof line. He's asked the dome maestro if he could work with him a little Saturday and Sunday. The dome is now about two-thirds finished and moving along nicely now that they've compensated for the two crazy time consuming corners. They are now talking about a complete dome, cupola inclusive, by Sunday and a start on the bathroom follows.

Back to hosing the garden. So far they are on schedule. Caught up with Gustavo. He will be by manaña to tell Umberto where we might set old brick, of greater import, and I hope he calls you tonight. I tried and missed. Do not buy Nogales tile. He was up there pricing last week to buy 50 meters, a lot, and said the prices were ridiculous. He developed a Dolores Hidalgo contact that will deliver to Álamos on the way to the Tijuana warehouse that supplies California. The truck driver will bring catalogs and samples. The delivery will cost $35, less than the price of one box of Nogales tile. Worse. Gustavo can order by phone and the tile truck makes a weekly run.

Peter left today and said that for the past week, he has been feeling chronically seasick and so back to San Francisco until spring. I'll sort of keep an eye on his house and exercise judgment if a pipe breaks or a brick leaves its 250-year-old home and drops, breaking on an equally old floor brick.

The crew is cooking some bean dish. I got back from Gustavo's too late to prepare hamburgers a la mexicana. I do the salad. Beans, here goes ... It can best be described as a bean and salsa dip with undeniable authority served silverware-less with a mound of tortillas. There's an art to eating this way with a number of variables I have yet to master such as: how big a piece of tortilla to tear off to get a mouthful of dip, how to get a mouthful of dip without the tortilla bending or breaking, unpardonable act for they stare at you and wonder how you can be falling in the beans, how to deliver to your mouth without having it drop off or sully your mustache, and on and on. I'm sure they don't want to be seen eating in public with me. But I'm observing and practicing.

After you overcome the initial shock, the food was delicious. A synergy occurs between the three ingredients, salsa, beans, and tortilla, that's unbelievable. Now I've got to figure out how to get them to take over the evening meal, cooking while I do the mundane eggs and potato bit with a store-bought pan dulce from the local bakery and the noontime "Caldo de Ramen." They love the stuff, can't get enough of it (or they're just being polite) because I'm pushing it and they douse it with my irreplaceable Heinz ketchup. (Please restock me; plastic bottles travel better.) Also, if you see a good buy on ramens, eight-to-ten for a dollar, throw in several cases when you come down. I love 'em and they make great gifts. It's about 7:30 so I head to my room. They'll be in bed before 8 and I'll read for awhile. G'nite.

Almost forgot to call Runner; he is conversing right now with two dome men watching him with fascination as he does his snap crackle pop routine on bloody, red, raw beef bones. Upon reflection, my life in Mexico seems to fluctuate between trauma and drama. But I feel very much alive. I hope Runner runs out of bone. It's almost 8:00 o'clock and the team is nodding. I'm going to let him take a bone to bed and let them crash. Nite again

Friday 6:45 a.m.

Umberto showed early to check work they completed after 4:00 p.m. Today may bring closure. What an apt word. I'm going marketing early. Got a lot of things to do before heading for the Navojoa dentist. More upon my return.

Back. They do a pound of tortillas daily per man. Impressive, no? Armida's beans will play out today and then I am on my own. Even Runner is going Mexican and developing a B&T taste. I may do the TGIF briefly at 5:30 since its being held at the Perkins, our neighbors from whom I copied the wall. Will have Umberto rip out the spot you disliked and re-do; will be easy with the brick-cutter available.

Going to change clothes and clean up and hope Gustavo shows before I have to split. All for now.

He didn't, I split. Had my teeth done by the dentist and not a tech. If you have a chance, see if Dr. Knochel can send me my records. Explain that I couldn't come back to the states four times a year for his ministrations and express my gratitude for the work he has done.

The dome is almost ready to be cupola'd. Checked the Navojoa domes, octagonal and great. Three windows, bordered in and out with black. White sides and brick top on the outside, or on the cupola where the mini-dome starts. Impressive. Also bought a bunch of food, coffee, and about five pounds of sawdust for Runner. He'll be happy. Also bought a bottle of wine in case I decide to do the TGIF around the corner.

Umberto's filling in the pool. If I can't catch Gustavo and locate decent brick, I'm going new. I can't hold up the schedule and the bathroom has to be completed before the dome men get rolling. Besides, it won't be used that much and we can shit in elegance under the dome.

It's almost 3:00 and the post office will be open and I want this in while it can still fit in an envelope.

Love, R & me

P. S. Victor came by to see the dome (Black Power). He said I need an electronic clutch component and a small part for a six cylinder '85 Ford 1.5 v. Also off-loaded the tile replacement for the bathroom. It's Saltillo, 44 to a meter, 30-cents plus per.

More love, R & me

December 1988

Dearest Joan,

The dome is done with the exception of the cupola. Learned that the orifice is determined primarily by the width of the mason's shoulders. Umberto's crew are shallowing the pool until I get roof brick. The dome men are off to get their tools sharpened and setting up to make an octagonal form.

Went to the TGIF party for about a half hour and the dome men babysat Runner. No problems whatsoever. There's a circus near the Dolisa Motel and a few fireworks. R was glad to stay home. Last nights' dinner consisted of the ubiquitous beans, this time with a garnish of chicharrones and salsa. Fortunately I bought some flour tortillas in town. We agreed that they are okay but corn is better. They are also harder to scoop food with and I kept losing food in my beard until I chickened out and used a spoon. The Perkins' house is mansion-like.

The local club secretary will be adding our names to the Gringo List, 139 strong. One died last week in a house in the vicinity of the Nuzums and it will be up for sale shortly. Met a major bass fisherman who said the lake was lousy this year because of the drought and will take a couple of years to recover to its former glory. In case you forgot I would like an on-sale yellow fishing rod and reel and some spinners. Advance Mart some money and let him get them. He'll like it. Also, if you can manage, check out the Bimco double sinks. And tell Ray that the heaters will be returned. Check Price Club and bring one or two down.

The weather has warmed up and I've been wearing T-shirts, sandals and jeans from dawn to dusk. Jackets and sweaters are unnecessary. It's getting close to 7:30 and time to do marketing. Will take one more shot at old brick and failing, get the roof going. The technique to be used is a drawing.

When the roof is on, I'll have doors and windows installed, get the fence completed, build the support pillar to eliminate the bathhouse roof sag, and dance around a lot. When the domes are done will deal with plastering and getting things set for painting, tiling, etc., will also get casita fireplace made or may hold off if you want a special number. I'm trying to see if I have enough work to keep my crew intact before I tackle the two front rooms. I think it would be better all around if I could defer until after the holidays. I will ask around, the custom might be to knock off work during that period. Off to el mercado and the daily tortilla run.

Got my tortillas stashed, picked up a handful of jalapeños and tomatoes and we are set. By the time the domers depart, our tastes will have drifted further apart because I believe that my hot food capacity is increasing daily and I like it. Didn't so much as scorch a hair this morning. Going to try my first pot of beans today. Hildy's crock-pot book didn't have a clear water-to-bean recipe and Gustavo claims that hers are lousy anyway so I'm going to improvise with the pressure cooker and see what happens. Then off the Pember for a quick swimming pool consult followed by brick checking. It looks as if I'll have a surplus of dome bricks which can be incorporated into a fireplace, barbecue, etc. Will quit now while I clean beans, do chores, etc. Later, Love.

Swimming pool crises. Ran down Pember to learn about steel reinforcing rods and recovered Sunset pool book. Hilde was by yesterday with a friend to look at the domes. They talked to the dome men. I told her that I laid out a bunch of bricks, also learned that you couldn't be reached by phone to abort the Nogales run re: tile. Hilde said she would track them down and bring them here and said I would appreciate an expense-sharing.

Came home to find a flooded floor re: dishwasher. One of the guys did something. It won't drain by itself so scooped it out. Mopped up and took what I could apart with the wrong tools, cleaned it up, but can't get it to run, said "fuck it." Paid off the help. Have 2M pesos left and will have to go to Tesoros to cash a check after I check brick, etc., and after I do a couple of other things. Took the dome men up to see cupola and they are hot at it again and wondering what's for lunch. Damned beans aren't even boiling.

Later, in a happier mood. Too much pressure today. More things are improving. Umberto, realizing I was broke, gave me 60,000 pesos in partial payment for his wheelbarrow and the beans are boiling merrily. I also have a $50 USD check for sand, cement and miscellany. I lent Gen Reynolds five for her driveway. Off to the P.O.

Thursday, December 8, 1988

Dear Joan,

Lalo came over last night and brought a bunch of homemade cookies. The Flying Doctors operated on his eye Saturday and for the first time since it lost sight, he has been able to see light. They told him that he should be able to see in about a month. His English improved greatly in Tijuana and he's going back to macramé owls. I forgot to show him the plant hanger.

Today started with the new maestro but no Umberto. He told me earlier on that he had to go to Hermosillo to visit a sick brother. The new guy will start plastering the wall, a peon will clean the dome and the domers will continue to do the bathroom. They completed three corners yesterday, will start on the most difficult one today to square things up, and then get rolling . The wind is the worst I've ever seen it and it is supposed to presage rain. If it does, work stops and time is lost on the dome. Shit!

At the moment, the new maestro is knocking holes in the wall to insert posts to erect a new scaffold. The plaster will run up to the lip of the dome. Think I'll leave the cupola natural brick. Wish you were here to advise on this one. We talked about lighting last night and the dome men got up a ladder and we played with a flashlight but could get no idea of placement. Before dark tonight we'll disconnect assorted extension cords and using Peter's lamp and the ladder, and take another try. I'm leaning towards corner lighting. The maestro, two side lights. We'll put it to a vote after tonight's trial. No critical problems looming right now. Just a matter of riding hard. Off to class, more later.

Back from class and shopping. Bought about a pound of quesadilla cheese and some kind of precooked beef. Came home to find the dome men struggling with the tricky corner and the new maestro muddying the wall directly over the stove, which cannot be used. It will be around noon when the stove can be uncovered for an hour for me and the dome men. Wind is still high and I'm hoping it takes the rain clouds away. It's a bitch to water the garden.

After lunch, which consisted of ramen noodles and quesadillas. Things are going great. All four corners of the bathroom are in place and the guys are flying. They are shooting for a Saturday completion date. It looks like the plastering will be completed on the window wall and maybe the short front wall today. Then the other wall gets done and they cut into the dome to extend the fireplace chimney. The dome should be cleaned and painted with one or more coats of varnish applied next week. The same procedure will occur in the bathroom.

Guadalupe Camarena comes by to check progress about every other day. He has an excellent (best in town) tile maestro that we can use for the bathroom and casita and eventually the kitchen. All things considered, when you come the domes will be up, the bathroom roofed, cabinets restored, dining room and possibly casita plastered and electricity in place. This will leave pool completion, fence work and the biggie—the two front rooms—and if doable, foam roofing and detailing and painting after the first of the year. I figure that I'm in for another two or three months before we can worry about furniture, landscaping, etc.

Screwed by the weather. Fierce winds and dust forced the guys off the dome. They told me that the cement doesn't set up properly to keep the bricks positioned properly. However, with decent conditions tomorrow they should be back on schedule. Their target date is to finish by the 22nd and head for home.

May go down to hear the mariachis later if the wind abates. Right now gonna start dinner. Tomorrow I'm going to buy piloncillos, those molasses-like cones, cinnamon and milk. The dome men are going to show me how to make something with the guavas. I haven't been able to figure out what to do with them and we have two large trees. All for now.

Rain came at 3:00 a.m. Thunder and lightning and lasted a couple of hours. It will slow things down. The sky seems to be clearing and the sun is coming out. Should dry things off. Both crews cleaned up and cement is back in use. The dome is about one-third done and one dining room wall plastered and paint ready. Umberto didn't show, along with one peon. Don't know what's happening. Theoretically adding more help should hurry things along. At the moment, this does not seem to be the case.

ALL HELL HAPPENED. A DELUGE HIT AND WORK CAME TO A SCREAMING HALT.

The completed dome, which hadn't been channeled and concrete-slicked to waterproof it, and the concrete between bricks had not hardened, so much leaking and leaching. The interior will have to be re-pointed, a couple of thousand bricks. Construction on the other dome is great. A few sunny days are needed to start drying before interior pointing and plastering continues. I don't know how much lime leached into the bricks and won't until things dry. If it looks too bad, can consider a brick-colored paint. Time will tell.

I've got one maestro and two peons sweeping out water and fallen mortar. It's been raining for five hours now, steady with an occasional cloudburst. The apprentice dome man is cleaning. I'm waiting for a break in the downpour to buy 25 pounds of black plastic and provide some protection. Cannot see the mountains. The garden is submerged. It looks like four lap pools. I haven't assessed the damage to the swimming pool, which probably has a few tons of fill in it that must dry out thoroughly before the bottom can be poured. Oh, woe is me! Leaving for plastic soon. Have a fire going and R is unconcernedly curled in his kennel. More later.

Just got back from downtown and there are rivers in the streets. There's a bad leak in the right-hand front room. The men swept most of the water out and built a sand barrier to protect the concrete. It's down to a drizzle and the mountains can be seen again poking out between low clouds. Everybody was talking about how unusual this rain was at this time of year and how the farmers and ranchers welcome it. All I can think about is limiting the damage and going forward with their work. It's not that cold but I've got a fire going for morale and bought a bottle of brandy to lace coffee with while I think sun. Be glad you are safe and snug and above all, dry. Will see what the crew is doing with the plastic I bought. More later.

Wet bricks, perhaps 2M, are being moved out of the bathroom. The hope is that not too much cement went down the shower drain. Plastic is going up. I hope it's not a matter of closing the barn door after the cow has escaped. Saturday and Sunday will be work days for the dome men to try to get back on schedule. Pity. They are agonizing right along with me.

An hour or so later. Still cleaning up. I've been behind a mop. The guys are using brooms, shovels and buckets. Kitchen cabinet bases have splattered concrete. The bathroom linen closet survived. Still don't know about drains. I'll wait 'til things are cleaned up a bit more before I check them out. The rain quit but the sky doesn't look all that great. My hope is that the worst is over. If it clears off, we should recover. I've got the new maestro and the dome man plus to peons hauling cement to try to provisionally patch the roof. All drains are go in the bathroom and a sand barrier is in place to keep any new rain out of the bedroom. Things could be a lot worse.

I'm going to check mail and pay for the plastic. When I bought it, I didn't have any money. Tomorrow, weather permitting, the crew will move and I'll play with mops and rags to get mud and cement off woodwork, stove, etc. The whole experience reminds me of camping in a field of mud in a leaky tent. At least, nobody is shooting at me and my bed is dry. The hatches are now battened down.

Went to the Post Office about 5:00; both R & I had cabin fever and would you believe, it started to rain ... and so it goes. Lalo came over with some takes of "Scorpion" and what I suspect is a Mexican-equivalent group. We are waiting for coffee to boil and looking at the fire. I reversed R's den so that he can be in it and we can keep track of one another when I sit in the dust-coated but comfortable arm chair. I dream of vacuum cleaners, big ones, commercial or industrial quality, at least two or three, going through the house, manned by fellow dust-haters, and attack in unison and gobbling up every last speck, nay more, of dust.

Saturday, 7:15

Clear and cotton puff clouds. Cement is being mixed, brick is being cut and mortar is being scraped and brick pointed. All is right with the world as it dries out. Life is better.

I've been going to school with Allen Pendergraft, a 70s former Episcopalian preacher who gave up the ministry and became an artist about 40 years ago, when first he came to Álamos. His Spanish seems good but he's trying to improve. Having him in class pushes me. He is in the process of moving from the guesthouse of the "Chocolate Palace" that belonged to the Mars candy bar family to a two room place in the country. He lived in Sedona for many years, did portraits in oil and realistic landscapes. He said that he's a second-rate artist but could produce prolifically a canvas or so per week, a portrait in a couple of months. He developed a following and made a good living at it. He tried living in a retirement community in Mesa but couldn't hack it so will remain here. He has a cousin, age 76, living in a house he put together many years ago and is an interesting old gent with a good sense of humor who knows a lot of things. Al ought to meet him. Apparently he did what Al (Lott) dreams of doing.

Runner came by and nose-poked me. He wants out and I'm not ready, so he went back outside to supervise. He'll be getting a bath today. Also met a young doctor who finished his internship and rented some rooms in the Plaza near the Portales Hotel. His English is excellent and he's having his shingle painted. I hope he's well-trained and makes it. His uncle, the local pharmacist, is helping with office equipment and expenses and he hopes to start seeing patients next week, after the painters leave his office. Of course, I discussed my problems with him and he told me that he'll give me a scrip if I run out of Valium and codeine Tylenol.

To expect a day without a critical problem is being too demanding. The brick on the new dome (one-third complete) is too wet to continue construction. We are now trying to figure out some way to wire Peter's space heater to force hot air on the surface so that the cement can adhere. If this fails, I'll have the scaffolding taken down from the kitchen where the new maestro is plastering and two peons cleaning and pointing and moved to the casita. They can re-rig and do the finish work next week. Dome construction comes first.

Guess I'll check to see what's up. The way these men move wire and electricity around is amazing. Using the cable I brought from the States, they poke two wires in a receptacle, connect to bulbs, heaters, or whatever, and it works. It's also dangerous. The dome maestro is checking to see if the brick edges are drying. Maestro Two is finishing a critical stretch of plastering so that scaffolding can be torn down and moved to the casita in a hurry if necessary. Out to check after I finish my coffee.

Also discovered a bad drainage problem at the casita that could undermine the foundation. After things dry out, will have to work out some sort of pipe or canal system to channel the water away. The heater works and we may have enough dry brick to complete the dome and cupola by tomorrow night. The interior plastering job is museum quality, to quote Dave Hill. All is right in the world again.

Off to the mercado shortly for Runner and people food, the Post Office to mail this, and to pay some bills. Will garden bath both R and myself later due to the inaccessibility of the shower. Umberto didn't show for work today; he's missed three days this week. Don't know what's up. To P.O. now.

Love, Us

Saturday, December 10, 1988

Dear Joan,

Back from Mercado. Runner had a little game of wolf ball going and is panting merrily.

One wall of the kitchen is done, smooth as could be hoped for. Another has a rough coat. Probably be another week before I can call it done and get the cabinets and furniture back. We'll see. The exterior dome will be gleaming with a new coat of concrete curing in the sun. Umberto showed to pay off the help, 208,000 pesos ($91 USD), smallest payroll since we started due to absences. He said he'll be here early tomorrow to leave dome-building and work along with the maestro. An interesting thing, he'll be off my payroll and on the maestro's, who is just as anxious to finish before Christmas and go back to his wife and children with a pocket full of pesos.

Bathroom dome, despite setbacks, is half done. They may reach the two-thirds point by dark, finish it off tomorrow morning and get the cupola forms in place and poured. It will set up overnight for an early start in the brickwork and both they and the scaffolding will be gone by Monday night. The guys in the kitchen should be done by Friday and shift their scaffolding to the bathroom. No other way but to leapfrog.

All for now. Must clean up the lunch dishes and decide whether to start a chicken or a pot of beans. My last pot was good for three days. Runner's been pigging out on Mexican food. It's fun to see him eat tortillas. He holds them between his paws and nibbles, then reaches over, again with his paws. Reminds me of people eating corn.

The day is done. Dome at two-thirds completion. I worked my ass off scraping cement with a spatula off tile and the stove and other surfaces where it dripped during the storm. Other people had problems. Allen Pendergraft dropped in and said his bed was surrounded by a small lake. As a consequence, he was afraid to turn on his electric blanket and froze his ass off, which exacerbated his rheumatism.

Umberto came by for payday. Says his ulcer flared up. As he left, he told me not to pay the maestro so he won't get drunk and be hung over in the morning. Guadalupe Camarina came by to check progress and gave me identical advice. I've heeded the admonishments and we're sitting around waiting for the pressure cooker to deliver a chicken caldo. Lalo is visiting. I made the discovery that my faithful pressure cooker comes considerably short of accommodating a kilo of beans, can do a half kilo, though, very nicely. I removed about two quarts of semi-cooked beans before I put them under pressure and ended up with a bit more than five quarts, peligroso, but in five days más or menos supply of refrito stock.

EMERGENCY: I "safe placed" my dental floss tool and Runner whistle. I have a spare of the latter; the best place to buy them is the pet shop on 22nd Street on the right hand side and past Reid Park. Could also use a flea collar. HELP!

Got to turn the pressure cooker off. Just ate. Lessons in Mexican Cookery and Social Observations: Got a very serious lesson on frijoles. Valentin, the apprentice, showed me the proper amount of beans, one-and-a-half cups, and oil, enough to cover the bottom of the pan. He's an Indian kid from the country an hour out of Tepic and proud that there is a road to his village. His mother taught him how to cook. He's mashing his heart out.

Lalo, the city kid fresh from Tijuana, sidles up to the stove and says, "It's better if you put some milk in it."

The kid looks at him as if he's out of his mind and says "Okay." About a tablespoon of milk is added.

"Cheese is good. Chihuahua cheese is best," Lalo continued to advise.

By coincidence, a big hunk of cheese was sitting in the fridge, left over from the previous day's quesadilla experiment. A little was sliced, diced and added. The mashing continued until the cheese melted into the beans. They were excellent but obviously the Indian kid preferred Mama's. They accompanied a rice-thickened chicken soup with half a chopped chicken floating in it. I used my standard method and localized it with one chopped jalapeño and no black pepper. Just a hint of it came through. A rule: stir-fried jalapeños retain their fire, pressure cooking (boiling) moderates 'em. They ate theirs with tortillas; I used a spoon.

Sunday 7:00 a.m.

Cement is being mixed as the dome men go into gear to complete it up to the cupola with its poured concrete and rebar base. I'll have a bit more coffee and head to the Tianguis for my Sunday ritual shopping adventure. Then I'll brush R first.

Umberto arrived. He'll work alongside the other maestro. If he learns to lay angled brick quickly, we'll be back on schedule. I'll try to keep him with the dome man to assure completion and let the new maestro and crew continue wall plastering and pointing. Then, I'll pull him off the dome for about a day to re-install assorted cabinets in the bathroom and kitchen.

The sun is shining and things are looking up. Later.

Ran into Hilde on the way to the Tianguis. She told me about an exhibition, slide presentation and lecture by an artist (Mexican, she thought). Then on my way home that kid who runs the museum stopped me. He was handing out invitations to the show. I asked, "What about Runner?"

He mumbled something about how he can stay in the office.

I said, "He's visited museums before."

"I'll tell my staff to let him in," he said. The invitation said refreshments, a bonus. Surely something other than beans and tortillas?

Went home and changed clothes. R is pristine and pure (brushed out an amazing quantity of fur; guess it will be a daily chore for awhile). Trotted downtown 20 minutes after the inaugural time, figuring this is Mexico. We passed through the museum and entered a lecture hall cum theatre. I missed the movie with about eight gringos. Bet Nuzum and a Mexican couple and teenaged son were there. The artist's name was Rascon, 50-ish, cosmopolitan, a ceramicist and professor of art at the University in Hermosillo. His presentation was on Peter Voulkas, the guy Bruce studied with and who was this guy's teacher. Interesting man. Had a mediocre pizza and raised havoc among the tuna fish quarters. Good coffee.

Came home and fixed lunch. Manuel Marietta was there to tell me about a 2:00 p.m. reception at Kendall Dawe's Hacienda. We went. Bill Preese says he spoke to you a week or so ago and you'll be flying back. I've yet to receive a letter from you with a schedule. Now I know. This is Sister City weekend so a bunch of people flew in from Scottsdale with clothes and toys. Had a couple of beers and came home.

The team quit early, not enough dry brick to complete the work. The maestro was also unhappy with Umberto's work. He said Umberto lacked the feel, the precise amount of pressure to use when cementing one brick to another, and that he never worked with this size brick and that he used too much mortar, the amount used when building walls. The maestro was very discouraged and talked about going home and completing the casita after January 1. I held fast on how important it was to me to have a December 22 finish. I know he'll give it his best shot and may use Umberto to see if he can help. The maestro said he placed four bricks to each of Umberto's.

Tomorrow will be interesting. The downtown festival ends tonight so I'll wear my cowboy boots to see better and go in about half hour. I'll give the crew $10,000 pesos (approximately $5 USD) for dinner and we'll make it a street food night. The maestro then asked for an additional 10 thousand and I said no. He smiled and said "cerveza?"

"Si" I replied and away they went in search of tacos.

I am only hoping that Umberto can discover the "soul of the brick" by tomorrow. [The dome was completed in December 1988.]

Back from the festival. Álamos school kids did dances, performed skits and sang songs. Pretty dull stuff except for the fact that Jose, Peter Brown's house-sitter, was the director. He looked beautiful in a white suit. Then I realized that he's the English and music teacher at the junior high. He plays great guitar. His English is worse than my Spanish, like Al playing athletic director. He comes from a no-road-to village tucked in the mountains eight hours away, much of it 4-wheel drive, from Álamos. Peter visited there and thought that he caught his premature return to San Francisco bug. If ever invited to his family ranchito, will politely decline.

Visited Armida and Bill briefly. She's in the middle of trying to clean up and repair the other half of the Las Palmeras restaurant. It is a four-room wrecked apartment which she rented to a Mexican couple who ran the ice cream and soda stand outside. She's doing a lot of the wall scraping herself with a one-legged worker who is an excellent worker but has ladder ascension problems. Tired and it's about 9:30. To bed preparatory to another week of testing, trials and tribulations.

Monday, Deember 12, 1988, 6:00 p.m.

Dear Joan,

Guess I'm in the habit of writing to you even though this particular epistle will be hand-delivered. Almost had a neighborhood confrontation. The people behind Gen Reynolds on her street and across the far wall side of our garden complained that during the deluge, our water flooded their patio and house and "what do I intend to do about it?"

I asked her, "Has this happened before in the past 50 years?"

"No," I was assured, "a few days ago was the first time."

Umberto came and checked, mucho palaver back and forth discussing pipes to the street, etc. The upshot was that I'll pay for the pipe and tap into their line running into the city sewer from the guesthouse bathroom, as well as use it to divert the water from their property. Perfect!

Your long-expected letter arrived. Glad to learn things are okay and impatiently await your arrival. It's totally dark and the dome man is still up on the roof finishing what should have been done Friday. Umberto is going to take another crack at it tomorrow. If he does better than yesterday, I'll use the new maestro to finish the guesthouse roof, and put the present maestro to work cement-sheathing the bathroom dome in case of rain. I learn. Then, I'll have him plaster kitchen and bathroom. Pull Umberto off of the dome (if it works) and have him install cabinets for an hour or two.

Contractors like Rudy deal with this shit daily. I find it pretty dicey. Call a spade a shovel. It is work.

Poor Runner. It is Guadalupe Fiesta Day. Big on firecrackers. He's cowering in his kennel. At about 9:00 the noise ceased and I was able to feed him by sitting next to his bowl. Then to bed.

Mortar mixing at daybreak. The apprentice gets things ready before the maestro, who joins me for coffee, then ascends the scaffold. He'll finish off the cupola, and new rigging will go in the guest house. The bathroom will still be hard to use because the interior scaffolding has to remain for the cleaning, pointing and varnishing. I have been looking forward to an honest, indoor, hot water shower. Maybe by the weekend.

School today. Holiday yesterday. One of my classmates dropped out to go the states and take care of some legal biz preparatory to marrying a local girl. I recruited a replacement. Gerry Hammer, a former contractor and Palm Springs friend of Ron (Casa Azul) Slaughter, who has been staying there and is trying to buy a house in Álamos in order to retire and paint. So I'll have two artists in my class. Maybe I'll learn about beauty in Spanish.

The crew arrived. Got to go out and count noses and make assignments for the day's activities. Also had to use the bathroom in heavy traffic. Just came back from an emergency cement run. Delivery did not come on time.

Now off to school. It is brisk this morning. Runner had a nice romp through the building supply store with the owner's dog, who has met him several times at the market or in the street where they dance around together. She's mostly a chocolate labrador.

Later: personnel problems. Umberto showed like a turista to ask questions about cupola building. When I returned from school, he was gone. One of the men told me that he had to go home to deal with a water problem. Then, the maestro and his assistant had a falling out. The latter will be on the bus tomorrow and I'll transfer my best worker, who is currently painting, to work with him. Then I'll hire a replacement.

I've pulled two men off the dome sheathing to set up a new scaffold to maybe get a corner or two blocked out in the guest house. The kitchen scaffold needs raising to complete dome cleaning and painting, but must remain at its present height to complete wall plastering. Will keep the bathroom at present level to expedite cleaning and painting and then lower it for plastering. The juggling act goes on ... the trick being to come out even, i.e. bathroom and kitchen clean and cabineted in about seven working days.

The lady that runs the neighborhood store (you took her red-dressed kid's picture a few years ago), called me in to look at a new puppy, only one and white. I never saw Runner mounting her and neither did she, though the two play together daily. It will be interesting to watch it grow. Runner took a look at it and I couldn't.

Monday, February 6, 1989

Dearest Joan,

R and I had a boys' night on the town. Went to the Tesoros and then to Polo's with Pember and Craig Hill. He just came back from Tucson where he drove his wife, Martha, to catch a plane to Worcester, Mass. We flipped coins for the tab and Pember lost and bitched and bitched. R is happily gnawing and chomping steak bones. Snap, crackle, pop and crunch. Dance at the Ganadero and they just went on set break and R is still eating, so I'll hit the bed in time for the next set. Shit.

Sunday 10:30. Had a lovely time at Tianguis. Shelled peas and fresh carrots again. Mixed with Mexican tuna, fish it makes the best salad niçoise I ever had. Strawberries also made their initial appearance and fresh corn is still coming, four weeks straight. The regular mercado does not have these things yet. Also bought 4000 pesos worth of roast pork and the man gave Runner about the same amount to snack on. It makes good sandwiches for lunch. Cooking and eating treats daily is part of my new program of self indulgence.

Weather is T-shirt weather. Planning on walking to the Cook castle. Ran into Mary last night. She walked in and said it took a half hour. Tom had a root canal done. Their car is in the shop. They're pretty flush right now after paying off bills. They run annual accounts at places like the hardware store (2 M this year) and clear debts when Tom's trust fund pays out each January according to his mother's will. Mary is talking new car but Tom loves his 20-plus year old classic.

Will also go to Gustavo to set up the car part thing. If this doesn't work, can bum a ride to Tucson with Craig Hill on Thursday when he's going to pick up his wife at the airport. If so, I'll call you immediately. Love Sundays. Will visit around, shampoo R, etc. More later.

Later. Didn't make it to the Cooks. Bumped into Kendall Dawes and his novia, Carol. They are down for a week doing things to the Hacienda. Pool pipe problems and he's going to rewire the whole thing. They flew down commercial. Apparently a new route just opened up that reduces the Hermosillo layover to two hours instead of 23, and rumor has it that the old route, Tucson to Obregon, will be re-established.

Also decided to get back to an exercise regime. All this creative eating and no smoking, getting gordo girl, fast. Walked a mile and a quarter and jogged one quarter. Plan on doing it daily and gradually build up both time and distance. Gustavo is leaving tonight and will be back on Tuesday gracias de dios. Did the Tesoros trip and off to Polo's for a t-bone. Craig and Pember came along. They didn't eat and when I finished, they went to La Caverna for tortas, which they took home. R. is gnawing again. Tomorrow it will begin: school, decisions, the whole shmear. Fireplace will be completed and work will be done on plumbing and wiring and window and door installation.

Monday

Problemas. My main maestro, Candelaria, the only man I've ever met with a five syllable name, didn't show this morning. And I had great things planned for him. The electrician that Pancho was going to deliver is on a long term job. I was going to have Ole Bill design the system and Candelaria plan, dig into the walls, run wire, add sockets and switches, all the good stuff, under his supervision. C. was also supposed to complete the fireplace. Don't know whether he's sick, hungover or?? Manuel, maestro number two, plans on being busy plastering the casita exterior. He's good and fast. At the clip he's going, he'll be finished this week. Still very much on schedule i.e., guesthouse complete except for floor and fixtures in four more weeks.

A minor adventure. Ole Bill and I drove Craig and Richard to the Mayo River in Craig's truck with the three dogs in back. Water was being released and the water was fast. They got their boat in. The dogs had a swim. We are to pick them up in Navojoa Thursday afternoon. About half the casita will be stuccoed by day's end. Moving right along.

Tuesday

Started out to be a beautiful day and then things went downhill. Fireplace, as per your design, has to be plastered. The far wall (Gen's property) is solid stone and cannot be chipped away for the angle. C. cut it as close as he could but the brick work is lopsided and he'll have to compensate with the plaster job. Gustavo is back sans part. The guy at the auto store said that the parts that were brought down should do the job if a man that deals with mechanical problems like piston firing order and timing worked on it. Gustavo has a local mechanic that works for the Dodge franchise in Navojoa that fixed his Jeep's electronic distributor problem. Gustavo is going by his house when he gets home from work to see if he wants to give it a shot over his lunch hour or after work tomorrow. Failing this, Craig has a local mechanic who completely rebuilt an identical motor on his truck last year. The mechanic is willing to tow the car to Álamos and fix it. Ole Bill, who sold his car in Mexico and will be going to Tucson to buy a new one, was told by the same mechanic to buy a VW, 4 cylinder Ford, Nissan or Toyota (shit) and he can repair them and can get parts in no more than three days. Gustavo also learned that the place where Tim bought the parts will ship them to Mexico on a phone call (Visa card) by bus and that delivery will be made in Álamos.

Now I find out. Just finished my run/walk and am cooling down. The front of the casita will be plastered más or ménos by day's end. Calalo will have most of the fireplace complete and will be taking the chimney through the roof tomorrow. Then comes the picky shit like plastering and setting windows and doors, plumbing, wiring, and setting up a sewer system. Gustavo will help me deal with City Hall on the latter and it may require a bribe to get the proper authorization to hook into the city system without hassles and time delays and muchisimas inspections.

Wednesday 7:30 a.m.

Bit of a nip in the air this morning. Manuel Murrietta was by for the first time in several weeks yesterday and pointed out a problem. When we did the bathroom roof, the bricks were V'd between the beams. This raised it about six inches from the edge of the dome cornice. Doors and windows are level and with the present two brick cornice there's still a gap. Guess gonna have to have the cornice ripped out, raise things with cement, and get it level. Shit. Time and money down the tubes. But may as well get it right.

Something strange in the street last night. Didn't provoke an outright bark but a lot of low, guttural, growling took place. It woke me up but if R wants to scare anything, he's got to raise the volume. I've noticed that he can howl very softly when he's in his kennel and belt it out when on the portales but that his growls are always subdued and gentle.

3:00 p.m.

Came back from class and didn't have time for coffee. Gustavo said, "Stay put. The mechanic will take you to Navojoa and fix the car." Cool. We went to Navojoa. Mechanic, assistant and son fiddled around for an hour. Borrowed a two chain from the Yanahari (plural i) and made it back to Álamos with a stop at El Caricol (mechanic's truck overheated and we needed water). It's now back in Álamos. At 4:00 p.m. will go look at Craig's motor and go from there.

Thursday

Day started out okay. After class came home and bought 70 old floor bricks, but not enough to finish baño, need 30 more. Mechanic came by. Couldn't fix truck. Hit me up for 200,000 pesos to buy a new distributor in Obregon. Will get it tomorrow.

Marsh Perkins came by for a visit, our diagonal neighbor, a retired anesthesiologist from Portland. Nice, laid-back guy.

Ole Bill and I went to the Rio Mayo to pick up Craig and Richard, dogs and boat. I was sitting on a log at the river's edge and R and his buddies were racing around up and down the bank, in and out of the river at full tilt. R bumped into me and knocked me off the log, partially into the river. One of the other dogs failed to apply brakes and ran over me. My pride was hurt, my ass wet, but no other damage. About 20 Mexicans watching the boat loading saw it from the bridge and thought it was the funniest thing they had ever seen and burst out laughing. I, of course, yelled at R and joined the laughter. It must have been pretty funny.

We stopped at a new place in Navojoa and had great, fresh strawberry hot fudge sundaes. I bought 11 pounds of goat meat for R and came home. Now waiting for chicken soup to perk and am cheezing Ritz crackers for dinner. Am getting pretty good at using mole sauce. I am learning to use the right amount and add about a tablespoon of honey and a pinch of salt before simmering chicken in same. Concoction is then poured over pre-cooked rice. Yummy.

Friday

Hooray, no more school. It was tough and I probably shouldn't have gone. The guys hit at 7:00 and have only an hour to deal with problems, make decisions, etc., and zap off to class. Life will be considerably simpler now. Progress: fireplace is complete with deco tile inserts. Major electrical problem in bathroom. The current entered the casita through what is now the inner wall of the shower. Gonna take some serious re-routing. Ole Bill will be by to counsel after 1:00 today. Made another unhappy discovery. The casita had a floor of scored cement and not brick. It is currently being sledge-hammered and crow-barred out. A slab will then be poured to serve as the base for a new floor.

Just got back from my two mile walk/run, keeping speed and distance way down and will get both up in gradual increments to avoid injury. Still a tad stiff in the ayem. Hit the P.O. and got your letter. Dreadfully sorry about the news concerning Gertie. Hope that when this arrives the breast lump is benign. I know how frightened I was about my lung spot. It was pure hell.

The romaine is getting ahead of me. I gave a bunch to Gustavo and have a good month or more left if it doesn't bolt or bitter up. Bill was by and we started the re-wiring. Calalo chopped a hole in the garage wall for the circuit breaker box and we'll make a stab at wiring. Won't move the current inside until Monday so I'll have light for the weekend, since Saturday is a half day and the job may take longer. The fireplace is gorgeous. In getting decorator tile, it makes it a piece of cake. We can do it to every fireplace in the house if we choose. Also, Gustavo said that the tile you bought is a better grade than the stuff he got for Merv.

Saturday

Bought 30 more old bricks. Can finish bathroom floor. Have two Sabino boards (the kind Bet used for shelving) lined up for Monday for bathrooms. Electrical wiring going okay. Floor cement base going okay. Sand-brick roof on bathroom is about finished . It has been a good week except that the truck is still dead. I want to get this in the mail today. R got rabies shot. They screwed up on dates at the reservation and I didn't want border problems. Vet said it was okay.

Love R & E

Monday, February 20, 1989

Up and at 'em early. It is now 2:00 p.m. and I just came back with three sacks of cement to hold the crew until we take delivery of 30 more sacks and 40 more of lime. Three courses of arched brick have been laid on the entry room. I think it's beautiful, good job of scrubbing and aciding brick. But you have to be the judge. Conferred with Pember re: pool and think I know the way to go. White cement the first year and then muriatic acid annually, says Pember.

He and Bet were off to the MD in Navojoa. He's having what they believe to be angina pains; hope it's gas. He had a pacemaker put in a year ago. Whilst having coffee with Bet and her to-be daughter-in-law from Montreal, who is studying at JFK Institute, we speak French.

Bill of Bill and Hector came by to announce the death of our neighbor, Zack Montgomery. He was part of the couple we met at the Pemex restaurant when I met you at the airport and you remarked about how sick he looked. Good diagnosis. They live around the corner. I was on my way to Allen Pendergraft's house; he's doing a portal and his air conditioning is in the process of being installed. Told him the news. He drove me home and we went to pay our respects to the widow.

Teri came by to call her husband; her phone was out about 2:00 p.m. and Snake Bob also showed. Apparently, when someone dies, the American colony goes to the funeral. I changed and we went to the cemetery. It looked like a TGIF but with a number of over-80 widows I hadn't seen around town. With the exception of Teri and Bob, I might well have been the youngest person there. Came home, jogged and did a bunch of exercise, started dinner, salad, and Teri showed and invited me to eat at her place. A little birthday party for a friend. I readily accepted as she's a working chef. Bob, Bill, a park ranger from Olympic National Park, Teri, R and myself.

On the way, it was about eight o'clock, Bob decided to stop at the Chocolate Palace to visit Delores Richy, who I know casually. We toured the place, a palace it is, and then off to Teri's with Delores and her houseguest in tow. Wine, dinner and back to our place. Teri wanted to call her husband again with some more things for him to bring. He's coming down for a few weeks in a couple of days and they're going to smuggle in a freezer from Tucson.

Delores Richy tagged along. She knew our house about 15 years ago and was curious to see what it was like. They just left; it's after 11:00, and I've had too much wine. Goodnight.

Tuesday, 7:00 a.m.

Bad, bad night. Up five times pissing my sleep away. Cannot drink more than one or two beers or wine and party with the crowd on work days when I cannot sleep in. Ole Bill is due about 8:00 to check some wiring, and then off to Minas Nuevas to look at old brick. I'm going to have to take a nap sometime today if I hope to jog at 2:30 and be in bed before 9:30. It's going to be a long day.

Bunch has happened since last sentence. Ole Bill came by to see about electricity. We have four ladders; three are incorporated into the scaffolding and the other is needed to get up and down the roof. As a consequence, no electrical repairs. Went off to Minas Nuevas, first village out of Álamos, on brick-looking. Saw 53 antique floor bricks. Guy thinks he can get another three or four hundred. We'll know Saturday. I can pay Gustavo the one hundred I gave him, patch the portal and maybe have a couple of hundred left over. Can maybe find some more in drips and drabs for the bathroom floor. I'm afraid it might take a lifetime to find enough to do the kitchen floor, but we'll take it a day at a time. Got to look at something, Calalo waving ... later, girl.

Wednesday, 11:15 a.m.

Quiet night of reading and bed by 9:30. No jogging. Ole bod too bent. Up at 5:45 , new morning. Day's going slowly. About half the roof is bricked and all four guys are busy cleaning more to complete the job. Wife of antique brick guy came by for 100,000 pesos down stroke and will go out to Minas Nuevas at 8:00 a.m. Saturday to see how many he has. Hope it is 500. Got to go to town and pay for yesterday's lime and cement, 455,000 pesos ($200 USD).

Went by Ole Bill's. Visited with Armida a tad and came home. The brick cleaning operation continues. Pain in the ass; no work being done on construction. Beauty not only costs a bundle, it takes a helluva lot longer. Snake Bob came by to invite me to stroganoff dinner. When the crew quits, will run/jog, exercise and go for a dip in the Hacienda pool. It is truly hot today. Hottest it's been so far. More later.

Thursday a.m.

Hooray, got your letter. Did not get papers to open an account from Schwab. Got a confirmation slip that our stock sold to raise money, and another customer service letter regarding someone asking if the Tucson broker was courteous. Maybe it will come tomorrow. If not, quien sabe. Went to bank this morning to have plenty of cash on hand in the afternoon to buy brick. Also picked up a gallon more of acid. One room is now covered with clean brick. Still requires clay, another type of brick and cement, a month to dry, and then the seal coat insulation. We seem to have enough brick to do the bedroom, but may have to use some new and take up the garden and replace with new. Will make a count this weekend and go from there. It looks great, say I.

Sounds as if you had a dandy time at the lake once Mart accepted the fact that he can't screw around with the boat. I can assume that Gertie is much, much better now that she's back to being bitchy and not worrying. Hope you and Mike Ryan (superintendent) have your confab so we can plan on a short term future or a little better. And also hope Al's problem is solved shortly. He's too old to be twisting in the wind.

Gonna crash for a bit, then jog, exercise and splash. No dinner invite tonight but Pat came by and asked me over for Monday. I accepted with alacrity. Teri and Rudy will also be among the chosen. May do the TGIF tomorrow if I can find out where the hell it is. More to come.

Crazy morning so far. Teri turned up at 6:15 a.m. to call her father-in-law and tell him that the Tijuana flights often leave a half hour early. She learned that last night. I gave myself a quiet night of music and reading and didn't answer the door. Couldn't find guts for R this morning, tried all five5 butchers. They were all overstocked with meat and didn't have to trim or dress out carcasses. Mañana. It's getting warm here and I guess meat consumption declines as temperatures rise.

It's a brick cleaning day. Calalo came by and needed 50,000 pesos ($22 USD) for more brushes. The acid eats them up. Tomorrow I make my final, final trip to get old brick. Ole Bill's at the door. Later, love.

Slept under a fan last night and under a blanket. A mosquito or two sneaked in and I figured that the fan would blow 'em off. It worked. Went downtown last night. Tourists are thinning out. Lalo has five owls to peddle and hopes to go to Tijuana to find work in May and maybe sneak into the States. He's scared shitless of the latter. The guys are still scraping brick. They've been at it for half the week. Next week they'll have them placed before covering up with cement, etc. It will be nice to move back to the bedroom.

Got to go get R food and then go to Minas Nuevas and load brick. Later, love.

Later. Bob dropped by to remind me of the Flag Day (Mexican legal holiday Feb 24) party at El Caricol. I needed reminding, too preoccupied—so it's the shower. Teri and Ricardo are also going. Mostly Mexicans. Should be interesting. Off to the shower.

Party didn't occur. Had two beers, came home and cooked supper for R and myself and, like an idiot, stayed up past midnight reading. Also forgot R's leash at Caricol so will wait 'til 10:00 or so to pick it up. My damn phone doesn't seem to be working. It may be citywide. Richard was by to make a collect call and couldn't get out. He went to Palmeras to try and will also call me to see if it is possible to take incoming calls.

Did speak to Skip Branin. He's getting some tax info for me and is alerted to the fact that I'm going to have to raise several thousand dollars. Richard told me of an American couple he helped yesterday.

Car clutch died. Toyota parts from US needed. I think it would make sense to write to GM, Ford, Chrysler, Datsun and VW and ask about compatibility of parts for a car purchased in the US and spending a great deal of time in Mexico. Their customer service departments should be able to get the info.

The crew is finishing the bathroom floor and running plumbing and sewer lines in the casita. Windows and doors are due on Monday and based on what I learn from Gustavo's expert, I'll be putting together a big material order and buying (ordering) a bunch more new brick. Gustavo is planning on using an octagonal, local floor brick on the new house he is building.

Time to get this in the mail. All my love, R & E

Wednesday

Yesterday had the blahs and couldn't get my ass into gear. Also had a touch of dire rear, my own damned fault for getting carried away by a cake and milk binge. Early to bed and up this morning full of piss and vinegar. Got the crew going on finishing the interior of the dome and just got the glazier, who measured all the glass that was needed for the cupolas, casita, etc. Ordered wrought iron interior framing pieces and will go look for brick to finish off the septic system. Would prefer to go to Navojoa tomorrow but may end up there today as my shopping list grows. Busy, busy.

Tried for Skip Branin but he was out. I need a bunch of money. Got your latest letter and don't know what to make of it. I gather that you and Lois had another knock down, drag out and she ended up as the downee and dragee. Ah power. Hope that somebody gets a second opinion if additional surgery is suggested. Got to go get an additional gallon of muriatic acid, some electrical plates and some other odds and ends so will continue this later.

Did I ever screw up. Went down to the bank to do money, waited on line about 45 minutes, whipped out my checkbook, discovered I'd brought the wrong one, rushed back home, snatched the right one, dashed back to the bank—too late.

Can't cover glass, so Navojoa tomorrow. Will go jogging shortly after a shot at picking up some of the needed materials in Álamos (hopefully). It's a little like reservation life. Everything you need is in Tucson. Couldn't find needed materials.

Just back from a run and trying to cool down. Got a pigeon problem. They are trying to nest on a portal pillar. Got to get rid of them or we'll have a season of pigeon shit. Snake Bob will be by later and zap 'em with a pea-shooter. Being humane. Don't want to kill them.

About half the interior dome is done. Still have old brick blues. The stash I wanted won't do. Pancho is searching as well as others and there's always a chance with Gustavo. but I'm getting antsy.

Thursday, February 23, 1989

Dear Joan,

Got two holes dug for the septic system, both over five feet, one square for the tank and the other circular for the drain. It will be easy to tap in the washer and darkroom. One slight problem: I'm short more old brick than I thought. A bad count. Now that I have the truck, I can do some more looking. Calalo knows of a cache of about 40 and I can dicker with Gustavo for the remainder if I can't come up with another source.

Calalo really likes the rubber tile set hammer. They don't have 'em in Mexico. Gonna get a bunuelo making lesson at 4:00 p.m. from Lalo. He'll be bringing down his mother's special equipment. Joan and Teri will be joining in. Lalo seems to have cut down on grass. The wooden door he was going to refinish was no good. Priced wooden doors for the casita, over $200 per and more for fancy according to the carpenter. Will go wrought iron and have the guy down the street (Egrin) make them.

Have to go to Navojoa for plumbing supplies on Monday and deliver Teri to the bus. She's going to Creel to visit the mission that virtually saved her life following the plane crash to bring them things and take some people who have raised money in Palo Alto for medical supplies. Bought about 30 books at the library used book sale and will take a bunch of them to read after I pay my help. Ron Slaughter had a garage sale which I missed. Too bad.

Really look forward to a restful weekend. Beautiful and warm. May go fishing in the Cuchujaqui or a 40 acre bass lake near the Caricol that I just learned about. Currently waiting for final phone installation. The guy said he'll be by to do the deed today. We'll see.

Manuel is finishing off the interior plastering for the front window. The frame is in place. One peon is still digging. The other is cutting floor brick on the machine. Poco a poco. Things are coming along. Been a good week except for the aggravation re: sewer hookup.

I had Manuel clear the debris out of one of the two channels leading to the neighbor's yard. It should improve the flooding considerably and keep our yard comparatively dry. She has no legal right to stop the water. She can French drain or divert to the sewer should she choose and at her, rather than my, expanse. Tra-la!

Took Teri to Tesoros, ate at Mansion, home by nine, feeding R and listening to an L.A. station while R finished and off to bed. Smoked cigarettes and it pisses me off.

A wonderful do-nothing day. To think that there can be more than one a week when the house is done is inspirational. Did Tianguis, puttered around, harvested and read. Afraid to go out. Don't think I can pass a cigarette vendor without stopping or meeting someone with a tell-tale bulge in their left breast pocket. Go a few days and backslide. Each time I tell myself that this is my last cigarette. Perhaps it will take an island plastered with "no smoking" signs and no cigarettes sold to accept me for a year's residency to finally kick the habit. Well got that off my chest and hope I've also quit smoking. Dinnertime—Bye.

Left for Navojoa yesterday morning and spent the day with a long list of plumbing supplies that ran about $500 USD. This will do the septic system, provide bathroom drains, spigot pipes, etc., and a drain from the rear shed. It got cold and rainy yesterday and it is still going on.

Went to the bank today to cover purchases and am waiting for delivery. While I was gone, one of my peons had an accident. Hurt his leg. Don't know how bad. Must wait and see.

If it's clear, Craig and Richard have planned to take Runner and their dogs to the Chalaton park arroyo, the acreage Al was interested in, for a hike. It's like a neighbor inviting your kid for an outing for the first time. I'm reluctant to let him go but I know he'll have a lovely time and I'll sit home and worry.

Got millions of squash blossoms and two-inch zucchini and yellow squash coming up. Will be inundated. Wish the clouds will clear off and things will get dry and pretty again. No major leaks but a few minor ones. It just hasn't gotten dry enough for the cement to cure and become totally water repellant. Ran into Ron Slaughter on the bank line. He said he made about $400 USD on his yard sale. He, with Pancho's aid, bought a bunch of 16-inch, round pine beams. Pancho located them at a nearby ranchito at 16,000 pesos per. He's planning on buying some for portales at his house and I went to check them out for palapas when they arrive. More later.

Pouring down again, pretty heavy. Guess Runner won't get his outing. The phone man is here. He was by about five minutes on Saturday, checked a few things out, but left. I ran him down at his house in Navojoa. Today may be the magic day. Gonna light a fire as soon as he leaves, boil a chicken and kick back and read. The maestro, Manuel, who took the peon to the hospital, hasn't returned. Hope it is not serious. He hurt his knee.

The telephone guy left to check something else after climbing the pole by Gen Reynold's house. Still no peons. The wrought iron man came by for 200,000 pesos ($88 USD) for materials like a glass, open-able insert with fancy bent iron. I will use a white glass to let in light. The insert will provide some circulation as well as light. I sure hope you like it.

Now I'm playing the telephone waiting game again. Shit. He just came back with a borrowed phone from Gustavo on a provisional basis. I called Mapco (the place where the Ford died) to find out about my materials. Calalo is ready to lay pipe. They said their truck broke down but they'll be here first thing in the morning. I explained that I had a maestro and crew waiting around with nothing to do, not true, but maybe I'll get early delivery.

The rain is not helping the septic system. Everything is mud. I'm waiting for the crew to quit in a half hour. Calalo will go by the peon's house and see how he is and I'll go buy onions. It's a chicken soup day. I got carried away by a two for $1.75 USD chicken sale at Sunday's Tianguis and I better do 'em. Had to cook 15 pounds. of cabrito for R in two batches. He really loves the stuff. I save the resultant broth for his breakfast, a cup of broth and half dozen corn tortillas.

No jogging for three days. Lots of pent up energy and dashing around Armida's yard with his buddies isn't enough. I don't know whether I mentioned it, but Craig bought a piglet about a week ago and is trying to train it. It does pretty well on leash and totally fascinates R. He pokes it with his nose and it runs away. Today he plopped down about six inches away from it in Bill's room and we couldn't decide whether he regarded it as something to play with or eat. We'll see what happens as it gets bigger. I don't' think he'll revert to the huff and puff school of wolf. Time will tell.

Wednesday 8:00 a.m.

It sure was good to hear your voice last night. Don't know what to make of Gertie, Lois, et al. I think the conservative approach being taken is the best way to go and hope that you're not caught in the classical jurisdictional dispute, i.e., surgeons want to operate, internists, never. I am very glad that Lois provides reinforcements to the extent that you can have some R&R. Sounds you have been stressed out by all the craziness going on. Sure wish you were here because decisions like where the washer is going to go should be made now that the drainage ditches are being done.

My peon is okay. Inspected the old brick floor and it looks good. The main problem is that the bricks are of slightly different sizes and still shy 100. Richard came by to invite R to go on an excursion with Jan later. He also checked the septic system and said it has about a 1,200 gallon capacity, much more than we'll need. He put in a 1,000 system, which was adequate for three people and has been in place, problem-free, for years.

I'm waiting for the Mapco truck and will then go brick searching and do a few other chores that require a truck such as check on a brick-maker that still owes close to 400 bricks which I've paid for and can use in the septic system, or run around and pay a few bills. I was glad to learn the peon is okay. He should be starting a six week internship shortly and then he'll find out how much he learned when he applies.

Coming back on or before the 18th looks like a good idea. I've got to do the VA bit on April 3 and can be reasonably sure that I can block out two-to-three weeks of work during my absence by April 3rd by asking Calalo how much he can accomplish while I'm gone. If I need surgery, I can probably hold off for a few days, maybe fly down, see what was accomplished, and return. I can estimate costs and leave payroll and materials money with Gustavo or hire Judy McClain (Judy and Mary) who does this sort of supervision for gringos over the summer. Ron Slaughter told me he used her and in one case, costed out materials in Álamos, thought them higher, got the stuff in Navojoa and saved him $100 màs o menos. I won't be able to travel for three-to-four weeks after surgery unless the VA is using the method described in the newspaper.

Waiting, waiting, all the time waiting. I search and couldn't find the tile layout. Will proceed and get everything done except for the final painting, fixtures and tile. The casita will certainly be ready for occupancy by mid-March.

1:30 p.m. Still waiting for the truck, pinned down. Craig, Richard and their dogs came by to pick up Runner. The five of them took off, Runner on leash until they clear town. He seemed to like the idea.

Sunday, 10:00 a.m.

Perfect weather, slept 'til 8:00 and it was wonderful. Just finished Tianguis. Hoped to find the pea-sheller stand. No show. No string beans, corn or celery but cauliflower made its first appearance. It looked great but I couldn't figure out what to do with a huge head so I passed. Ran into the mechanic. He could not locate the part in Obregon. He will be going to visit a brother who has a garage in El Centro and will get the part there. He assures me he will have the truck running in a couple of days. I sure hope so. I hate having to rely on other people.

Heard that all kinds of cold records are being shattered in Alaska. Met our new neighbors (Don and Dorothy Wilcox) on the street across from Gen Reynolds. Alaskans and delighted to be here. Called their kids at home to learn that it has been minus 30 degrees for nine days running. Next year, Mexico will be inundated with Alaskans, those who survive the winter. Had a Tesoros drink with Bill Preece and later, dinner at Polo's. He's got two planes in for the weekend. Learned that he spent 20 years as a Navy pilot and took early retirement, worked for Motorola in Phoenix for five years before striking out on his own. He's very pleased with the way things are going and looking forward to six months here and six months in Arizona.

Got to get moving. Put groceries away, eat and cook R food. Goat guts. Good buy in Navojoa. Cooked half—five or six pounds—yesterday and will finish it today. Must find out if goat meat has to be cooked like pork. I'm doing it to be safe, but would rather freeze it and feed it raw.

Monday

And so, another week began. Base for brick is tile (concrete) finished and wiring for casita started. Ole Bill was by and we marked off places for switches, power sources, etc. Spoke to Gustavo, who is supposed to contact city electricians to run in a new wire for 220 and appropriate meter.

One window is in place and needs two panes of glass. I am in a bind without wheels to go to Navojoa and deal with all the glass work. The other maestro is redoing the cornice so that we have a clean roof line. Just getting started but he's fast as hell. After these two things are done other windows will have to be framed, made, or both, and the plumbing roughed-in waiting for your tile placement i.e., shower walls, countertops, splash board, legs, etc., as well as fixture selection and purchase of same. Things are really moving along. I may go back to the pool or put a crew repairing the front of the house.

I want to put off roof removal for awhile longer because of rain, and painting has to be deferred until I get to the States. One American told me that Mexican paint is great for one year, US five. I prefer the latter. Also holding off on roof framing until the front rooms are complete and I haven't ordered floor brick because of lack of transportation. We also need shower tile, which Ron Slaughter got at Price Club along with all plumbing fixtures.

Moved up to two-and-a-half miles walk-run and will keep that distance for a week before moving up to three miles. Feelin' good. Richard was by on his bike and pumped up the tires. R is a problem. He's trained his dog, an Australian shepherd, to ride behind him on a platform made of a small serving tray. We were talking about getting a bigger tray such as busboys use in restaurants and mounting it on the rear for Runner. It'll look silly but it might work if we both learn how to balance.

The guys are hard at work. One team is busy wiring the guesthouse and the other is replacing the cornice to square off the building. I had the original cornice torn down 'cause it didn't look right, which I believe I mentioned. Runner just came back in from supervising. He is fascinated by the cement mixing process. Also, when both peons are mixing and R is on the portal watching, the three of them howl. I've been unable to tell whether R starts it or one of them.

The Larson card was delivered in yesterday's mail. Nellie, the maid, bounced in so R and I will be clearing out to the mercado, a daily ritual, and then to Armida's to socialize Runner and later, accompany Ole Bill up here to check the wiring progress. It's only about four blocks but he has to rest twice to make it. Your father is in infinitely better shape and a dozen years older.

Just got back from visiting Armida. The roof line is three bricks high and coming level with the bathroom. The electrical wiring is coming into the garage and a slit has been cut in the casita wall for entrée. These guys are really moving and my problem is "what's next?"

Guess I'll put a pair on some more interior dome cleaning to get rid of cement streaks.

It should have dried out sufficiently to get the job done. Marsh Perkins was by and said that it is pretty important to seal overhead brick to avoid constant flaking. That'll take a couple of days. Place looks real spiffy after Nellie's cleaning . R and I will have it messed up in a couple of days, bet on it.

Time to start lunch and soup, a pair of chickens I bought at Tianguis. Later.

Big decision: an outlet over the bathroom sink, assuming some sort of minor arrangement. Front cornice is four bricks high. One more will bring it level and then the side needs doing. Quality and speed are amazing. He (Manuel) is twice as fast as Umberto. Lost, strayed or stolen—one billfold with $125 USD gone. Had a $100 bill which I was saving for the States. Have to find a gringo who needs pesos to buy US effective. Maybe it'll show but I've looked. Think I lost it at the mercado but where? Shit!!!

It occurred to me that the magazine Sunset some time or another must have done an article or two on brick floors. Why not contact their readers' service and see if they can pull copies for you? They know the best and do an excellent job of researching things. The guesthouse now has a clean roof line and Manuel is in the process of plastering same. Now we have to decide whether we want to have an exposed brick cornice or do it all in white. We also have to decide whether we want chimneys plastered. I've looked around. Some folk plaster, some don't.

Good news and bad. It's starting to sprinkle and I found my billfold. Would you believe, I put it in a safe place when I went walk/jogging in response to your admonishment, "don't leave money around"?

Manuel is continuing to plaster the wall despite the drizzle. We may be in for one of those chipichipi three-day deals which test the best of roofs. Guadalupe was by to check progress. Calalo, my honcho, is his son-in-law. They were on lunch break. He told me Calalo knows electricity as well as plumbing. He too is fast. Ole Bill laid out two days' work and I think it will be done by quitting time as will the roofline.

Plumbing is another matter. I was told by the city water and sewer guy to get something in writing from my neighbors because they are poco loco. They hassled the hell out of Gen Reynolds, forgeries, lawyers, the schmear. The job is going to involve a deep trench from the casita under the common wall to their sewer drain.

Calalo, who knows the people, is going for the paper. The city guy lives in the house next to Micha's and I had a few beers with him when I was living there. Gustavo believes that I have a legal right-of-way for access but prefers cooperation to hassle. One more thing to be concerned about. Been out cornice-gazing. They all have overhangs, some plastered, some not, some single, some double and a few triple. More gazing to do.

Wednesday, 7:30 a.m.

It looks like a chipichipi. Sullen sky, mountain's obscured but gracios a dios not cold. Gonna slow Manuel's brick-laying down considerably. Think I'll move him and peon inside and let 'em cement-scrape the dome some more to clear out cement streaks. Calalo can continue the wiring. Hate to send them home. They need dinero and we need the work. We'll see.

One of the snakes, the heavy-set one, visited me last night. I may revise my opinion of him. He was a stockbroker in Tucson. His blood pressure sky-rocketed, his heart fluttered., he fainted a lot and spent a month in TMC, which scared the shit out of him, so he quit his job and came to Mexico. He thinks the hunting operation is stupid but it gave him something to do. They are not making any money due largely to poor airline schedules. He's got himself an old school Mexican girlfriend and has as yet been unable to take her out without a chaperone. He's pretty serious about her, but he's getting horny as hell and is afraid of prostitutes. I empathize.

Damn it, the rain has picked up. He is staying at the Hacienda and supervising a rewiring. Says he's afraid that Kendall has a white elephant on his hands and that there isn't a comfortable room in the house. Bad traffic flow and more like a multi-bedroom hotel, but the grounds are gorgeous. His car, a new Buick, lost a belt and he searched for six days to find the right size. He's going to get rid of it and bring down a '67 VW he bought for conversion to a dune buggy or see if he can find a VW Thing, which he claims will be a fun car (convertible) for local travel with a ready supply of parts.

He has an extra refrigerator which he offered to lend me; may take him up on it for freezer space for R. I'll use it for goat meat. Due to the lack of storage space, I only bought 12 pounds. I could have gotten him 50 and he really loves the stuff.

Brought Manuel, the gardener, in to scrape cement off the tile in the dining room. Whoops. May have another burst pipe running from the city water in the street through the bedroom and under the bathroom floor. Heavy, heavy. Hate to have to tear out bedroom brick. Calalo is right on it and left the casita with his peon, pick, crowbar and shovel. We will see.

We saw. They checked the water entry—"nada." Now we're waiting a bit to see where the water comes through the bathroom floor to localize where to dig. You didn't like the bathroom floor anyhow. Big deal. Guadalupe dropped by and consulted. Slight leaks in the domes that Umberto sealed. He apparently didn't use the right mixture or press down hard enough. No leaks in the casita dome which Calalo did. This doesn't trouble me because they will all be foamed soon.

It is new pouring hard and the guys are finished plastering the casita interior. They were smart to leave it undone for wet weather work. This is going to be an interesting day. I filled water jugs, pressure cooker and both sinks in case I have to go for a few days s without water. Christ, just when I was beginning to live in style. Now I may have to go back to camping.

Manuel's philosophy and commentary: "I am a poor man but I'm lucky. I have a job. I have friends that are brick-makers. A rain like this means lost brick, wet clay and as much as two weeks without a paycheck. What will they do? What a shame. Life is hard."

Mountains still obscured but rain back to drizzle. Got to make a bank and Mercado run. R, wet of course, sat in brick dust and his tail and rear sport a fine pink patina. We're off.

Back. No rain for awhile. They are opening the floor by the hopper so I will have one final shit. With Peter gone, it's going to be more than a day. I'll have to find another place to use that is not too far away. The guys are on lunch break and this afternoon's activity should reverse the problem. Little did I envision when it all began that my life would be centered around: 1. Saving an old brick floor. 2. Finding a leaky pipe. 3. Wondering where to shit. And the list goes on.

Visited Ole Bill and Craig. The latter is in front of a fire reading, the former watching it and adding wood. The dogs are snoozing. R's visit was the big excitement for the day. Ran into Tom Cook at the Mercado making his daily, on foot, grocery run. Waved at Emily Preece in passing; she looks pretty incongruous down here with her blonde hair and heavy blue eye shadow. Also ran into Stephanie at the bank. She believes that she can be wholly self-supporting down here as a full time rare seed gatherer doing what she likes to do best. She knows what she can export and how to decontaminate them to satisfy USDA import requirements.

Think I'll get a fire going shortly and cheerful up my life whilst awaiting the plumbing verdict. Will break now for a P.O. run. To be continued.

Well, the toilet just left and they're digging down to see. It may be possible to run in new plumbing if a cutoff valve or T could be located under the kitchen, but at the moment this is still conjectural. It's a puzzle and I don't have a clue. Haven't ordered floor brick yet, which is just as well because they'd have been ruined. The old brick is safe in the garage. Think I'll need you to look at floor brick. They come in all sizes and shapes and I refuse to make a decision, not being as conversant with beauty as you are.

Pouring again. Mountains have vanished. An hour or so later, maestros and peons swam home and I'm all alone in the world, sina qua inside. Had it cut off at the street to avoid further damage. The search will continue tomorrow. Snake Bob came by. He'll drive to the Caricol for dinner. I'm in need of a treat. He's keeping to one meal a day to shed weight. He's still huge. Wonder what he weighed before hospitalization. Gonna get out of wet clothes, kick the fire up, read and think the good thought. First clear day, our pink wolf gets a shampoo.

Thursday, 6:45

Waiting for the crew to show. The deluge is over and I've emptied pans and buckets, one in the bedroom, three in and around the stove area. Will have the guys on the roof, patching. Not worried because foam will cure the problem. Still have the under-the-floor leak. Sky looks iffy. All Álamos prays for sun so people can dig out and clean up. Good dinner at Lou and Dee's. Snake is no snake. He's a self-styled wheeler-dealer and his stock brokering is "penny stocks." I also suspect that in spite of his health problems, he's an alcoholic. Poor bastard.

It is possible to run pipe through the roof. This would be a good time to do the kitchen revise but it can keep for another day. Let's first locate the leak. May still go for roof if it's under the bedroom floor. "Dig we must" and dig they are. They showed a trifle late, first time. Problems dealing with mud. Right now they are assessing damage. The entry room roof dribbled on some loose cement and they want to get it up while it is still damp. The baño roof held up perfectly and Manuel is very proud. There was a miniscule leak in the casita dome; we spotted one moist brick. Will wander up to Gustavo and see about the possibility of foaming domes and glass rooms and then doing front rooms at a later date.

I'm sure Hilde is pissed because her kitchen leaks and between both places, there should be enough work to get a crew out of Obregon. Just don't know. No damage was done but it's a nuisance. The worst thing that happened was that I started smoking again and that truly pisses me off. Must stop today.

Must have rained four-to-five inches. Pool is flooded again so any work on that must be deferred for maybe a month and then we'll dig down to make sure all is dry. Sand affords great capillary action and sucks water to the surface nicely. The sun is actually appearing. Praise to the highest!!!!

The pipes where the hopper sat remained dry. They are replacing it rapido. It is a question of whether or not they can do it in time to save me a mad dash to the back of the garden. It is much too early to bang on a neighbor's door to do the deed of defecation. "Hi Gen, gotta shit. Where's the john?"Won't contribute to my reputation as "that nice Earle Winderman," will it?

Need to go back to boiling water for a few days. Professor Medellin claims that after many rains, sediment gets stirred up in the city supply. Crew quit. Finished. Roof patched and now to deal with shower. Ran into a neighbor and he said that every room in his house leaked. Couldn't locate the under-floor leak. Didn't open floor to try and localize it from usual seepage rather than search and destroy. Started trenching for plumbing. Sky is clear, blue and beautiful.

7:00 p.m.

Went Gustavo-hunting to check foam and more important, home. Should have been here last week and I would like to know the status before getting very, very, nasty. It will have to keep 'til tomorrow, and now for a leisurely, solitary dinner, reading and bed. Until tomorrow.

Friday

No change in bathroom. Could be seepage. The side of the casita is half corniced and should be completed today. Wiring, switches and boxes are in place,

5:00 p.m.

No TGIF for me. Too much of a hassle. Cooling off from a jog/walk. The cornice is complete. Have ordered one ton of lime to coat the exterior of the building and the big project for next week will be trench digging for water and sewer hookups. Progresso poco a poco $125,000 pesos ($55 USD), not at all bad.

Saturday, 7:05 a.m.

Great adventure last night. Long about dusk, I tried to turn the lights on. Nada. Checked my jerry-rigged wiring, good. Decided to go to the corner store to buy candles. Gen Reynolds and one of her sons were in their front room using candles. She offered me a couple. I declined, being confident that the corner store would have them. She said, "You'll be back."

I was. Lit 'em and waited. No light. Changed clothes and figured I'd better get downtown to eat. R and I left, flashlight in hand. The whole town was blacked out with candles flickering in windows. Kind of pretty. Made it to the square and Snake Bob called me from the Portales where he was having a beer. He told me he had a day-old Tucson newspaper he picked up in Navojoa which he was finished with. I joined him and Lorenzo, a computer guy that was in my Spanish class, and left for a month's consult caper in Phoenix. He bought the place with the smell of sewerage across the arroyo we looked at a couple of years ago.

Met my periodontista, a member of the Yanahara clan and hardware store. He and some of his friends took three or four days off to take a workshop in soft stone sculpture at the museum. They invited me to join them for beer. In addition to Yanahara were two orthodontistas, a 28-year-old businessman and a cattleman, all totally turned on by "ART." I had seen and liked the orthodontists' work at the show a couple of weeks ago. They all said that their respective families thought them loco for their interest in ART. They all hoped that they could become good enough to do it full time some day. They were all sent to the States (U of A mostly) to learn English and obviously enjoyed practicing it. They all had candles issued at the desk of the Mansion where they were staying.

We all ended up eating at Polo's by candlelight. It was packed and R got the residuals of six steaks. I agreed to see their work at the museum Sunday. Eleven students in the class, no gringos.

Just looked up and saw R lying down and supervising Manuel at the far end of the garden. Hope he doesn't offer to help with the digging.

The lights came on about 9:30. We had another beer and they left. I invited them to the house at noon on Sunday for a graduation case of beer. I think I ran into the local art cell. You'd enjoy them and we'll get cards to Mexican "openings." Wonder if they do cheese and wine?

The crew is busy. I just authorized brick trim on the cornice. I've been checking other houses and it adds a nice decorative touch. Calalo is truly moving. He laid a full brick course on the side of the house and will finish up (probably) by noon, quitting time today. They moved the landscape rock from the side wall to run the darkroom-laundry drain when the pipes arrive and now they're cutting cleaning and laying more brick.

Have a bug infestation killing chard and cabbage, broccoli, sprouts, etc. Must buy a plastic spray bottle and spray for Manuel to use.

I've got to go downtown and pay for the lime order and post this episode of going crazy in Mexico.

We love and miss you mucho. R & E

Thursday at 3:50 p.m.

The PAPCO truck checked in to make sure of the address. Have to off-load some other stuff since ours is at the rear of the truck. Runner is due back from his outing with Richard and Craig between 4:00 and 4:30. It's a little strange to be without him.

He's back. When I let the gang out, he tried to trot along with 'em. He must have had a great time and they're planning on doing it again so he must have behaved himself. He's wet so I assume he went in for a dip.

They also invited me to an elk liver and onion feast tonight.

Elk liver is great, a new experience, liver texture, different flavor. Craig's theory is that beef, calf, steer, etc., livers come from animals who have been fed growth hormones, chemicals, antibiotics, etc., all of which is liver-stored and not good. Quien sabe. R was still fascinated by the piglet. He'd stand three-to-four inches away while it is eating and give it a nip (gently I hope) the minute it stops. The pig squeals and runs with our guy staying close.

Stayed home and supervised. Woke up with an almost overwhelming desire to smoke. Knew that if I went downtown I'd either bum or buy cigarettes. I know that withdrawal symptoms will diminish, but when, Oh Lord, WHEN? R and I just got back from a three-and-a-half mile jaunt, one mile jogging. Piece of cake. Just cooling down before showering and will more than likely stay home. Having a nice quiet evening leisurely fixing dinner for R and myself and listening to L.A. radio. The end of an uneventful, peaceful day.

Friday

Got your letter, which was redundant with the phone call, and leaves me in the air. It sounds as if they got rid of Gertie's cancer and the endometrial infection seems to be responding. I'm amazed at the costs and always thought that the medical professionals were in on the monetary rate of Medicare, i.e., they would be happy with the government money paid. It is a federal program. The state program is for medically indigent only. Of course, MDs charge what the traffic will bear, i.e., the price for three stitches on the patient with a Chester address and unemployed would be a fraction of the cost charged to a Bryn Mawr lawyer. When Marge was practicing, the County Medical Associations also maintained lists of MDs who accepted Medicare as total payment, as do most proprietary hospitals. The problem is that most people are reluctant to ask MDs and hospitals about costs up front for whatever reason.

Snake Bob came by and checked out the plumbing. Said Calalo does an excellent job of pipe fittings. He also selected a place for a hot water heater to service both the laundry and guesthouse and will figure out a way to pressurize the system. Have to have our well water analyzed if we want a pressurized system in the house. He's in the process of doing one with the Hacienda's wells. I'm going to check the local laboratory for a sterile sample container to see if they can either run the test here, in Navojoa, or send it to you in the States with somebody who is leaving. Kendall Dawe is supposed to send Bob a plumbing supply catalogue to order parts for his job, which should be in the mail shortly, and then call him to fly them down next week when he's due for a few days.

Ate barbequed corvina at Armida's and smoked a few cigarettes. Shit.

February-March 1989

Dear Joan,

Did the TGIF last night. Got a BBQ chicken which I chopped, covered R's water bowl with lettuce, dumped the chicken in. It was a success. The Lambs are back for three months, the academic-type house-sitters we met a few years ago. She's great. He's a pill. Party was at our neighbors, the Perkins, and R behaved perfectly. Stayed where I put him.

Richard, Craig's partner who braids horsehair, came home with me for a cup of coffee. He and Craig know a lot of Mayos from their river trip; they buy and will look for strings of rattles. They've seen them in people's homes and will try to locate a source. How many do you want? They are going to float on the river next week to check it out prior to taking tourists.

Spoke to Tim's wife and he's due in tonight, car part in hand. She said he's been busy as hell because of the fierce cold in Nogales. A number of the TGIF folk asked about you. My crew quit a little late today. It's been a good week with lots done. They started out cleaning cement off the final dome interior and finished the final plaster coat on the outside this ayem. Presuming I have wheels, will buy thick glass in Navojoa and get the cupolas sealed next week. Still chilly. Hoped to wash R but too cold. Maybe it will warm up tomorrow. Hope so.

Learned that the brick across from the Mansion, June and Joan's house, was finished with a heavy duty grinder before sealing and varnishing with clear US spar varnish. Will also look at another brick-floored house up the hill (new) that belongs to some people named Walworth. He used one of the better contractors in town but no more. Too many cut corners, 25 percent markup on materials such as cement, etc. He thinks I'm doing the right thing. If what my contractor told me was accurate, I face about a $27 labor cost for 15 weeks. Have no idea of what materials will cost. Bricks, cement, wood, re-bar, fixtures, etc. We'll learn as we go along.

Sunday, 7:30 p.m.

Tried to sleep in but Tim woke me up with car parts. He rode the night bus down and wanted to give them to me before he crashed. He was very apologetic about not coming last week but his boss sent him to Flagstaff to some meetings. Said there was snow all over the place. Went to the Tesoros last night. Bill Preece was there with three of his pilots. This is the peak of the hunting season. Bet Nuzum will be flying up with Cammie in a week or so and wondered if you might want to fly down with her on the return. Dates were uncertain. She was going to work it out with Preece today. He said that flights are pretty regular at the moment so I imagine that a long weekend is possible.

Ate at Polo's with the Tesoros group. I bundled up (five layers including thermals) and was toasty warm. Everybody else was bitching about how cold it was. The Cooks are out of the slave quarters and back in the main house. I don't think they are going to rent it again. Too many problems. Pember was trying to convince them to play their band at San Carlos but Tom wants stay home and do his own thing in his studio.

Going to Tianguis, the biggie on Sundays, and long about noon plan on shampooing R. He's still shedding and bathing loosens things up for brush removal. Now that roofs are sealed, things are lots cleaner and less dusty so I may as well keep the wolf hair down. To market, to market, more later.

Bought carnitas, corn and hand-shelled green peas. A guy sat there with a sack of green peas and shelled kilo plastic bags full. Used a handful in a ramen and will do a salad niçoise tomorrow. Carrots are fresh. Buy a bunch and they cut off the greenery before bagging them. They're great.

Went to a sidewalk art show yesterday. The couple we met from Navojoa New Year's Day was there. She was showing and made a sale, a really fine picture of an Indian girl and a tree. We would have liked to own it. The price was about $150 and the lady was pleased with herself. A sculpture class in stone will be starting next week in Álamos under the auspices of the museum. Hilde mumbled something about enrolling but also added that working with stone is hard to do.

Monday

Will go to Navojoa to deliver car parts and then go to the phone company with Gustavo . He has lined a phone up for me to buy for under $1,000 including installation charges. We'll see. I don't believe it until it happens. Was told that phones in Guadalajara cost $2,500. Ouch!

The crew is finishing the casita dome interior and working on the exterior cornice. It's beginning to look good. Your retirement income looks great. Does it also include your years of servitude in Pennsylvania? Heard some chit-chat the other night and it might be possible to set up the house here as a rental property. Remy would have to set up a depreciation schedule and all repair and replacement can be deducted. If doable, it'll save us an awful lot of taxes.

Things are finally beginning to warm up. T-shirt weather during the daytime. Tim and wife will be heading for the States. She has a job lined up with Head Start in Nogales and intends to work on an Arizona teaching certificate. I wonder how many of her Mexican college courses will be accepted and how many requirements she'll have to take?

Wednesday 5:00 p.m.

Not a glorious day to remember. Left with Gustavo for Navojoa. Bribing three different people plus regular contract brought the phone up to about $1,000 but I finally got one.

Left the parts at the Yanaharas to get the truck rolling after I completed the phone flummery. But such was not to be the case. We may still need one small part. Shit. Gustavo took off and the guys fiddled and diddled to no avail. They had one more idea but it was 3:30 so I thought I'd better start for home, hitchhike—walk—bus? Adventura. It ended up bus. There's a rear luggage compartment that R sat in and could look out the window. Jose Medellin spoke to the owner last week who said R can ride when the busses aren't crowded. They weren't. He rode.

Yanahara was super loquacious. Wrote out the Japanese alphabet, gave up on trying to teach me to count to ten, and invited us to dinner some night. Then he asked me what I thought of his daughter-in-law. We must have gotten great reviews from his son, Geraldo, but—no car. Will call tomorrow. There's a chance that it will be fixed. If not, more parts from the States. Gustavo may go in the next day or two. Will go up to his house about 6:00 and give him the news and see if his schedule jelled. More later.

Back from visiting Hilde and Gustavo. He doesn't know for sure whether or not he'll be leaving. If he goes, it will be Friday or Saturday and he'll find out tomorrow. I'll find out what part as well. Guess I'll fix dinner and spend a few leisurely hours reading. 'til tomorrow.

Thursday

Today's adventure involved another trip to Navojoa. They could not find the critical part. Decision—send the pieces Tim brought down and buy a new mechanical distributor. Hopefully, Gustavo will be going tomorrow. We wandered all over town part-hunting and got back at 2:30. I got some sawdust (five pounds) for R. Saw parts of Navojoa I never saw before and spoke a lot of Spanish. Interesting day so far. but still no wheels.

Gonna have to close the window in the guesthouse for structural purposes and cut a hole someplace else for the air conditioner since it is adobe and not as solid as new-laid brick. The interior walls of the casita bedroom are pretty much plastered and the maestro is preparing to start the fireplace according to your design. I'll go straight brick. If you don't like it we can easily plaster and tile as per your picture.

Just did my first huevos rancheros with a mild prepared sauce. Good stuff. Checked with Gustavo. He'll be going up to the states on Monday and can get the necessary parts at that time. So we wait.

Up bright and early and went to class. Ole Bill and Craig came by with Rye, the chocolate lab. She and R really play well together. They seem to take turns chasing one another until exhaustion sets in. We'll take them to the river when it gets warmer to give them more room to romp and where R can play steal the Frisbee. T-shirt weather the last couple of days which is as it should be. Hope it keeps up.

I am satisfied with the way the casita is going. The exterior cornice is complete and the entire thing is plastered. A bit more brick cleaning in the dome is necessary (damn that rain) before they seal it.

I'm trying to quit smoking for the 100th time and so will avoid TGIF and Tesoros for an evening at home with Runner.

Crew's busy working away. I'm sipping coffee and thinking cigarettes, which is to be expected according to the quit smoking booklets Marc successfully used. This is a situation, morning coffee, where I've always smoked. I can deal with it. My real problem is frequency of urination, which the books mention as a short term side effect. Up six or seven times respectively the last two nights. Pisses me off (pun unintentional). Craig and Richard offered me a half price river trip (see enclosed brochure), which would be fun for me and Runner. They'll bring their dogs along. But as things now stand, I won't get any sleep, having problems using a bed. The ground would be worse.

Gonna have to get Manuel more interested in stagger-planting. I think it offends his sensibilities to have the same plant at different heights and ages in the garden. He believes in having everything come up at once and then start over again instead of trying to sustain the harvest for a month or two. The present radish glut is a case in point. There are over 1,000 ripe radishes out there now. I eat about six a day and that's saturation. I can't cook them, jelly or jam, jar or freeze 'em. Runner won't eat them and in a week or two they'll have to be pulled. A similar thing is happening with romaine and I think there is enough cabbage to organize a sauerkraut festival when it heads. Next time around, will go for three to four plantings a couple of weeks apart at the risk of hurting Manuel's feelings. Runner is bugging me to take him out. Will stroll to the P.O. and mail this.

Love, Us

Friday, February 24, 1989

Spent the day in Navojoa with Gustavo and Pancho . Returned six-ish totally wasted, just like a long trip and shop in Tucson. Bought all the glass but had to wait around for two hours of cutting. Don's stuff is Saltillo, bought in Guadalajara. We looked at some that came on the same truck, okay but not great. Did get a good idea for finishing the cupola—plaster the supports and create inches at the tops—much better light reproduction, so gave Calalo marching orders. It will take a few days.

Gustavo has a sufficient number of amapa beams of the right length. He has a pile of about 100 and has been sorting them out. He needs 14 footers. We need 16 footers. If time permits, will go out today to check and measure. Will also pick up the critically needed used brick and replace them when I can. He's a long, long way from flooring. Feel good about this. We'll try to off-load the glass later today. Need to scrounge up gloves. We drove back with the picture window enveloped in corrugated cardboard, blankets and sleeping bags very, very carefully and made it with no breakage with Runner and three of us in the front seat. Every time we stopped people looked at us and smiled.

Had our neighbors, the Wilcoxes, native Alaskans, over for coffee,. He's a retired mining engineer and I believe that she taught school. An interesting couple with great stories. If we can find out where it is, we'll do TGIF. Snake Bob came by right after I returned with some Kendall's apricot nectar, tequila and two ice trays because I never have any. It makes a nice drink. I kicked him out about 7:45 with some books he borrowed. He's on a weird schedule. Reads 'til 3:00 or 4:00 a.m. and gets up at 10:00 a.m. and seems to go through a book a day.

Had hoped to get about 50 pounds of R food to put in his freezer yesterday but couldn't. Maybe on the next trip. It would sure simplify my life to get a backlog because it's so iffy in Álamos. Much like trying to get it at Basha's in Sells, AZ, a pain in the ass.

3:15 p.m.

Just got back from loading the needed old brick to finish the casita. Worked up an honest sweat. Jogging doesn't count and I'm afraid that it's impossible now with slight Achilles pain. Now I have to worry about my back. Aging is such an ugly process when a bod that you depended on for years and served you so well begins to wear out. I've left the off-loading to the peons.

Gustavo will be by tomorrow with a designer contractor who is handling the old hospital re-do for Merv Larson (Desert Museum director in an earlier life) to give his final word on how to do the roof in the front rooms. One critical problem again is a sufficient supply of whole, old brick. Much of the brick up there has been cut to meet the curves, knots and shapes of the amapa. We also have no idea of the shape and condition of the heads of the wood up there.

Got to stay loose on this and may have to go concrete. I want these guys' best estimates of the best way to go and Gustavo claims he is the supreme authority. While gone, Snake Bob left a note to come by the Hacienda. Will, as soon as truck is empty. More later.

Thursday, April 13, 1989

Dearest Joan,

Finally, things have settled down so that I can get back into a writing mode. Trip down was uneventful. Border bribes totaled $13. The Scottsdale/Álamos sister cities folk were in for the weekend. Big party at Kendall Dawe's Hacienda. Food prepared by the socially prominent (?) women of Álamos. Absolutely spectacular food. I truly pigged out and R was perfect throughout.

Goofed around on Sunday and visited the Cooks to give them flea and tick collars for their dogs, who R truly enjoys. He went swimming. I drank coffee and visited. Folks are pulling out for the north country. Alaskans are going fishing if oil spill hasn't put them out of business. Went to a party last night. Ginger's novio's birthday at her house. She's in New Mexico studying therapuetic massage. He'll be joining her in a couple of weeks to get married. They had the Tesoros' mariachis for entertainment. I left at 10:30 and don't know how long it continued.

Progress on house is good but to get maximum production you have got to be here. Lost electricity in the bathroom and back half of kitchen complex when roofs come off. All but one concrete beam is currently in place. And it should be in today. They have to cure, constant wetting down for two weeks before bricks can go up. Salvaged enough for one full room and part of another, so will mix the new and the old. Hope the effect is interesting if not beautiful. Still need a couple of hundred old floor bricks, 100 to repay Gustavo and the rest to repair and replace on the portales.

Ricardo, the mining engineer, came by yesterday to invite me to the party and figured out a good way to do the pool. That'll be the next project, after the roofs. Flowers are up. Finished the rest of the string beans. Lettuce is gone. A week's worth of spinach is left and lots of chard. Phone dead. Waiting to go to Navojoa with Gustavo to buy some wood, 16-foot boards, because they've only got 14-foot in Álamos. Shit. Will be taking delivery of 1,500 brick tomorrow and scrounged 200 from Pat and Don. They are re-roofing. They're new, damn it, but I'll find some use for them. Will load them in my truck mañana. Got to get ready for Navojoa. More upon my return.

1:30 p.m.

Back from Navojoa. Wood should be delivered tomorrow. Also bought three gallons of muriatic acid and the crew is busy cleaning brick to get them ready to pop in. Laid the corned beef on Ole Bill and Armida, complete with turnips and cabbage from the garden. It was excellente.

Been at it early this morning. Took delivery of 1,500 bricks and picked up 100 salvaged brick from Pat and Don's house. My two peons tossed them down from the roof onto a sand pile so they wouldn't break. My job was to load them in the truck. They weigh over 20 pounds per. It was damned hard work. Also had to pick up another six gallons of muriatic acid. Brick cleaning is time consuming and costly in terms of preparation. Only one more short beam is needed for the roofs and we can start covering as soon as he brick is cleaned.

Recap of last few days. Bumped into Don Coleman in the bank on Thursday. Joined him for dinner. He barbecued steaks; we do eat well in Álamos. He never got the rest of his tile and has been searching.

My new brick arrived and the guys are finishing the rim to support the roof. All beams are in place and curing. Wood arrived from Navojoa yesterday. Brick cleaning has been the major enterprise for most of the week. Next week they start covering.

Snake Bob came by last night. He had gone up to Tucson for three days, taxes, business, signed over titles to his Porsche (old) and VW for his sister to sell and will buy a new truck with the proceeds. He came back Thurs. and missed me.

I'ved started walk—jogging again. Will use the Hacienda's pool this weekend and mostly loaf, do a little housework and review about 50 annual reports, sign and make vote

authorization forms. Phone fixed yesterday. Gave the repairman 5,000 pesos. He was happy. R is doing well. May take him to the Cooks for a run later. All for now and all my love,
R & Me

Monday, April 24, 1989

Dear Joan,

Had a lovely, do-nothing weekend. Got about 400 old brick, my best score so far, and am pretty confident that I'll be able to come up with enough to finish the roof and do the bathroom. They are coming from an abandoned hacienda. Loaded the truck with about 5,000 pounds Saturday morning. Still a little stiff. Ordered a bunch more. Loaded a bunch of Sabino wood, pretty beat up, though, and won't serve. Still looking.

Did see a lot of old, hand-wrought bits of iron attached to wood. Figure that when you're down here you might wish to check it out and we can dicker for some. It's lying in a junk heap. Also, some of the wood could be cobbled together, I think, to make a table. We'll let you be the judge.

Took Ole Bill to Tianguis yesterday and I over-bought. Great bean sprouts showed yesterday, first time, so did a wok bit with pork. Also used chard stems and green onions. It worked. Made my last tomato buy yesterday. Will rely on garden, since ours are pinking up nicely. Went running and swimming. R dances around the pool but won't go in. ??? Will shampoo him today since we're invited out for dinner.

Weather cooled off abruptly. It was downright cold last night and I ended up with two light blankets.

The guys are dismantling the scaffolding and will do the other roof. Anticipating no problems and can deal with a brick shortage, will know if more are needed. Will cannibalize the garden first and replace with new. I realized why old brick cost so much. A lot are lost when they are taken up and the brick salvager partially cleans them. The guy had his wife and kids chipping off cement with chisels and axes. Tedious, slow work. Then my guys scrape and acid them. Scarcity also adds to the price. They are rarer and rarer as existing supply gets incorporated in restoration jobs. All for the moment. Got to make a food run for R, more later.

11:30 a.m.

Been a rush morning. Rudy Hale wandered by with his father and kids and Don Coleman popped in five minutes later. I'm coffee floating and cooking chard like spinach for poached eggs. It should work.

Don's traumatized. Got home last week and found out that his wife ran away and left her daughter, whom he can't stand, behind. He doesn't know where or with whom his wife is living with. At the moment he is trying to sell one of his hospitals quickly. He hopes to move to Mexico ASAP but has no idea when and his lawyer has yet to make a damage assessment. I set up arrangements for him to buy 2,000 new brick and am helping him to rent a truck to haul same. Poor bastard. A victim of the Pygmalion syndrome, I'm afraid.

The chard was lovely with a fresh egg addendum and a dash of salsa. Think I'll do it three or four times a week. More later.

Nice time last night. The Hales were there, as was Stephanie, the seed lady. We talked about landscaping. She knows native stuff and a bit about landscaping and what does well on minimal water. Invited her by Wednesday to check our place out and make suggestions. The guy she uses to locate seeds also digs things out for gardens in the hills. Be interesting to learn what's available and does well. Hilde has Manuel installing a drip irrigation system for her trees. It will make it a lot easier when we get around to doing it because he will have some experience.

Off for R food. He looks great. Washed and curried him yesterday. He's going through a shedding period. I have a big bag of hair (fur) for whatever. It would be nice to get a wolf Kachina similar to the Xerox you sent, and use his fur instead of fox for the ruff.

Wednesday

Ah, the wild social world of Álamos. Dinner tonight at Don Coleman's, tomorrow the Hales. The rest of the roof will be covered today and, miracle of miracles, we had enough brick. Linc Reynolds, Genevieve's son, bought the old repair yard at the end of the street and offered me a bunch of brick from his floor ruins. Several hundred that would do about half of the kitchen, added to what I can scrounge, it may be doable. I don't understand my crazy brick obsession, must be the challenge.

Off to Navojoa this morning to the periodontist. Will take Ole Bill; he appreciates little junkets in contrast to watching the cathedral from Armida's portales for many hours every day. He says he has to keep people from stealing it.

Back from Navojoa. Bill was bitching about the fact that Armida gave him a big shopping list and also told him she needed plates. He said he bought $40 USD worth of plates three months ago and asked her where they were. She said she gave them away. He also claimed that he bought $300 USD worth of groceries three week ago and saw Armida feeding her family on his steak and chicken and he never got a steak. As a consequence he bought nothing. I guess she's been milking him a bit but the ride is over. Be interesting to see what happens. I'm holding my own according to the periodontist, with the exception of one tooth. Pity. Still salvageable, though. Will work on it. Mouth tender, so chicken caldo for lunch, aspirin and siesta. More later.

Thursday

Had a good time at Don's. Cooks made salad, Don BBQ'd steaks and I did strawberry cajete dessert: cake, rum, strawberries cooked with piloncillo with sour cream topping, and a big hit it was. Drank two bourbon and sodas and two small glasses of wine, and got up five times during the night. Guess I'm not cut out for the Álamos alcoholic set. Sleep is too sacred.

On way to bank I ran into Bill Preece tooling around on a bike. He had just come back from Yecora, the town Frank Valenzuela mentioned. He said it is gorgeous. He explored it to the north Arizona mountains. It sounds like a great place to check out to maybe do a cabin in the woods by a brook.

Later ran into Emily in the bank line. She was also impressed by the beauty of the town. Three thousand population, great, spectacular vistas. One hotel and one restaurant. She didn't know the rates. They stayed in cabins built of slabs from the lumber mill that result from squaring the logs. Varnished bark on the outside and varnished wood on the interior. She said that Jerry Criden (Marie's relative) has let a few people put these up on his land, interesting. Lunch time, will jog later.

Roofs all on, getting on cornices and insulation, etc. Next week, get the air conditioner installed and do wiring. Then cure the pool and can probably get portales done before you come down. Need counsel: shall I go with Bobida-type roof or flat, like existing portales? My inclination is to go with the Bobida since I already have all the lumber I need for forms.

The old brick lady just came by; they have 130 more and expect to have at least 70 more by Saturday when I'll go by to pick them up. They've also located some Sabino that needs looking at. Now have enough brick to repair the portales and complete the bathroom as well as return 100 to Gustavo. Praise be—later. Came in from a good walk-run and must shower and get ready for dinner.

Just got back from shopping and let Runner race around and play with a friend. They danced around sand piles and he had a good workout.

The crew is beginning to sheath the roof and reconstruct the fireplace chimney. Should take another week to finish up and then we move to other things.

Real chilly this morning. I needed second blanket. Had a good time last night. Limited myself to two beers and had a good night's sleep . From conversation, eating out on sort of a dinner exchange is a premier pastime down here to a far greater extent than in the states. Teri had two pretty chicas to serve and clean-up for ten people. Took Ole Bill home and came back and read.

Looks like today will be an easy one for me unless something breaks. I have a good supply of materials and a little cleaning to do and not much else, so will take off and do a little visiting and look at a roof staircase. May even do the TGIF, haven't been to one for a couple of months. More later.

Saturday, April 29, 1989, evening

Dear Joan,

When I went to get the mail and mail a letter, I noticed that Runner was behaving weirdly. He wasn't dashing around with his usual enthusiasm. Got home and watched him carefully and checked his walk. He seemed to be limping badly and in discomfort. Cold nose, no fever. Got the truck down and made him wait in the entry and had to help him, a boost, in to the front seat to find Jorge, the vet. I was told he had a sick in-law and went to Mexico City. Back in the truck to see if I could catch Don before he flew. He had already flown.

Back to the house for water (R drank) and I checked his foot and found two small ticks attached to the webbing between one paw. Was in the process of extracting same with alcohol and forceps when a young (Lord, she looked young) girl appeared in the doorway, introduced herself as Dulcie something or other, a veterinary physician subbing for Jorge. After determining that R wasn't going to eat her alive, she took a history and performed a physical. She believed that the ticks caused the limp but could not account for his listless behavior. She asked questions and I realized that I forgot to get him wormed when I was in the States when she asked about intestinal worms, and thought that that was probably the problem. We got into the truck. R jumped in this time (no ticks) and went to the animal pharmacy. We ordered de-wormer and he'll start tonight.

We went back to the house and she left to see a cat she's been following in the neighborhood. She makes house calls on foot as does the new M D. Anyway, R is staying cool and quiet and we'll start the pill tonight. I have the new vet's phone number. We wait and worry.

Sunday

Awake and frisky and feeling fine. Whatever he had disappeared just as quickly as it came. Did Tianguis with Ole Bill. He's going to do his own cooking (he says). Problem is, he'll buy a dozen steaks, get one and Armida feeds her family with the rest, so his food bill, he claims, has been running 300 pesos per month. Who knows? We walked one-and-a-half miles and jogged half, then went for a dip in the Hacienda pool. Dined at Caracol, no prime beef but carne asada and stuffed veal gut, absolutely delicious. R is busy eating and it's beddy-bye for me. Mañana y más.

Monday, May 1, 1989

Crew is working away. To preserve authenticity, they are running the antique dirt (clay) salvaged from the old roof through a screen and putting it on the new roof. That's real detailed restoration, baby! One guy screens, two carry it up in a bucket and Calalo spreads.

The ant army attacks. The tomato glut is upon us. Manuel proudly brought in half a dozen Big Boys proudly. I don't think they grow them locally since I've never seen any that size in the market. He's impressed by them. I've got to get some fertilizer going this week. I'll see Gustavo to see what can be done later. Want this in the Post Office so will conclude with Love, R and Me

PS: Exciting stuff. We salvaged quite a bit of the old square brick from the roofs. Combined with what I bought I believe I have enough to do the bathroom, portales repair, possibly the front room and a start on the kitchen area with a good chance to scrounge more. Lincoln Reynolds, Gen's son, has a couple of hundred in an order he's considering to make into a swimming pool. I'll just hold off doing anything until you get here to help with the decision on the brick. I'm off to the P.O. and then will place an order for 1,500 roof brick. Love again, Us.

PPS: Just invited to a Cinco de Mayo dinner party by Stephanie, the seed girl. Will also be stuck for holiday pay and no work due to the holiday.

Still more love and wish you were here. Me

Tuesday, May 2, 1989

Dear Joan,

Most things were closed yesterday, May Day, but Álamos is not a proletarian town so there were no parades, fireworks, etc., as there is in Europe. Nellie showed today. Missed yesterday due to a small scorpion bite over the weekend. Pancho is back. He spent two weeks at Ron Slaughter's place in Palm Springs. It's going to be a day of running the brick yards to locate new brick fast. Weather is good and Calalo is confident that we'll come up with some.

Back from banking, letter mailing and shopping. Ole Bill was by and gave me a thermometer. He had a spare. It's 80 at noon. Still stalking brick. No success. A brick-maker is supposed to come by this afternoon. If he's got 'em, great. If not, have to have 'em made and it takes a minimum of two weeks.

Wednesday

Still no brick. Insulation dirt is going on the roof and I feel frustrated. Just have to hang in there and keep looking. Rain would be devastating at this stage. Ole Bill just left, as did Pancho and Ron Slaughter. The latter invited me to a barbecue on Saturday. He added that he also invited Pancho's entire family. Should be fun. He and Lovey are planning to summer in Guatemala. He hopes to buy a bunch of stuff for resale in the States. He also mentioned that he would like to visit Sells FOR O'odham stuff. Got to go now and see if I can line up some brick. Later.

Hooray!!Got my brick from two separate sources, a bit more than they would cost if I had them made but well worth the price difference to set my mind at ease regarding a rain disaster. Life is beautiful again.

Thursday

I imagine that now you are savoring chicory coffee and beignets and trying to decide whether to go to morning sessions or explore the New Orleans at the National Reading Conference. Calalo came in this morning with a pound or so of steak bones that Teri and Rudy left outside my door last night. I visited Snake Bob at the Hacienda to borrow his blender to make vichyssoise. He had a bunch of steak bones also that he had been saving for Runner. He really lives well down here.

The water tank was moved and reconnected, but one critical part is worn out so I had to hose off in the garden and wait until the stores opened to do last night's dishes. A minor pain in the ass. The brick is due in about an hour so the crew is busy packing and grading the insulation dirt. I would imagine that it will take about four more days to lay the brick and apply a final coat of cement. I will then have Manuel and his crew apply the water proofing and insulating paint on the dome areas, and Calalo play with the wiring so that 220 will be available for the pool and the casita air conditioner. Just stopped to pay for a delivery of 350 bricks and it'll get them started. More are expected shortly. Later.

More came, but only 442 so I'm still short 770. Off I go to look.

Shit! No luck. He has one good possibility, will find out tonight, and if it is a go, will deliver tomorrow. Rudy just came by to invite me over for dinner. His father and kids got off yesterday and had a good time here. Some kind of hummingbird showed up today and has been hovering around and looking at me through the windows. This is my day off from running so I'm heading up to the Hacienda for a few laps and will try to convince R to join me to rinse away some of the accumulated dust. Later, girl.

The contact man jut showed with a sample brick for Calalo to examine. Can relax a little now because it looks okay to me. We'll see. Off to splash. Later.

Had a dandy dinner at Teri and Rudy's. Then they came down here to use the phone. Believe I've got the brick situation under control. Can hear the beginning of the Cinco de Mayo parade so will move on down. Later, love.

Watched the dancing horses, had a beer with Lincoln Reynolds and then wandered back up the hill together. Spoke to a relative of Armida's, a young cop, who said things are pretty quiet now (3:00 p.m.) but the whole force will be working all night. At 6:00 p.m. there will be horse races in the arroyo and a major dance at the Palacio. May watch the racing, go to the party at Stephanie's (beats cooking) and maybe wander by to take a look at the dance. I've yet to go to one but the cop said it would be okay. Can sleep in tomorrow. The crew knocked off at noon and won't be back until Monday. Off to jog and then to swim. A further report to come.

Slept until 7:00 a.m.—the luxury of it all. Cinco de Mayo is over and I think the whole town is hung over. Hardly anybody in the streets when I went to the market. The party at Stephanie's house was kind of boring. I ate and left at 8:30, went downtown and visited Ole Bill. The only fireworks were when we were a block or so from the house and R ran on ahead and couldn't wait to go inside. I'll have to forget about the firecracker holidays and plan to stay at home with the stereo on. We know that New Years Eve is one of them. Hope that the P.O. is open and so will sign off with Love, R & Me.

June or July, 1989

Didn't mail this yesterday as I had cramps and nausea. But hauled 218 old brick and damned near upchucked in the process. Came home and crashed. Drank a couple of glasses of tea, ate a bowl of cream of wheat and a soft-boiled egg, and stayed home and suffered. It was not turista but the result of my own food. Fine today and getting ready to do Tianguis and enjoy Sunday in leisurely activities.

Insulation and dirt is going on roof now. Start was made yesterday. Got your last letter. Think it is great that you'll get to go to New Orleans. Elaine will be fun, too.

Looking at trees loaded with mangoes and limes too small to eat but truly thriving, same goes for the weird kumquats (locals call them yo yo mo trees) that fruit before they leaf. Still nothing from school. My Visa card is way overdue and I have still to receive the application to open a new account. Can you buzz them and let me know the score, por favor?

Sunday

Been a perfect day: read, did a laundry, visited with Gaspar and five friends who came by to play wolf ball. When they threw it, R ran and got it according to regulations. Then they had to run him down to get the ball. The kids got the idea that they would play catch and try to tease R. He dashed back and forth between them, but they always caught the ball. Saying the lupine equivalent "this sucks," he stopped running, watched them play catch, picked a cool spot and quit. Gaspar asked, "How come Runner doesn't want to play anymore.?"

I told him that he never got a turn so he quit. Gaspar acknowledged that, under similar circumstances, he'd do the same.

Made concentrated chicken bouillon with three pounds of meat, including three pounds of chicken feet, and peach cajete with four pounds, eight ounces of peaches found at Tianguis. Couldn't be passed up. Added one piloncillo, some honey and a bunch of cinnamon and when cool, some brandy. Superb. Froze some and jarred the remainder—about one-and-a-half quarts of pure deliciousness.

Dinner: pollo, pasta, ensalada con salsa francee. Writing to the less than romantic strains of "Don't Mess with my Tutor." Took a stroll downtown to ogle the chicas in their Sunday finery. Either they're getting prettier or I'm getting hornier or both. Hoped to get to bed early but the band started up. Fixed dessert, read a bit and turned in. Turned on the radio. Maybe it'll drown 'em out

Summer 1989

Sunday

Dearest Joan,

Today is what the good folks at Lincoln would say is going to be one hot mother. It is 86 degrees at 10 a.m. Hotter than late afternoon on any previous day. Was up and got my shopping done early, put things away, will run-jog shortly and pool loll later.

Went to Ron Slaughter's yesterday. Mostly Pancho's family, sister, brother, kids, etc., no Lalo. Ran into the latter on my way home. Pancho's pissed off at him because he's not helping to support his family and is high most of the time. Pancho (Lalo's brother) and Ron have been visiting the ranchos and buying everything in sight. Old tequila bottles, furniture, rugs, etc., in copious amounts. He's talking about perhaps opening a gift shop and is building inventory. The guy's got good taste and knows antiques and crafts people. He's planning two months in Guatemala, mostly antiquing. We could learn a lot from him. I just wish I liked him better.

Did a laundry early this morning. It dried in about two hours. Well, it's off to jog and goof around. Snake Bob invited me to join him for barbeque pork chops later., and so it goes.

5:00 p.m. My world has been destroyed. A tropical storm came out of nowhere, much like line squalls on the Chesapeake. The roofs are unprotected and naked. One room has brick over the clay, the other is exposed and washing away. Could fuck up the entire interior of clean, old brick. Pool is flooding. Has to be drained manually, moist sand removed and spread to dry, muchos problemos. A malign deity is afoot to punish the gringo who dares violate the sacred rites of traditional Álamenses remodeling and restoration, and so it goes. The rains continue and I watch muddy water spew from the drainages. Shit!

Damage control report: The plastic sheathing over the new roofs held, no leaks. Minor leaks in the domes which we know about and planned to correct after the roof completion. Pool soaked. Has to be mucked out. It will probably take a few days to dry out and apply additional clay before brick work prior to the cement, then about one month's cure prior to application of sealer insulator. PITY!

Tuesday

Eighty degrees at 6:00 a.m. Went out and got my shopping done early. Runner food is a daily chore unless I go to Navojoa, where I can usually buy a bunch and take home to freeze. The guys are busy cleaning up the mess made by the rain. It is not as bad as I thought it would be and may only cost me about a day. Everybody in town was bitching about the fact that the rain was totally unexpected and nobody was prepared to deal with it.

Am stiff and sore from yesterday's run. I guess that I better quit jogging. My body just can't seem to take it anymore, and substitute walking and swimming. Found the calorie expenditure chart interesting. When I got back my weight was at 165. I've dropped about six pounds.

Tried calling you several times over the weekend. Assume you were in New Orleans or up at Coolidge. I quit after dark because it seems to be impossible to get a line out Sunday night.

Hot dry wind going for us. Just what we need for the roof. Have enough brick to keep going until Thursday when the balance is coming. I'm tempted to add more crew to hurry things along. There's still so much that needs doing around here: plumbing, electricity darkroom, roof coating, floors, painting, and on and on. I feel as if I have a tiger by the tail.

Wednesday, 6:15 a.m.

Ran yesterday too fast or both and am stiff as hell right now. We've moved the workday up a half hour due to the heat. We now begin at 6:00 a.m. and knock off at 2:00 p.m. The drain spouts (five) are now being positioned and progress continues. The peons are mixing cement and playing "howl" with Runner who is out there supervising.

Tried calling last night but couldn't get through. Curious about your New Orleans trip and Ryan's (Sells school superintendent) response to your letter. Also, no account application from Schwab and no credit card. Goose 'em if you get a chance.

Ole Bill was by for a visit. I was walking him home and ran into Candy Joe, the guide who also runs the shop around the corner from us. He wanted to show me some crazy new masks made out of javelina skins that he just got in for a buyer from Tucson. Very different.

He's married to a Mayo Indian, has five kids and worked at the Phoenix Botanical Gardens for four years, cactus department. Hence his English. We got to talking and he knows an Indian wood-carver. He came by my house and I gave him the Wolf Kachina picture and a handful of Runner's fur. The back of the picture indicates colors and materials which he will translate and we'll see what he comes up with. I'm sure it will be interesting. A contractor also came by looking for amapa beams and would like to buy them all. We'll have to decide how many we wish to keep and I've got to find out the price. I will be taking Calalo to look at a palapa-type portales and count beams. I'll also have to determine whether they can be used on the roof structure. If so, I'll hold out the best for ourselves and get rid of the others. It will help clean the yard.

Candy Joe also wants to take pictureS of the house to put in the tourist information center. He said that almost all Americans who come down here like to look at restoration projects and that ours is unique.

Snake Bob came by. His phone is down again and he wanted to call Kendall, due here in a week, to have him bring some plumbing parts. He also checked our system. We need new controls on the pump and possibly some new lengths of pipe. Replacement should not be a major undertaking but Bob suggests we hold off until we decide what to do with the kitchen, drainage, sink position, etc. Good idea. He did fix the shower so that it is considerably better.

Think I'll go for a real slow walk now and swim a bit later. I didn't feel up to exercise, so took a siesta instead, have a slight gut ache, my own cooking, too. Kendall called and I got Bob and told him to re-call in ten minutes. He's bringing us down some plumbing supplies and will call again at 5:00 p.m. tomorrow. Bob went up to the Hacienda to get some tools to dissect the dishwasher and order parts for Kendall to bring down. I'm off to shower before he turns water off to check pumping mechanism. Later.

Thursday, 5:45 a.m.

Waiting for the crew. Tried calling you again last night. Consummate frustration: first you dial the international operator. Sometimes you get a busy signal. Hang up and try five minutes later. Sometimes it rings. I counted 20 unanswered rings. Hang up and try five minutes later. Sometimes you get the international operator. She tries and you get to hear some weird electronic noises for awhile. Then she tells you that either all the lines are busy or that the circuits to the States are "blocked," whatever that means. Hang up and try five minutes later. Repeat entire process. Hours go by, nothing happens. I believe it is easier to call from the States here but "quien sabe". Coffee time.

Just got back from my marketing chores. Ran into Candy Joe and he asked me if I would take him to an Indian village where he has to deliver some javelina and deer skins to be made into masks. The village is called Masiaca and is regionally famous for rugs. We tentatively planned to go after work (2:00 p.m.) on Monday. This might be a good place to use Runner's fur and have it incorporated into a rug. Be interesting and sort of wish you could come along, but there will be other times.

Later, walked four miles today. Bod recovered. Also swam seven laps in Kendall's pool. Skip Branin called. First news of the market I've had since leaving Sells. He called to let me know he sold some stock, hence the enclosure. On second thought, so what the hell. I'll trust the mails since I'm not sure when I can get out of there to pick up some paint sealer. He also told me that Schwab said that they are sitting on my visa since they are not allowed to mail them out of the country. He was going to call Schwab from the States and advise them to mail it to Sells as well as mail me an application for a new account or tell me that the transfer can be made. Copies of portfolio to Skip, which he will continue to manage until the stocks can be reincorporated in my portfolio.

Will try and phone later. If can't get through, well, just one of those things. Or maybe it's not our destiny to speak tonight. Anyway, I'll finish this epistle and ready it for an early morning visit to the Poste around the corner before going to the butcher.

Love, R & Me

P.S. Runner prefers to swim in rivers, streams and lakes. Pools don't really turn him on all that much.

Soccer Trophy for Los Lobos

August 1989

We just got back from the soccer game. Lobos won by 3-0. Doug's eyes are okay. Saw showers in Navojoa. A storm passed through Álamos and the soccer pitch had mini-lakes. A bucket brigade dealt with goal mound puddles. Centerfield seas were handled by a pickup truck with 18 kids piled in the back dragging an eight foot chunk of railroad track, much like a rear-end plow. It co-mingled and spread a combination of mud and water somewhat equally over the field. Looks like more rain's a-coming, so will stay home tonight. Also have a summer cold, mild sore throat when I woke up, and now nose is running. I have been known to feel better. Will take aspirin and kick back more than usual tomorrow and also dedicate a chicken soup to the cure. Still no broker's statement; it's not the sort of thing I want floating in the mails but ain't nothing I can do. R food cooking and I may as well fix something light for myself. More to come.

Summer 1989

Dearest Joan,

Well, we survived the night and it was lovely. The return trip was uneventful. Keeping busy. The holes in the portales walls have been patched. Getting the paint off the fireplace is a bitch. Will take hours and hours. Soledad hasn't shown. Laid the "no grass at work" law down to the boys gracefully. Think I made it stick by expressing my fear that the smell carries to Gen's yard and she might call the cops. We'll see if it works. Calalo is working on dining room and Manuel is finishing off the bedroom plastering. Power's off on our street.

Alberto came to measure the fiberglass pool part and R decided to go for a swim. He promptly lay down in mud so I hosed him off and he's lying on his blanket in the middle of the room. Doug and Bill came by for coffee and limeade. The latter will be looking for houses for friends with Hilde later in the day. Had the pool balanced nicely and hope the electricity comes back soon so I can filter. All for now.

Guys are still working. Calalo is wiring away and preparing a list of electrical things needed. Spoke to Bob. He's been at Angel's place peddling three wheelers, etc., and playing "Big Man," I assume. Hope Angel gets some of the dinero when he returns from visiting his folks. The world is beginning to cloud over. I hope it doesn't rain until I do my walk and swim. Electricity is on again. Added water to the pool as it was down a tad. Wish Tom Cook would come. The pump seems to be laboring, i.e., pushing water out of the two front jets with force. The deep jet doesn't seem to be doing a helluva lot and I'll check it when I go lapping. More later.

6:39 p.m. Did my swim bit. Deep jet not working. Others breaking their hearts for us. Turned everything off and removed the filter. Absolutely caked with mud. Spent 20 minutes trying to get it clean. Put it back. Added a cup of diatomaceous earth and we'll see what happens. Don't like what's going down and don't know what the hell I'm doing. I hope I haven't fucked the system up. Will hunt Cook down tomorrow and see if he'll make an emergency call or give me some advice if I've got to climb the goddamned fence. I worry about the pump and motor. Tomorrow we'll know.

Tomorrow. When I started the pool up, I checked everything and noticed that the clear plastic container on the pump was not thoroughly sealed. Fixed. It works fine. Douglas

(Reisborough) was by. Hilde showed him the house, Prison Hill, past Cammie and Chacho's and just before you descend to Pancho and Lalo's place. The view grabbed him. He's going to buy it as his getaway from his townhouse to look at sunrise and sunset. The panoramic view must appeal to his muralist sensibilities.

Paid the crew. Soledad on fireplace brick, looks good cleaned. Still no bank statement. Maybe Monday. No Kendall money. Fronted Jose (gardener at Hacienda) 100,000 pesos ($44 USD) to cover the weekend and too disgusted to call his boss. Shitty, shitty!

R and I went to the soccer game. We were behind 2-0 in the first half with our star player (sober this time) in defense. We moved him to the front and he scored four goals. Carlos got one. We won. Lalo was doing laps before the game and Snake Bob and Slime John showed. Car problems on the highway. Left R with Lalo and pushed them to a garage. Lalo said R howled the whole time I was gone. I didn't want him on the road. Later, lost my door key. Bob got me a ladder and he and Ramon, half owner of the Tesoros, helped me break in. About the time I opened the front door Bob found the key next to my truck. I had separated it from the bunch when I went running. Gave 'em each a couple of beers and sent them off. More mañana.

Did Tiangis with Bill. The good fish and clam man was not there. Went to soccer game at 10:00. Álamos Allstars vs. Navojoa. Navojoa won 6-3. Our goals were all made by Victor, sober again.

Goofed on the pool. Low on water and turned it on and overfilled. Am siphoning it off now and should get it down to where it should be before going to El Centro for street food with Don. It will be his first time. More later.

9:15 p.m.

Picked up Don in a drizzle and one friend at the Tesoros. Drizzle stopped. A Navojoa group was there with their own musicians who sang Norteños. Then did tacos, tamales and cake and went home. R's eating, and pool level is where it should be so I pulled the hose. Temperature is perfect and will need a blanket before the night is out. Another great night in Álamos. What do you think about cutting arches or shells above the electrified wall recesses in the front room? Off to bed, more mañana.

Monday 6:30 AM

The week is upon us and the guys are all busy. Calalo is wiring with peon, Manuel plastering and the boys scraping their hearts out. Added chemicals to the pool and am waiting patiently (one hour says the book) to see whether it needs another shot of acid.

Saw Suzanne at Saturday and Sunday soccer games. Gordon , her English friend, is down and refereed. He's recovering from heavy-duty surgery; they put a wire in his brain to alleviate unbearable headaches. Interesting guy, a civil engineer who has built bridges all over Africa and is trying to figure out how to get a job in Mexico. Had surgery three months ago and looked as if he would collapse after the games. Beginning to revise opinion of Suzanne ever so slightly. There may be something there beneath the blub and fluff. She's all hot to sponsor girls' sports in some way and is searching for a vehicle. Women's lib??? She also has a D. E. filter for her pool and the instruction manual which I will check.

Still no Tom Cook. Pool looks great. Slime John came by yesterday. Bob let a bunch of chemists use the Hacienda and he said he had enough partying. I threw him out so I could meet Don for dinner. He did tell me that he used a good cabinet maker in Navojoa for some work he needed, a man about 65 who speaks some English. I'll locate him for you to talk to when next you come. All for now.

Tues. 7:20 a.m.

Big personnel problem. Astrobeto didn't show. Caught him rolling a joint yesterday and told him it's a no-no. Explained that it slowed his work down and if he wished to continue to smoke, he could do so days, which would be the equivalent of eight hours straight, or stop smoking, or get less money i.e., six hours pay. Lalo says he is a heavy user, about 12 Js a day, and a no smoking rule was too much for him to handle. Lalo, our reformed smoker, went at him with missionary zeal. but Tibeto couldn't handle it so he didn't show this morning. Lalo said that his habit also got him an academic probation, understandable.

Feel sorry for the kid, know he needs the money, but can't keep him on the job if he continues to smoke. Perhaps he'll show tomorrow. If not, Lalo will finish up. L is no longer talking Tijuana. He's on a health kick and is watching his diet, running daily, practicing soccer and trying to get back in shape. He said that before his illness, he was the Sonoran county champion. I had heard this before. Hope he keeps at it.

Getting that paint off the beans is tough. They tried, and I guess they did, to save me money and used an old beam that came out of the kitchen on the assumption that we were going to plaster all the wall trimming. I'll shift them to the bathroom. Alberto finished the pool part, a perfect fit with five layers of fiberglass to paint them all white. The electrical work goes well and should be finished tomorrow. Will vacuum later today. Haven't been able to raise the Cooks. They're hiding out. Couldn't catch the Santaella broad. That's what mañanas are for. Water is still clear.

Tuesday, 7:00 p.m.

Fixed kedgeree for supper. Read about it in a British book and looked it up in the cookbook. Not bad. Used up frozen fish and have enough for tomorrow. Goodnight.

Lalo is putting back the armoire doors. Manuel is working on the white beam. Took off what we could and chipped it, and we hope the skim coat of cement works. Otherwise we'll need a cement-colored paint to match our beams if it takes.

Calalo is busy wiring and one peon is scraping flaked paint off portales pillars. Chlorine level was low so added both powder (granules) and new cakes. We'll see what happens. Will also try to get more in-flow re: the filter and D.E. Snake Bob and Slime John took off for Navojoa and then Tucson. The latter is feeding and beer-ing the former.

The place is a mess from cement drippings to install new wire. Will talk to Armida to find a new girl to clean house and brick. Off to get R food. Wish you were here. Still no bank statement form Schwab. Concerned because I need to know my balance. Shit!!

Back from P. O. Got the joint account statement but the 11:50 a.m. Biggie isn't here. Maybe tomorrow. Got caught up with Tom Cook and now know how to D. E. the pool. Will wait till Saturday and try my luck.

They're having a rough time. Still using neighbors' electricity and I gather that Mary is in the pits of depression. He said, "We're hiding out." He's wondering whether to go to the States for six months, but has serious reservations re: leaving his house. They had to drain their pool due to lack of electricity. Muchas problemas.

Calalo is busy dismantling the bathroom. We will get it tile-ready for your artistic placement. Had Lalo put doors back on armoire and kitchen cabinets to protect them from dust resulting from wall chipping. It just started to rain, real early in the day; everybody is hoping for floods which they claim we need.

Present shower may ground my jog because I prefer dirt roads. Lunch time, more later.

3:00 p.m.

Rain just letting up and Lalo took off to change clothes and run. I'll wait and maybe skip. When we took the bathroom closet out, we ran into a bad stretch of wall. Calalo will very carefully dig out the crumbling adobe and reinforce with cement.

Thursday

Back to the days of dust. Put all the doors and windows in the casita to protect them. Had a spectacular storm about 3:00 p.m. Looked like and sounded like war. Just took a break to move everything out of the cabinets so that the electrical work can be done. Think that while they are down, will have Lalo scrape them. Find myself living around heavy construction again. Pain in the ass but it simply cannot go on forever. Am glad you are not here for the nonce. The casita stinks of linseed oil and the glass room, etc., floats on dust.

Took a break and got mail. Still no word from Schwab so have no idea of bank balance. This particular statement is important because I must check to see if my annuity interest is flowing into my account. It was supposed to begin on July 1. Two little kids came by selling tamales at 500 pesos a copy. Bought a half dozen and will see if they can be frozen and then microwaved. With a salad, they'll a quick and easy meal.

Friday, 7:15 a.m.

Martin, the flying miner from New Mexico, showed up. He had been checking his mine, a shoe factory in Los Mochis of which he has a piece. He has a six-seater new plane that was flown by his son Brian, who just completed flight school for commercial aviation and now must go to college for two years and be 21 years old before the airlines will look at him. They'll be back down in October to bring more equipment and were talking about hiring about eight guys from Álamos—mechanics, mine foremen, etc., and then fly them in and out every weekend. Only a 30 minute flight and no roads. He's also working on improving the landing field. I'd like to see it when the latter is accomplished. It'll be the Copper Canyon by air. He told me, in confidence, that he was a pot smuggler for 12 years, making two flights a week at $20,000 per until he got caught by the feds and IRS and did three years in jail and two on probation 15 years ago. He says that now he doesn't even try to cheat on his income tax.

Lalo has just about completed the cabinet. He's doing the hard part, i.e., has to sit down to get at it, and then will go back to doors. The last few he did were great. Solid, old Sabino. He wants to continue working so I'll put him on brick cleaning when he's done with wood scraping. Looks like it will be a relatively slow day. Will make a hardware store run for electrical tape and get some R food now. More later.

Just checked the P. O., still no balance from Schwab. Called them. Bad connection, frustrating, and they agreed to send a duplicate ASAP. Did learn that my annuity payment had not been made. All the papers, phone numbers, account number, etc., are in the desk in Arizona. Great. Could you call them and find out what's going on? I left instructions to start payment on July 1. Also, do not cash the five thousand dollar check. There is not enough cash in my account to cover it and leave me a margin of safety to meet construction expenses. Pain in the ass. All for now.

Just finished playing with the pool. Acid is marginally okay so added a pint. Still high on chlorine. Threw about a cupful in and it was high for two days. Hope it subsides by tomorrow. A learning process. Tomorrow will also change D.E. according to Tom Cook's instructions and give the pool a thorough vacuuming. A slight yellowish something is appearing at sides. Suspect old paint peeling through. Will let it go and wait and see. Can always repaint and drain pool. Suspect another coat can cure the bottom.

Doesn't look like Don will come today. Martin spoke to him from El Paso and the former wasn't sure. Martin's new plane is the same as Don's.

Payday. Chlorine still high, acid just dandy.

Douglas is having an eye problem so will take him to Navojoa after 11:00 and hopefully get back in time for the soccer game. The crew is busy plastering over the new wiring. Don't expect to use kitchen much for a couple of days, then everything will be put back and living will be easier. I sweep and dust daily when the crew leaves but it's a bit like shoveling snow in a blizzard. It's all back the next day.

Kendall called. He and Bob will be down about Wednesday of next week with an electronic pool tester and some wine vinegar. Harvested first ear of corn yesterday and getting inundated with beans. Finished the last of your vinegar ones yesterday and do fresh ones in microwave with butter, bacon grease and parmesan. Sabroso!!! Glad the weekend is upon us. Need some rest and lazy time tomorrow. Off to the P.O. to get this in the mail.

Love, R & me

Sunday August 20, 1989

We are 64 years old. I feel ancient. Still couldn't sleep in. Now waiting on coffee to boil. The sky is a solid grey with mists obscuring the Sierra. R escaped and one of the girls that runs the neighborhood tienda told me he was visiting a tiny bitch in heat, looks part Chihuahua, across the street from her. I got him and he must have been in a fight. Mt. Álamos, because of fog patches, looks very Alp-y. I'll have to keep R close and confined for the next few days. Today will do pool, just vacuum and back off filter until this afternoon, assuming it doesn't rain. Nose running but no sore throat. Kitchen is depressing, shrouded in cement, streaked plastic and counters full of things that belong in shelves. This is no shining hour. Tianguis later should perk me up and then soccer against Navojoa at 9:00 a.m. More later.

Álamos lost by a ridiculous score but next weekend is the biggie. We play the Campana for the local trophy. We beat them once. They beat us once and there is a tie. Did some laundry and spent one-and-a-half hours diddling with the pool. Still doing something wrong but figured out what it is after the fact. Filter was not near as dirty this time. Water is okay.

May take a shower or go for a brief dip. My cold is full-blown. Will get some Contac later. Time to put the chickie on. Don Coleman just popped in. He brought pump and R stuff. We drank some beer and he went home to change. I guess I'll join him for Sunday street food and will figure a three hour time frame to do R in the afternoon. That's how long he said it will take. I'll have some concentrated chicken soup as a nightcap.

Really feel rotten. Couldn't get Contac Sunday; thought aspirin would do it. It didn't. Now waiting 'til 8:00 a.m. to go to drug store. Albert Einstein said, "Summer colds suck." I concur. Don invited me to dinner at 7:00 p.m. Rabbit, yummie, but as of this moment I may decline. Soledad came by yesterday, claimed a bad stomachache but promised to show today. I'll have her excavate the kitchen and sweep and mop and then go back to doing brick. All for now—collapse time in armchair indicated.

Got through the day with an extra long siesta. Did soup and a drug Joaquin recommended. Did dinner at Don's. He forgot one necessary piece of medication so he'll have to do R next time. The electrical work is virtually complete as is the front room plastering. Soledad didn't show. Once the kitchen plastering is complete I'll have things put back and out of shear sloth see if I can get Nellie back to a one day a week schedule. I just don't seem to have the energy to cope.

Looks like Lalo will finish the woodwork this week. I'll also check with Don on further refinishing. He mentioned that he used three coats of matte finish urethane on his walnut dining room table. It looks great. Will hold off on pump installation. Kendall (Hacienda owner) is due this week and will take samples from both his and our well to the states for analysis. According to pump instructions, wells should be treated with chlorine to kill a rust-thriving algae. The latter would affect test results. Wish I felt better.

Big excitement: R hopped on the washing machine and over the neighbor's wall and off to his true love. We're putting up boards to contain him on a temporary basis and I'm going to be better about keeping him with me at all times.

Did my rounds and hit the P.O. and got all the TIAA annuity stuff. Spoke to Schwab and will send them the bank paper for a quick turnaround and am trying to phone the girl in NY to get the dinero rolling in by September. As is, I've missed July and August,—800 numbers don't work in Mexico but I'm in there pushing. If I have to, I'll mail them my passport as proof of age, a problem unless they'll accept a Xerox copy of my birth certificate, which is all I seem to have.

No tile order confirmations. Be just my luck to have the mail on a train that crashed last week. Shit! Bob McKay just called to say the acid man's in town. He's sending him by. I'll pick up six gallons. What with brick and pool, stuff goes fast. Acid man came and scrounged up containers for nine gallons.

Rudy Hale arrived in town with a new plane. Took him 10 hours from Palo Alto. Teri had her operation and has not quite recovered enough to come down. He said that she'll be coming with her mother and sister for eight months in October. Still can't raise the TIAA girl but will get papers in mail now and hope money rolls in come Sept. 1. Off to the P.O. Later, girl.

Back, been doing a hell of a lot of running around and am feeling better. The drug works and I'm virtually symptom free. Progress report. Calalo has five courses of brick laid in front room (sala). Should be finished this week and will use garage for in and out until the varnish coats dry. Won't go out nights for a couple of days. Manuel should complete kitchen, dining room plastering today and will get furniture off the portal, probably tomorrow. Then I can enjoy a few days of comfort and cut the crew loose in the bathroom as a prelim to the kitchen job which will be a biggie.

2:00 p.m.

Peace. They're gone.

Lalo's run into some pure cedar doors. Hardly any two are alike in the house. Interesting. Visited Douglas's (artist) house on the hill. Amazing view. Then took an ever more amazing walk downtown on a path. Ran into a number of thatch houses, village style, two blocks from the Palacio and was titillated by a café-au-lait teenaged beauty pulling up her drawers as she left the privy.

Still struggling with my water bill. Brought receipt to show that the bank pays mine monthly and my house was purchased from the long dead Smollens, who they insist on billing monthly. I think I told them that they can cut their water off for lack of payment but don't do it to me because I collect receipts. We'll see what happens next month.

It was great talking to you last night and getting some things squared away. Rudy came over wet to call Palo Alto and the monsoon hit, complete with cloud bursts, thunder and lightning, and he was worried about how his new plane was holding up. During a lull in the storm he rushed home to close windows, etc., and then came back to try his call again. No luck. I didn't feel like going downtown, so fixed dinner. The storm came up about 9:00 and I swept out casita and house of water and went to bed.

At 2:15 a.m. either R or thunder woke me up and the biggie hit. Did some more sweeping. The pool filled to within a half inch of the coping. Went to bed and the storm subsided. It's pouring now. I've got a hose going to siphon out the pool. The skimmer hole is completely submerged. Developed a leak in the casita window which I will get repaired if and when the rain stops. Also some slight leakage where portal and new roof joins. Will also get that sealed. Understand that the arroyo is a roaring river much like those in Sells (Arizona) several years ago. The storm seems to be passing and rain diminishing. I've got a lot of pool debris removal ahead of me and Manual has a bunch of broken branches to get out. Hope the sun shines. More later.

Still pouring. Pool seems to be filling quicker than the siphon sucks and until I get the water level down the skimmer is inoperable. Lalo and the new peon, Martin, have not shown up for work yet.

Spoke to Don about wood finishing. He recommends a polyurethane sort of finish for exterior doors and some Danish imported polymer stuff for the rest. We are too late for polyurethane since the linseed oil would have to be sanded off. I'll have him bring the other stuff next trip down and have it applied. He said that there's nothing you can really do against termites. Let 'em eat and when doors are too bad, replace same. Most of ours are Sabino or cedar and termites don't like that kind of wood. Check in the States about termite-proofing furniture; surely something can be done short of injecting or total fumigation.

I see a patch of blue and the rain quit. This storm came from the west. I'll be heading down for R food and survey the damage shortly and take a look at the arroyo.

Got back; streets are flooding, dirt and debris is all over the place. Everybody saying "mucha agua". Have to get to the bathroom. Discovered old brick under concrete tile floor but it cannot be salvaged. A shame.

Been out and water is draining but will still be a couple of hours before I can crank up the filtration system. Played with the pool and got come chlorine and acid going. Snake Bob said their rain gauge shows seven inches, mucho, and that he thinks a minor tornado hit La Hacienda, five trees down, furniture on portales scattered, flower pots dumped, etc. I haven't been up to see it.

Lalo has not shown; he took three hours off earlier in the week when I went to get R food. He's lost interest but I need him to hang the shit because I don't know where they go or where the screws are stashed. It looks like the whole god-damned bathroom is going to have to be torn apart, sink stand, floors, etc. I'm sorry I started. Much, much more than I anticipated in time and money.

Got your letter and don't feel as disgruntled as I was earlier. Caught up with Cammie and Chacho and they just left so I'm fixing dinner. It's going to be beddy-bye before nine. I'm beat. It's raining again, but I doubt that we'll have the violence of yesterday's storms. Chacho also said that a little over seven inches fell in less than 12 hours. Guess I'll build a salad, eat and go to sleep. The bathroom is no longer operable so am using the casita exclusively, more mañana.

Thursday

Thanks for the caution in your letter. I visited the bank today. They had not paid taxes or trust account. Went to City Hall and paid taxes. Ran into Gustavo, who said the city never mails bills, got to be paid there and yes, penalties can run into big bucks. He said the Banamex Trust will mail me a bill in April. He also said that the next time he goes to Hermosillo I can join him and we can start the procedure to remove the trust in favor of direct ownership.

Visited Don Coleman and paid him about $450 USD for the pump set-up and he will pick up a quart of Watco wood finish, which is rubbed on and gives better protection than linseed oil. Ask Ziggy about it, particularly for exposed doors. About all for the moment. Until later.

If you want to do something beautiful in the bathroom, call me and tell me. I'm having it totally gutted, shower stall, sink base, the whole schmear, or I'll just replicate the previous design and do a relative repeat of the casita. Let me know your ideas by phone.

Don Coleman just left after a swim. He noticed some tile discoloration and said, "A result of lotion and potions." Easily remedied by some stuff called Breeze which he gets at Price Club and uses exclusively in his hospitals. I'll pick some up tonight since we'll be (R and me) going there for dinner and drink. All for now, got to get R fed and put some clothes on. Later, lass, later.

Couldn't find pepinos (cucumbers) for my daily salad. Don't know if Kendall made it down with the fine steel wool. All the pipes are unearthed in the bathroom. Will have Bill or Bob check and see if they need immediate replacement, and so it goes. Manuel is preparing the exterior wall, plugging cracks, etc., with plaster to get it paint-ready. Calalo is finishing up the electricity. Checked the pool. It is absolutely perfect. Lalo is busy working on another door and the two peons are busy hauling brick and trash. And so it goes ever-so-slowly. Off to the P.O. Hope it reaches you soon. R and I do miss you, Love, E&R

Monday

Dearest Joan,

Well, the weekend passed with style and ease. Didn't do a damned thing except take a short mile or two walk on the trail up to Mt. Álamos. Would have gone further but didn't bring water and t'was pretty hot. Craig, Ole Bill, etc., are on a three day rafting trip. Allen Pendergraft came by with the latest issue of Reader's Digest. White wolf on the cover and a so-so story with good pix about Arctic wolves. Runner will lose his anonymity for a spell, I suspect, much as he did following the National Geographic story a couple of years ago.

Kendall and Dave arrived with the plumbing parts manual. His ex-wife runs a tile export business in Tucson. He looked at the sink and recognized it. When I told him you bought it in Nogales, he knew the place and the people that run it. They wholesale to his ex's business. He has been scuba diving down here since the 50s and said that in about two months the man o'wars come into certain areas and he recommends tennis shoes, long sleeve shirts and jeans for protection. He said that if you do a fast shuffle there's no ray problem. He also told me of a small, deep water port for tuna and shrimp not too far away where a boat could be kept, just a couple of miles away from great beaches. I'll get a map so that we can explore the area.

A walk today, no jogging until leg is totally pain-free. Stuff still to come. Visited P.O., no mail last week and no letter today. What a bummer. Crew just left. It looks like another one-and-a-half days to arch, plaster and gloss the interior domes. However, it means mess, cement dust, etc., in bathroom and dining room, but I've had good training in living with dust. Just realized that I'll have to have screens made for guesthouse (Navojoa, I guess) before I can move in. Will see if Allen needs a lift. He came down in an old Dodge which is "in shop" since Friday and may or may not have parts, ugly problem. Exercise time, more to come.

Sunday

Too, too much excitement this morning. R started howling at 6:30 a.m. There's a bitch in heat followed by a pack of 15 or 20 males that wants to get it on with Runner. Ran into them yesterday. Had R on leash and tried to hide in the CONASUPO until they cleared off. Headed down town and she showed up again. I had to be rescued by a Mexican who ran into his house and chased them away with broom.

On my way to get meat for R, no problems but on the return trip ran into them in from of Micha's house. I had the stud collar on R to control him. It was tough. Again, I had to be rescued by a neighbor who pitched rocks at her and her train. They disappeared to catch us again in front of Gen Reynold's house. She offered refuge and the yipping and yapping attracted Don Wilcox, who chased them with rocks.

If I go out again, I'll carry gravel and maybe a stick. Don't want R mixing it up. Many of the males are bloody from fights. The bitch goes right up to R every time. She likes him. I'm afraid of hurting my back handling R. What a weird situation. I'm a prisoner. Guess I'll use my truck to get food the next few days. Pain in the ass! Maybe the other dogs will cool her out and leave us alone. Even with the stud choke collar, R is incredibly strong and can jerk me around with ease. Poor horny guy. I empathize but ....

Both maestro's doing cupola work. Maybe Navojoa for screens after a bank run. Right now I feel as if I want to get out of town.

Wednesday

No more problems with Runner and bitch. Maybe the owner or police picked her up and confined her. Life is easy. Cupola done. Can't decide whether or not to do interior panels. Guys are cleaning and doing finishing plaster while waiting for septic system cover slabs to arrive before placing and covering.

May have located approximately 400-to-500 old floor brick, enough to replace those destroyed on portales, and do main house bathroom as well as repay Gustavo. Calalo has to check them for quality. Expensive (three-and-a-half times new brick price). But I seem to be getting into an old brick mode. Maybe it's the challenge of locating stashes as the existing supply disappears forever. Found these by talking to a Mexican who was salvaging a ruin. Hope they are not "salt" brick. Gustavo is going to Navojoa today and will see what can be done again about my phone.

Thursday

Manuel is finishing up the floor. Calalo is finishing up the Mexican laundry. Peons are hauling shit out front to be picked up and I'm trying to find Pancho to get the sander back for Manual, and getting ready for brick hunting. Candy Joe, the guide who has an artifact store, asked permission to take tourists through to look at the domes. Much oohing and ahhing.

I will be coming up on the 11th. Craig will keep me company. He's going up to get his teenage daughter and bring her down for a week.

Bad things have happened the last two days. One fellow I know was shot in a hunting accident, not fatal, but enough to keep him from returning. He hunts with a three-legged Doberman, a pal of Runner's, and has been coming down for a month or two for 20 years. The son of the Markanthonys (Leo, Alaskan University professor I think you met) was in a head-on collision outside of Magdalena. In the ICU, status unknown. A nice kid (Robert) that was building his own little house and trying to develop a mine. Bad action. Gustavo and the Wilcoxes (I suspect) have gone up to see what can be done. The Wilcox car is gone and the Markanthonys are somewhere between Álamos and Anchorage and haven't been located as of last night

Got Calalo estimating re-bar, cement, sand, lime, etc., for roof and we are changing the work schedule from 7:00-Noon, lunch, 1:00-4:00, to 6:30-2:30, then lunch in anticipation of the heat to come. I'm planning to leave a bunch of pre-dated checks to cover payroll, etc., and open credit accounts all over the place. Gonna go and check a pile of used brick now. More later.

Wandered down to the P.O. and got your letter. You are having such a wonderful time with your job that I worry about you ever coming down here. Don't know what to make of the "where will Gertie stay?" problem since I gather that she can't be left alone. With Lois, it might be tough because of Arizona MDs and I know it will be tough with you or Gene because of the job. Down here would be equally hard. Have you thought Coolidge and live-in housekeeper? No word about Mart. How is he bearing up?

Craig took his Dad and brother fishing. Came back with 50 or so off the coast about a mile or so out.

Major engineering today—moving concrete lids over septic system. I can see how Mexicans build pyramids; it's in their blood. The slabs must weigh 1,000 lbs. My thinking now is to defer surgery, if the new technique can't be used, for a couple of months and finish off down here. ASAP pool, roofs and the landscaping to start to take advantage of the summer rains. What do you think? You need a break from post-op anyway. I am also thinking of spending a week in Arizona, coming down and then going back for VA appointments. Gonna need a couple of truckloads of stuff anyway, paint, roof asphalt, etc.

Just got back from martini-ing with Allen Pendergraft and Runner is limping. Can't find thorns or glass. Poor baby. Light is bad. Will look again in the morning and if I don't see anything, will go to the vet. I felt bad about this since I can't help him. Now dinner because it's "más o menos" 5:30 on our new schedule. This goes in the mail so it precedes me to the States.

Friday, 6:35 a.m.

Guys have started. Manuel is busy sanding and aciding the old brick in the casita. The plans are shoveling dirt on the septic system Calalo is putting the finishing touches on his "Mexican Washing Machine." Runner seems to be okay. Limped a little bit when he got up this morning. Examined him thoroughly, some small cuts on his paw. I went to the Mercado; he danced around a little, played with some dogs en route and the limp disappeared. It must have been a muscular thing. He was out romping at the Cooks for about an hour yesterday and was totally winded when we left from a swim, which he dearly loves to do in their swamp pond. About it for the moment, breakfast and the P.O. See you next week. Love R&E

Wednesday, September 6, 1989

Dear Joan,

It is bitching hot today. Thermometer reads 85 degrees and I suspect that the humidity is about the same. Álamenses say, "It's Navojoa weather." I was there yesterday to get a new tailpipe for the truck and deliver Patrick to the bus terminal for the airport. He'll be mailing important papers, check, etc., to you, which should arrive way ahead of this letter. Took Ole Bill with me. He seems to enjoy little excursions.

Swam 20 laps yesterday. A big mistake. My leg is bad. I am aching. I saw Joaquin. He said, "Take Ibuprofen and stay off your feet for a week." Well, I'm tired of this shit. Ole Bill walks (oozes) faster than I do.

The bathroom is coming along nicely. No word from the tile people. so will call Gustavo and once again, seek his assistance. When the bathroom is done, will get sink and water heater going, as well as a new pump installed.

I just spoke to Skip Branin. He got a call from Schwab re: transferring stock back to the portfolio. He's sounding a note of caution vis-a-vis investing new funds at this particular instance. He mentioned that he signed a new client last week with a bunch of cash, which he's feeding into the market on a highly selective basis. I asked about unloading and he pointed out that you're better off in stock than cash since, until the capital gains tax is revised, regardless of what your income bracket is the government will claim 30 percent tax on profit up front. He also said that there is generous bipartisan support to change the law. It used to be a maximum of ten percent. Big difference. Time to eat so can take pills and prop leg on heating pad. Later.

Thursday 9:00 a.m.

Leg a little better. Can walk with scarcely a limp and pain is down some. Still in the rest phase and taking pills. Pool's in good shape. Breast stroked five laps yesterday. Did not use legs at all. Still fighting the tick battle with R. Picked eight off this ayem. It's clouding up some, unusual this time of day. Perhaps the rain will come and break the humidity. If it doesn't, we're in for a hot one.

Lalo didn't show. He was late every day this week and when here, didn't accomplish a helluva lot. When he does show, he's going to have to decide whether or not to continue. If not, I'll have Calalo find someone. It will be easy. 'Bout it for the moment.

Did my banking and met the Moores. Two kids and a large poodle, professional photographers who live in the Gould house on Prison Hill. Made it to the Post Office and as I turned the corner to come home, the rain started. Talk about perfect timing. Also saw a plane but without binoculars couldn't tell whether it was Don's, Mart's or someone else. Time to elevate foot and apply heat. More to come.

Awfully good talking to you last night. Thanks for processing papers. I sure hope the annuity people get their shit together and that it was just a typo. My leg is a little better. Guess the older you get, the slower you take to heal. Lalo is a no-show again today. The broad beam is complete on the closet and Calalo is framing with wood and iron to go on up. Ran into Gustavo. He'll be by tomorrow morning to call Dolores Hidalgo for tile.

Also, ran into Alan Bacal (sp). Gave him your phone number, which he will pass along to Chrissy. He thinks the 4th of October will be a good time since she is recovering nicely from valley fever.

Got one-and-a-half inches of rain, so I siphoned off some pool water so that the skimmer works better. Water is crystal clear and electronic pool tester is fun to use. Plan on laving R when the guys leave. He's been mud-romping. Also, Cindy, the shepherd, is coming into heat so I have the guys keep the front door closed at all times. And keep him on leash. Micha keeps Cindy fenced but R likes to hang around.

Also saw Ole Bill. He's spending an awful lot of time in bed. While I was visiting, he had to go lie down because he was feeling a little dizzy. Suggested he go see Joaquin. He may. Lord, he is slow and frail and he's ten years younger than Mart.

I hope the trailer at Apache Lake goes at the price you put on it. Try to remember all expenses, etc., and even consider an ad in an appropriate newspaper or list it with a realtor. Remember, there is no hurry to sell it.

Just washed Runner and have him in drying under the fan. When the sun sets a little, I'll do some kick-less swimming and some other chores. My laundry of two days ago finally dried; kept getting caught in the monsoon. Got the mail, note enclosed as curiosity got the best of me, so opened and read the enclosed. Do not lose the recipe; sounds like a great use for cabbage, pickled and blanched or frozen , and black-eyed (infants) peas. Don't know how to acquire smoked hog jowls so will substitute bacon and pretend it's New Years and use a peso instead of a dime. Since I'm the only one who will be eating I'm assured of good luck. More later.

Up 5-ish and did the pool. Douglas showed up about 6:30 and we had coffee and talked. Told him about ordering tile from Dolores Hidalgo so he got Gustavo on the phone and wandered off to look at the catalogue and measure floors and will be back at 9:00 for the phone call. No Lalo, which is surprising because today is pay day. Now I'm wondering if he's sick or something.

Brushed, curried and fluffed R. Extracted four ticks from his fur and put stuff on his forehead and ears. This is where they congregate.

Bathroom problem. Can't curve because of door jamb angle. Calalo put a base in to set up the wall between toilet and sink. He's ripping it out. I caught the mistake before he erected the wall. One door, 900 pesos or slightly under, jamb is pretty well left. We ordered the tile. It came to $1,731,900 pesos, or slightly under $760. Don and I will meet at the bank Monday, change dollars and then go to the telegraph office. They will notify the tile guy that they have the money and the stuff will be loaded. When we pick the stuff up in Navojoa, the money will be released in Dolores Hidalgo. Gustavo figures we should get the tile late next week or by Monday. Perfect. Off to the P.O.

Love R & Me

September 1989

Skip called yesterday. Mortgage payment arrived at Schwab. Cash the check and let it draw money market in the trust. He's got no inspirational stock to recommend at this moment but will let me know. I'll give you another five thousand when you come down in October and discuss suitable investments for both of us with Skip the next time he calls. I'm also thinking of depositing $20,000 US in the local bank to take advantage of 30 percent interest to offset and input, the loss of 11-½ percent mortgage money I was getting.

Need information on Mexican income tax, the most effective way to transfer funds. Know it's got to be in amounts of less than 10,000 USD. Would also like to reduce the one percent the bank takes when it cashes checks.

Visited with Pember yesterday. He looks good, all things considered, and is changing his lifestyle. He takes a two mile walk daily and has an exercise bike, no booze, cigars or salt, the latter a problem when eating out.

I seem to be becoming a morning person. I start playing with the pool at 5:30; it takes about ten minutes to sweep down and skim. I use my hose siphon about every three days and figured out a way to avoid mouthfuls of water. Saturday will deal with a filter cleaning, but will have to construct a few parts to plug pipes. Spoke to Tom Cook about it. He forgot to tell me of the need to do this. It'll make the cleaning operation infinitely more effective.

Gammy just called; another $140 USD is due for a month. Will stop it now. Gustavo came by. He was on his way to Navojoa and forgot to turn off his pool pump, easy to do, so he used the phone. He says that there will be a devaluation before Christmas premised on the fact that pesos flee the country to buy presents, etc. in El Norte and advises against considering a peso account at this time. He said the peso is becoming increasingly unrealistic in the world market and an adjustment must be made. We'll wait and see.

He also told me that it is possible to get an Álamos truck that delivers to the border, pay short term US insurance to pick up a load in Sells and then, through prearrangement, re-cross the border and deliver to Álamos. Will pursue this.

Interesting afternoon. Sammy came by to sign paper to pay the current SS statement. He told me the guys get off Saturday because the statement only covers actual work. I asked about last week's holiday. They had not heard the President speak. They agreed they'd like this Saturday off. I said, "Cool, but don't expect to get paid for it. You got your holiday pay last week."

"But we need the money."

"No problem," said I, "No trabajo, no dinero, solimente si tus trababajo sabado,"

We work nine and ten hour days next week or Sabado is off. I scared the shit out of them and they became most solicitous, particularly Lalo, who earlier in the day was caught dawdling. He picked up a tool, I timed him myself for five minutes, and he did no more than a quarter of what it took an hour to do. He snapped fast the rest of the day.

We are in the middle of a cloud burst. Heard something about a hurricane moving in and heavy rains expected inland for two days. This must be it. Getting hungry. If I have the energy left after cooking I'll write on.

Friday

Been busy as hell but will write about it later so you can get going on the check. Tomorrow is a holiday. Want this in the mail.

Love R & Me

Joan,

I'm in a rush to get the mail out in a hurry. I had to hunt down Patrick, who is flying to San Diego tomorrow. Armida and Bill helped. Located him and he'll mail the papers and both installments of present epistle to you from the airport so you can get the notary and stuff to Pennsylvania this week by the fastest means possible. Express mail if doable in Sells or ?? This is just an addendum and the meat is on another page, as well as more letters in the white envelope. All for now.

Oh, spoke to Martin and Mary. They may be flying down this weekend and will be coming again in October, open dates, to get their mine going again. A possible lift and a big plane to carry stuff. Also, Kendall and his friend Caroline will be coming in early October. He's only going to be here five-to-seven days and Sells is en route. Another possibility if dates work out okay and it'll be a round trip. His number is 994-5917, office number, but he's never there, or 264-2952 (Caroline's). Check timing. Also, he'll be back down here for a weekend or so in three weeks. Martin's going to call Don in San Diego to see about this weekend. I gather that they're pretty good amigos; both have the same kind of plane. If Don comes, we'll deal with stinky old Runner. All the news for the nonce.

We still miss you, E & R

Saturday, 1:00 p.m.

Dear Joan,

Slept 'til 6:00 this morning and then did the pool while it was still cool. Ran into Dan en route for R food and stopped in for coffee. Came home and Manuel Murrietta came by. Threw him out so I could fix something to eat. Then Candy Joe arrived. An Indian who ordered ten masks from three months ago showed up with 14. Did we want the excess? We sure did, two male and two female, four bucks apiece, no profit for Joe. Then he told me that there are four different style Mayo masks depending on regions. These come from a village on the Mayo River and look almost Chinese. The men are black and white, the women kind of mud colored and white.

He said our friend Benigno makes a good mask representing the Masiaca, 50 K south of Navojoa, but has a drinking problem. Joe has been trying to get him to make a few wolf Kachinas for his shop, as well as get some masks. We bought the ones that Joe had paid an advance on. He said that when Benigno has money he doesn't carve and Joe's afraid that he's somewhat embarrassed to bring him things right now. Joe also said that in terms of craftsmanship, the best masks come from the San Bernardo area and are made of cedar. He also said that they make superb instruments, drums, some kind of harp, etc. There are also some excellent furniture makers there. Better and cheaper than anyone in Álamos, all cedar.

Anyway he'll probably be going there on a buying trip when the monsoon season is over in October. I offered to provide transportation just to look-see. He has been wholesaling deer, javelina and goat skin masks to some guy in Tucson. The guy was here to pick up a load last week and rejected the javelina and deer skins because he was not allowed to cross the border with them, only the goats can go. So instead of making 2,000,000 pesos (approximately $900 USD), he only got 800,000 ($350 USD). He figures he'll sell them individually when the tourists come. He says he pays about $15 USD for them wholesale and sells them for $50 USD. Not a bad markup but some work is involved since he buys the skins one at a time and then delivers bundles of ten or so to assorted craftsmen and prays for timely delivery.

Right after he left Pat Siefert, the artist showed. During his absence, one painting was sold and another one stolen from Polo's restaurant where his work was displayed. He'll be coming by later to go to the soccer game and go for a swim. The soccer game is the final 35 minutes of last week's championship. The game had been called because of rain and darkness. We're ahead 1-0 and Alan will be back in the lineup on defense. Carlos came by on a bicycle to tell me that we have nothing to worry about and to still plan to accept the trophy tonight at the Baila de Futbol. We'll see. I'm going to have to squeeze in a siesta early evening if I'm to stay up beyond 10:00 p.m. All for now.

Álamos update: The Lobos won, score 2-1, scary. Tacubaya, the rival team, tied in the first ten minutes of the 35 minute playoff, but Los Lobos (named for Runner as the mascot), through a truly beautiful play, made the winning goal, four players involved in setting it up, picture book stuff.

Kendall and son Gregg flew in. I picked them up and now am getting ready to go to the victory dance with Gregg as soon as R finishes eating. Kendall bought the pool tester but no steel wool. He came down to fly his broken-hipped father back to the US on Monday. Bob Dunn should be down Thursday so will call him for steel wool. Off to dance and trophy presentation. More manaña.

1:25 a.m.

Have no idea why I'm awake at this hour but we have the biggest fuckin' soccer trophy you ever done saw. I'll have Kendall ship it to you from Phoenix so it will probably beat this epistle. If my handwriting is poorer than normal, 'tis because of mucho, and I do mean mucho, cerveza in celebration of the great victory. Everybody and his brother kept buying me cans of Tecate. When you come we'll have to take in a dance; it looks like fun. Bunch of kids in their best clothes are bopping around. Teddy, the guide who works with Bill Preece, was there and acted an interpreter when I stammered too badly. Mario, the guy who used to own the little organic food market a few years back and took pictures (Arco Iris), was there for the ceremony. I'll try to get copies as well as the newspaper pix. We got a big damned trophy which will probably reach you before this epistle. More manaña. Wish you were with us.

Sunday

Lazy Sunday. Slept in 'til 7:00, got up , did the pool with the electronic tester Kendall brought down. Then did Tianguis with Ole Bill and Kendall. No car when you fly. Angel, back from visiting his folks in Minnesota, reclaimed his truck from Bob. Then came home to a leisurely coffee, a full pot, and read the Phoenix newspaper. It was grand. Went for a dip and along about 3:00 wandered up to the Hacienda and visited Ramon, co-owner of the Tesoros, who was there with his family. Learned that you can rent a fisherman and panga for 30,000 pesos a day ($13 USD) at the beaches. Do we want a boat?? Returned home and went for another dip, more waiting for dusk to do another Sunday night in Álamos and it's getting there so, more on next page.

Friday, September 15, 1989

Dear Joan,

Benigno just left (Mayo Indian who made the Runner Wolf Kachina). Bought six small car window dangles at two dollars per and one large six-dollar mask. He'll be back next weekend with more. Maybe you can become the mask queen of Tucson. To both hurry and improve production (we'll trade them for masks), can you buy him a jigsaw with extra blades and a Sureform file with different attachment blades? I'd get him a power carving tool, but he has no electricity. Before I bought the masks we hunted down Candy Joe to give him first crack, but he didn't want them. However, he did buy two Kiva Wolf Kachinas. We introduced a new product inadvertently. Occurs to me that if you could locate a few cheap or nickel-and-dime Kachinas, Benigno could reproduce same out of wood. They'll still be authentic Indian.

Got a phone call from Monterrey, Mexico. TIAA CREF sent by Express Mail a bunch of papers for me to sign. Wow! They wanted to know what bus lines go from Monterrey to Navojoa to Álamos.I told them to put everything in the mail. I'm beginning to wonder when, if ever, my annuity check will come. Also didn't get my bank statement from Schwab. Called them to see what can be done, a true pain. Finally drained off excess water and cleaned rain-produced debris from pool. About two inches fell and I learned that for effective surface skimming a precise amount of water is needed. And so it goes. More later.

The guys are going to work tomorrow. Shit. I was going to siesta and maybe go Tesoros-ing with the gringo colony and then scare up a Mexican party, but with up at 5:00 or 5:30 can't hack it. Needing sleep.

Well, tomorrow's the day to hang which I will do during the daytime festivities. School kids have been out on the street practicing marching, and beer cans are being filled with kerosene to go on roofs and torchlight the plaza. When I went for dog food, watched a guy rehearsing his dancing horse near Micha's house. Candy Joe tried to interest me in an Indian-made violin. I didn't know what to do with it. When I saw him today he said he bought it. Incidentally, I 'm starting to walk only one-and-a-half miles slow (sort of) and am now up to 25 laps in the pool. Don't like it much but may learn to. I'm off.

Saturday

Everybody showed except Martine the musician. Rain, about an inch or more, put somewhat of a damper on last night's festivities. Later, about 8:00 p.m., it starts to rain. Two nights in a row and I am stranded in the main house, so crash on couch and wake up about eleven and R and I wander over to the casita. Spent about a half hour on pool skimming. Am now lowering water so skimmer will work and will re-charge and clean filter today. Much trabajo. Will leave for arroyo at noon and watch festivities: horse dancing, races, parades, mariachis, etc. I have no firecrackers as all bets are off. More later.

Just back from getting R food. The butcher was closing early and gave me two pounds of steak meat. Tempted to eat it myself, but won't. Peddlers (rich ones) have card tables with cheap plastic toys and dolls, poor ones spread their wares on the pavement. Three ballooneros strolling. Can hear several fife and drum corps practicing.

Been busy all morning setting up a system to clean filter. My God, there's a bunch of stuff coming out. Be a lot more if I used the vacuum which would drop the bottom dirt in the skimmer hole instead of siphoning and getting rid of silt. I'm afraid to admit it but I'm getting to enjoy pool maintenance. Will enclose some photos, two taken by cameras on different occasions.

The Ketchums came by, John and Jackie, to check progress. R and their dog behaved perfectly. They sat about two feet apart and communed while we talked. They left and at 11:00 o'clock the Slaughters popped in. They just got back. They had to see progress. I ushered them out the door.

Stripped down and was mucking out the filter, washing R's security blanket and misc. bedding with occasional dips, and lo and behold, Don Coleman arrives, bathing suit and a couple of beers in hand. I'd been working hard because I wanted to get things done to hit the arroyo festivities. At that point, Don provided a good excuse to quit, so beer we drank and then some more. John arrived all upset because his $20,000 USD, plus 12 passenger van's electronic system wasn't working. He was looking for Snake Bob who allegedly knows something about wiring. A few more beers and I hustled him out the door, completed the swim and hit the arroyo. All Álamos on horseback, drank some beer, watched crazy contests, heard some music, good and bad, ate a hot dog, more beer, and off to Elsa's for food and home about 7:00 p.m. Didn't have the energy or inclination to go downtown for the evening's festivities. Maybe next year.

Up at 5:30, shit, had my morning's trauma. The problem: how to remove one or more coats of varnish from old brick in bedroom. Heat didn't work, straight nitric acid didn't work, paint remover sort of worked. I mentioned my problem to Lincoln Reynolds. He suggested that I try some of the super paint thinner Alberto uses on car enamels and lacquer finishes. It works. Now I've got to buy a bunch; we are using it in conjunction with acid. Old brick problem, no two alike. Even those from the same source are different.

Want this in the mail so off I go. Gave Gen the cartoon for Pancho. She got a kick out of it.

Love, R& and Me

Tuesday, September 19, 1989

Cleaned up pool mess. Don pointed out the beginning of black algae, the enemy. Dumped some stuff in last night and it totally zapped it. Had to add water to bring it up to the level of the algae. Now I'm draining it so the filtration system is more effective. Don's been to a lawyer, temporary spousal support at $2,300 per month. Marie is back in school. She wants to be a writer and is taking appropriate courses. Don has no idea what the final settlement will be.

Learned one thing from Snake John. He buys three or four coolers in the States, stuffs them with chicken, bacon, hamburger, etc. Stuff that's either very expensive or unavailable, loads his freezer, and then sells the coolers for about $10 more than he paid for them. Very interesting. He brought a big freezer down to stuff with doves and lucked out, 80 M in pesos. He also told me of a Kentucky Fried Chicken place that sells pesos at more than 100 pesos per dollar than the local bank and generally, he claims, picks up $300-to-400 USD worth. Good idea.

He also told me that the US government sells Mexican-tagged cars that were confiscated for dope, wetbacks, etc., every Christmas in Tucson. They cannot be licensed in the States. He claims that a friend of his went and bought a US-tagged, confiscated Ford truck at auction, mostly US used car dealers and for private buyers like himself, but that three Mexicans bought all the confiscated Mexican cars, all made-in-Mexico vehicles: Ram Charger, Ford trucks and VW vans, and all '88 and '89s. Smugglers don't drive heaps and all sold for about half US prices, since Americans couldn't bid on them. This is worth doing some research on.

Getting on towards 8:00 a.m. and Ole Bill Tianguis time. More later.

Today's Sonoran adventure is over and I am beat. Picked up Don Coleman, went to Huatabampito. Splashed a tad, R even swimming, then off to Yavaros. Prior to leaving, I went by Casa Slaughter to repay Ron 20,000 pesos I borrowed when he was here yesterday and told him we were going shrimping. He returned the 20,000 and said two kilo. Then went to Ramon, who was on duty at the Tesoros to cash dollars, no pesos left for the day's activities, had him draw us a map, and away we went . Don wanted a bunch of shrimp to fly back to San Diego and give to his help. He ended up with 18 kilo. I ended up with five in three packages. We got there late and that was all we could buy. We got slightly lost and ended up in Navojoa and not on the highway near the government place. Ate at Plaza Bruja, great!

Back to Álamos. Parked in front of the Tesoros and got Ron and Lovey to divy up the loot. Ron borrowed a scale from the Tesoros and took his two kilo. Ramon wanted two kilo for the restaurant and I kept one for you.

We stopped for one beer and Pember and Veronica, the gracious Brit who lives next door to the Tesoros, arrived. Pember talked about his robbery and Veronica, a lady of a certain age, asked Don and I to escort her home. We did, lingered briefly to look at a painting (old) of Don's place before it became a ruin, and home. Loaded Don's shrimp in his truck, sorted yours into three packs of 24 each, fed R before freezing stuff and off to bed, read a tad, rested a lot, more mañana.

And so the week begins. Been hitting it hard since daylight, 5:35. Playing with pool, relieving R from salt and sand, cleaning his dog home before putting in fresh (cleaned) bedding, etc. Lalo showed up sick and went home after returning my bike, which I let him use for the weekend. He couldn't get a horse. Discussed a bunch of stuff with Don yesterday. He has many gallons of grey beam paint which he would like to sell if you want the beams painted. He also has red brick paint which I can think of no reason to buy. I will give him $100 to buy wood carving tools for Benigno.

He's also interested in establishing a non-profit bowl turning operation. I heard of a woodworking shop set up by the government to provide employment and export products in Álamos. Now defunct. I'll find out its status and let Don carry the ball from there. He told me about a singles weekend he went to at Big Bear, all over 40, all divorced, women 300, men 125. Good odds but he said they were all too freaky for him and could understand why they were divorced. Must go for R food; more to come.

Back from the Mercado, a real rough time with R. The same bitch that followed him around six months ago is back in heat. She goes into the butcher and hardware store after him with several other dogs in town and I've got to wrestle R on his leash. May start driving to market to avoid problems. Damn. I worked up a sweat and my stud collar is at Don's. They're closed today so may go mañana with Don for dinner. Also have to commence R's surgery. José just came by to borrow a tool. Calalo couldn't find it. Thinks Lalo knows where it is, no Lalo, and so it goes.

Wednesday, September 20, 1989

Bet and Pember just wandered by. Showed them progress, poured coffee and sent them on their way. She's pretty anxious to see you and mumbled something about picking up books. Pember approves of my pool maintenance. High compliment from a pro, so there. R just happened to be howling when they arrived. Bitch in heat. Guess if he brought everything, Don'll do R. this afternoon. I've got to go see him about 8:30 to take his truck to be fixed and leave him mine for awhile.

Also want to pick up 100 feet of copper pipe to do hot water shower, etc. He advises against hot water for washing machine. I'm not sure why, but I'll run it over because the darkroom may need some.

Lalo's back, cheery as ever. Manuel's finishing "detailing" the front rooms and Calalo is still on the bathroom. No word on the tile, but Gustavo is due back from Hermosillo today. Think I'll put the hot water heater in the rear wall storage shed and on Don's next trip down in two weeks, get my pump installed. I've hesitated to do it because it takes all four guys to build scaffolding and haul the old one out, as you may well recall. I really want the bathroom ready to accept tile upon your arrival.

Don's going to bring a wood carving tool down to let Benigno pick what he wants and then bring the stuff in on another trip. But he mentioned that June Marthens has a great roof-top palapa. We'll take a look when you're here.

Ran into Ramon at the Hacienda yesterday and we were talking about cars. He said that the government has lifted a 40 percent or more tax on new cars because people were going to the US to buy 'em. If this info is correct, we can check out the Datsun dealer in Navojoa.

Friday, September 22, 1989

Not much happened last couple of days. Shared dinner with Don Thursday and we both went to the Caracol last night. Excellent, couldn't have been better. Don departs today, back in two weeks. Will do R then. Didn't have proper antibiotic. I'd rather wait than take chances. He's also buying some tick repellant cream which I hope is an improvement on the present stuff. Got metal choke collar from Tom. Need it to control R with hot bitch.

Snake John moved his car to the Hacienda. The whole thing burned to the ground yesterday. Were I his insurer, I'd be suspicious. Gustavo back from Hermosillo. Will be here at 9:00 o'clock and we'll birddog tile in Navojoa. Doug's (Reisborough) got his movie neighbors coming down from Hollywood Hills and will move to the hill. He's got a phone up there which simplifies life. Los Lobos has a game Sunday with a Cuidad Juarez team Sunday morning. I've also agreed to join the boys for poker Saturday afternoon. Arnold came by to invite me yesterday. Also Pember, Craig Hill, who just got back, the Reynolds boys. Should be fun.

Pool was a mess this morning. A wind was up and skimming took a long time. If I don't do it daily, leaves sink and they're a bitch to get out short of vacuuming, which I hate. Also, a minor well problem in town. Bless our well!

I bought a sander from Don, infinitely better than ours, and will be picking up a scaffolding rig he invented to paint the front rooms and will return same before he gets back in about two weeks. I'm making a list of what I owe him because he never wants to be paid in cash when I want to clear things up.

No Gustavo. Ran into Doug and he hasn't seen him yet. Candy Joe came by with four

Guarijio Indian masks of a different style, more elaborate and possibly better workmanship. Gay showed up with 10; Joe bought four. We now have 14.

Well, we're starting to paint the sala. Handed the scaffolding over, bought brushes, etc. Calalo is plastering the bathroom and should have it tile-ready upon your arrival.

Worked hard on pool. Some fluffy stuff floated on the surface that took forever to skim off. Still no word on whether or not the tile arrived. Gustavo will check again today and Doug and I will go into Navojoa Monday to inventory and sign off.

Went to Tesoros last night, the usual crowd. Ramon , the co-owner , invited me to his home for lunch today. He's really proud of this wife's cooking. She's a nice lady. Don hired her to train his maid. He hired a girl from the Indian settlement next to his property and it looks like she had never been in a house. Doesn't know how anything works, i.e. hot water, use of soap on dishes, mopping floors and on and on. He was discussing the problem with Ramon, who volunteered his wife. Could you bring that housecleaning book from S. F. down? Don is thinking of getting it translated. Good idea. For us as well, assuming one gets a maid who can read. Pix taken by Bob Dunn.

I'm heading off to Merv's after I finish this letter to see Gustavo and look at an antique brick floor configuration Merv is installing. Then back here in case Benigno shows, payday. More pool work, lunch, poker, siesta and on the town. May shampoo R if I have the energy and timing is okay. So until ....

Love R & Me

Monday, September 25, 1989

It was downright chilly this morning. The pool was a piece of cake. Not much debris. Made an omelet with a new kind of cheese. Bought a loaf of bread at the corner store and saw one of the neighbor ladies carrying five slabs of white cheese and assumed she bought it there. Asked and was told she got it at the market. Offered to sell me one. It's called panella and is bland. They use it to top tostados, beans, etc. Have got to find a good cheese with a little zip to it.

Am bushed and am putting together a "things to bring" list. Re-reading O'Flaherty's Informer. That guy can write. Written 60-odd years ago and absolutely current since the tribal warfare continues in "the old sod." Time for market, more later.

Ran into Alan. He came by for coffee and croissants, a new discovery, 750 pesos a pair and good. This is part of the treasure hunting aspect of Mexico Alan told me that goat stew or curry is indistinguishable from lamb. I'll experiment before you come. Had the tinaco thoroughly cleaned. It's something I should have done earlier, like when I bought the house. More, I want to sterilize it with chlorine but must research the amount to put in. Have to go downtown for things so will ask Pember. He knows about water treatment. On my way, more later.

Pember was out visiting so went to the Tesoros to pay Gamy some money I owed. Discussed my problem with him and Ramon. The latter told me to add a little copper sulfate, which he gave me. Let it sit for a day, drain, scrub the sides with a cup of Clorox, rinse, fill, enjoy. He also said he heard of people using epoxy paint, which restricts algae growth. Must learn more.

Kicked back and beginning to worry about dinner. Just need to boil some rice. Did chicken and veggies earlier for microwaving. Later.

Also have solved hot to trot. Will hit the Tesoros for a drink and wander home to eat, to be continued...

Thursday

Lots of company Bill, Don and Pat for coffee. She and Don are going back to the States because of problems with his leg. Benigno came by, ordered more leg rattles and added five masks. No work on tile. Will check Gustavo later. Will be sending this with Don and Pat.

Love, R & Me

P.S. Mailing this from the States will give you a little more time on the enclosed "Thing To Bring" list. Nothing is essential; do the best you can.

Late September, 1989

Dear Joan,

Sunday is here, hooray, hooray! Played four hours of poker yesterday and won $7.00. Got to eat some smoked salmon and tongue. Houston Walt, the big winner ($43), has a smoker down here. Came home, changed clothes and did the Tesoros. Craig Hill, Pember and the Reynolds boy bitched and moaned about losing, particularly Doug ($1.00 lost), who makes his livelihood as a professional Vegas dealer for five years and occasionally see hundreds of thousands of dollars change hands when the high rollers come to play.

Ate at Polo's. Biggest damn $7.50 steak in the world. Slept 'til 6:30. Diddled with the pool for a half hour, did a bunch of wash, mostly T-shirts and skivvies, picked up Ole Bill for the Tianguis run. Got him home, got R food, and went to the soccer game. Hung around with the team for about an hour. The opponents from Juarez never showed so the baseball players took over. The new soccer field should be ready in a couple of weeks.

Visited Pat and Don. He's still in a cast and may go back to L.A. for doctoring early this week. They may be back when you come and you and Pat can play at Mocuzari or the beach with her Sunfish. Temperature hit 95 degrees, hottest for the summer. Got some food on the stove that's about ready. Then plan on taking R walk/jogging immediately to give him a change today. May then go to the Hacienda and put him on the grass to complete the job. Nothing but rest for the day. Tomorrow we hit it again. Later.

Was fun talking to you. Was sitting and reading and waiting for dusk to spend Sunday at the Plaza, my ritual. It was special tonight. They had a band in the gazebo that did commercials like "Eat at Polo's," etc. Met Bob Dunn there and we did the taco/cake and coke ritual. Ogled pretty girls, a glut tonight, and on the way home stopped to watch a dancing horse perform to live music. Further along the route, ran into Balthazar (The Crooked Chicken), local head of the electric company, who wants a screwdriver from the States. He's also a palm tree trimming magnate since he controls the only tree climbing grips in town through his company affiliation. R's eating. I'll go to Navojoa this week and look at Datsuns: price, style, date, etc. R has dined. Think I'll read a bit and crash early.

Met Allen Pendergraft, whose just in and at the unpacking and cleaning up phase of life. We'll get together in a couple of weeks. Also ran into the Slaughters at the Plaza. They were attending the grand opening of a new gift shop which had been priest-blessed, mariachied (Tesoros quartet), with Linc's ex-girl, Marie Antoinette, on vocals. Also ran into Linc, who said Craig Hill was by my house (I was jogging) to invite me to his place for Tuesday poker. I may pass on this one because they start at 1:30, out of the question for me, and the Hills have two dogs. Don't know what kind. Linc suggested that I see if Don Wilcox would babysit Runner. They love each but—off to casita, more momento.

People Mentioned in Earle's Chronicle

MARIO, (OWNER OF ARCO IRIS ORGANIC FOOD)
MARTINE (PEON ON HOUSE JOB AND MUSICIAN)
MARTIN AND SON BRIAN, (PILOT AND MINE OWNER)
MARTHENS, JUNE AND JOANIE, DAUGHTER
MCCLAIN, JUDY
MCKAY, BOB (SNAKE BOB)
MEDELLIN, JOE (PROFESSOR JFK INSTITUTE)
MENDOZA, ARMIDA
MENDOZA, UMBERTO
MESSINA, JOHN
MEYER, STEPHANIE
MICHA (LANDLADY WHEN FIRST IN ÁLAMOS, RETIRED NURSE)
MONTGOMERY, ZACK
MOORE, SUSIE AND HUSBAND
MORRISON, TIM & LORRIE
NAVARRO, JOAQUIN (MEXICAN DOCTOR)
NUZUM, PEMBER AND BET (ELIZABETH)
PENDERGRAFT, ALLEN
PERKINS, MARSH
PREECE, BILL AND EMILY
QUIJADA ALMADA, MARIE ANTONIETA
QUINTANA, RAMON (HALF OWNER OF TESOROS)
RASTON CERAMICS
REISBOROUGH, DOUGLAS
REYNOLDS, DOUGLAS
REYNOLDS, DAVID
REYNOLDS, GEN OR GENEVIEVE
REYNOLDS, LINCOLN
RITCHY, DELORES
RIGGS, GERT AND MART (JOAN'S PARENTS)
RYAN, MIKE (SUPT. OF SCHOOLS, SELLS, AZ)
SCHNEIDER, RICHARD
SERRANO, MANUEL, (MANAGER OF OLD HACIENDA UNDER DAWE)
SIEFERT, PATRICK
SIQUIERAS, BERNARD
SLAUGHTER, RON AND LOVEY
SMOLLENS, MRS. (EARLE BOUGHT THE HOUSE FROM HER AND HUSBAND JIM)
SOLEDAD, MAID
SOTO, VICTOR
SUTHERLAND, DON AND PAT NICOLSON
TAYLOR, WALTER (SW ARCHEOLOGIST)
VALDEZ, CHACHO AND CAMMY (BET'S DAUGHTER) AND THEIR CHILDREN, CHRISTINA AND GASPAR
VALENTIN, APPRENTICE DOME MAN
VILLASEÑOR, RICARDO (MINING ENGINEER)
VALENCIA, HECTOR
VILLAREAL, ALSTROBERTO
VIVIAN JUAN, O'ODHAM QUEEN
VOLLERTZÓN, MARGARET
WALWORTH, BOB
WEITZMAN, LOU AND DEE (CARÅCOL)
WILCOX, DON AND DOROTHY
WINDERMAN, MARC (EARLE'S OLDEST SON)
WINDERMAN, MARGE (EARLE'S SECOND WIFE)
YANAHARA (PERIODONTIST)
YATES, GORDON
WILKERSON, BILL
WUG (CALIFORNIA ENGINEER)

R getting ride to Navojoa.

Photo by Joan Gould.

Epilogue

Photo by Joan Gould.

Earle Winderman lived to be 90 years old, finally leaving this world on February 28, 2016, in Tucson, Arizona. His beloved Joan recalls that his photographic memory was starting to fade toward the end—he'd quip, "I used to be smart"—but his friends still had trouble keeping up with him. One of his Bronx Science High School buddies told me they all used to do whatever Earle wanted to do, he was their leader. He started early.

R.I.P. 1925–2016

Painting by Robyn Tinus.